RWANDA AND THE NEW SCRAMBLE FOR AFRICA

Robin Philpot

RWANDA AND THE NEW SCRAMBLE FOR AFRICA

From Tragedy to Useful Imperial Fiction

Baraka Books

Montréal

Cover and book design by Folio infographie

Photo credits:
Robin Philpot, pp. 15, 77, 81, 127, 197, 215
Jacques Godon, p. 213
Africa International, p. 71

ISBN 978-1-926824-94-9 pbk; 978-1-77186-005-5 epub; 978-1-77186-006-2 pdf; 978-1-77186-007-9 mobi/kindle

Legal Deposit, 4th quarter 2013
Bibliothèque et Archives nationales du Québec
Library and Archives Canada

Published by Baraka Books of Montreal.
6977, rue Lacroix
Montréal, Québec H4E 2V4
Telephone: 514 808-8504
info@barakabooks.com
www.barakabooks.com

Printed and bound in Québec

Société de développement des entreprises culturelles Québec

Baraka Books acknowledges the generous support of its publishing program from the Société de développement des entreprises culturelles du Québec (SODEC) and the Canada Council for the Arts.

Canada Council for the Arts

We acknowledge the financial support of the Government of Canada, through the National Translation Program for Book Publishing for our translation activities and through the Canada Book Fund (CBF) for our publishing activities.

Trade Distribution & Returns
Canada and the United States
Independent Publishers Group
1-800-888-4741 (IPG1);
orders@ipgbook.com

CONTENTS

To the memory of Juvénal Habyarimana and Cyprien Ntaryamira and their staff whose shamefully trivialized assassination led to a terrible human tragedy. They will not be forgotten.

ACKNOWLEDGEMENTS

This book would not have been possible in the original French version and in this new enriched English version without the support and participation of a vast number of people. I sincerely thank them for their understanding and contribution through aid in research, interviews, comments, criticisms, and more. Thanks are due to the original French-language publisher Les Intouchables in Quebec and later Duboiris in France. They withstood unbelievable pressure to ensure the book would be available. Thanks also to Phil Taylor at Taylor-Report.com for posting an earlier version in English—and in German—when all other English-language publishers chose not to touch the book or the issue. Thanks to Ed Herman for insisting that I update the book and publish a hard copy. Thanks also to my colleagues at Baraka Books for supporting this publishing adventure and to Josée Lalancette for her skill and devotion to book design. Any errors are entirely my responsibility.

Robin Philpot
November 1, 2013

LIST OF ILLUSTRATIONS

INTRODUCTION

Until lions produce their own historians
the story of the hunt will glorify only the hunter

African proverb

"The genocide in Rwanda was one hundred percent the responsibility of the Americans!" Those are not the words of a political leader who has been marginalized like Robert Mugabe, Fidel Castro or Bashar al-Assad. Nor are they the words of a nostalgic African activist bewailing the fall of the Soviet bloc. Former United Nations Secretary General Boutros Boutros-Ghali made that statement in July 1998, and he repeated it to me in November 2002 and again in 2004. People in the White House liked to call Boutros-Ghali "Booboo Ghali" or "Frenchie," while they methodically ejected him from the United Nations, an operation conducted by then United States Ambassador to the United Nations Madeleine Albright who vetoed his re-election on November 19, 1996.

His analysis flies in the face of all the clichés and accepted ideas about the Rwandan catastrophe whose effects have spread well beyond the borders of that small African country. The story of Rwanda is so littered with clichés and blind beliefs that a modern Flaubertian would be well advised to draft a new *Dictionary of Received Ideas*.

Throughout his life Flaubert wanted to compile a dictionary containing all that should be said in good company to be right and proper and to laud the things the right thinking agree upon. What should be said about Rwanda at cocktail parties in Europe and North America—which Boutros-Ghali obviously did not say—in order to be well thought of among the right thinking? If your ears perk up at such events where Rwanda is mentioned, you are sure to here some or all of the following statements.

- Rwanda is a beautiful little country perched on a plateau in the heart of dark Africa where horrible Hutu *génocidaires* massacred a million defenceless Tutsis after a plane crash killed an African dictator on April 6, 1994.
- The United Nations and the international community hopelessly failed to respond in time despite the clear warning in a fax sent on January 11, 1994 by the valorous Canadian General Roméo Dallaire and the numerous warnings issued by devoted and neutral human rights workers.
- In a predictable return to its iniquitous and colonialist past, France flew to the rescue of *génocidaires* and dictators by deploying its army in the Opération Turquoise.
- The Rwandan Patriotic Front led by the brilliant military and political strategist Paul Kagame, now President of Rwanda, put an end to the genocide when he swept down from the north and marched into Kigali on July 4, 1994, taking power on July 19, 1994.
- Pressured by impartial, non-governmental, human rights groups and in light of the trustworthy information they provided, the international community got its senses back, established the International Criminal Tribunal for Rwanda, arrested and indicted the bloodthirsty *génocidaires*, and brought these big fish to justice in Arusha, thanks in particular to Canadian Prosecutor Louise Arbour, who later became judge on the Supreme Court of Canada and then head of the UN Human Rights Commission.
- Thankfully after centuries during which rape has been a weapon of war and domination, a man was finally convicted

Boutros Boutros-Ghali
The former UN Secretary General declared that, "The genocide in Rwanda was one hundred percent the responsibility of the Americans!"

by an international criminal court of rape as a war crime. For that crime and other crimes against humanity, the brute is now serving a life sentence in a Malian jail.

- The *génocidaires* fled Rwanda while African dictators in the region continued to protect them. As a result Rwanda rightly launched a defensive war of aggression in the neighbouring Congo that continues to this day. Nonetheless, thanks to Jean Chrétien, his nephew, Ambassador Raymond Chrétien, and Canadian General Maurice Baril, the international community came to the rescue of the Rwandan refugees, liberated them from the *génocidaires*, and made it possible for them to return freely to their country. Since some remained, however, Rwanda was and is justified in pursuing its defensive war of aggression in the Congo. Unfortunately, more than four million people have since been killed.

- On behalf of the international community, President William Jefferson Clinton and his Secretary of State Madeleine Albright apologized for their timid reaction—and ours—during the genocide and promised never again to tolerate such crimes.
- And because we failed to listen to calls to protect Rwanda, we—the international community, NATO, USA, Europe—are entitled and obliged to invade Libya, Syria, Iran, Mali, Sudan, and any other country we choose.

Who has not read or heard such descriptions? Is it possible that they are just clichés or fashionable misconceptions? Does the truth lie somewhere else? Was Boutros Boutros-Ghali right to lift the corner of the very heavy rock of American responsibility to see what lies beneath?

The problem with the Rwandan tragedy is that nobody dares to look. It's like the tale of Blue Beard who sweetly hands his wife the keys to his castle but warns her that one door must not be opened. Unlike Blue Beard's wife, we have all obeyed the tyrant.

The goal of this book is to disobey, to use that key or those keys to open the door and find out what lies behind. Reams of paper have been written on Rwanda and the African Great Lakes region. The space taken up in libraries and bookstores is measured in metres but, except for fine points, all these books and reports say the same thing.

As is often the case with unanimity, dissidence is not tolerated, factual omissions and errors signalled are simply drowned out, and silence about crucial events is imposed. In the case of Rwanda, these problems are compounded by a shameful servility towards those who wield real power in the world, as well as a profound contempt for Africa.

The unanimity begins with the cavalier and abusive use of the term "genocide" and all its derivatives, such as *génocidaires* borrowed directly from French, accent and all, thus making it even more sinister. The road map that led to its widespread use tells us more about the goals and policies of big powers and the parties at war than it does about the crime itself. The term is a bludgeon, a gag order for millions of Rwandans and for anybody who dares ask questions. Its continued blind use will do more to perpetuate war than to render justice. As Noam Chomsky wrote in the preface to *The Politics of Genocide*, "As for the term 'genocide,' perhaps the most honorable course would be to expunge it from the vocabulary until the day, if it ever comes, when honesty and integrity can become an 'emerging norm.'"[1]

The most deafening silence concerns the worst terrorist act of the 1990s, the assassination of President Juvénal Habyarimana of Rwanda and President Cyprien Ntaryamira of Burundi on April 6, 1994. That tragic assassination of two African heads of state became a "plane crash" in official international newspeak and more recently has been buried under six feet of official reports aimed at preventing us from finding out what happened.

Why have Louise Arbour, Kofi Annan, Madeleine Albright, and their superiors from Jean Chrétien to Tony Blair, Bill Clinton, George W. Bush, and Barack Obama, not insisted that the killers be identified and brought to justice? After all, the "international community" solemnly promised to do so on April 7, 1994. The answer is obvious. Any serious investigation of that assassination would destroy the narrative that has been so carefully crafted to explain the Rwandan tragedy.

Equally astonishing is the silence about the three and a half years of war in Rwanda, starting with the invasion by Ugandan troops on October 1, 1990, leading up to the assassination of the two presidents. A close look at that war conducted by the invading RPF army between 1990 and 1994 and thereafter would effectively shatter the official narrative. That war heralded other wars that have torn up and terrorized all the neighbouring countries, particularly the Democratic Republic of the Congo. The victors of the Rwandan war, the Rwandan Patriotic Front, have been the main aggressors in the Congo yet have remained the staunchest allies of the United States and the United Kingdom. (For example, Paul Kagame was the first African head of state to back the United States' invasion of Iraq. Rwanda under Kagame broke with the African Union to back the invasion of Libya and in September 2013, Paul Kagame spoke in New York City calling for international intervention in Syria.)

Starting in 1989 power in the world was concentrated as never before in the hands of a single country. One might have expected that with the fall of the Soviet Union criticism of what used to be called "American imperialism" would have become sharper and stronger, and more people would be digging up information, and pointing out the interests, misinformation, manipulation, and covert action of that superpower. That certainly did not happen with respect to Rwanda.

Whereas France has been portrayed as being riddled with motive and guilty of the worst sins, the United States and its faithful sidekicks, mainly Canada and the United Kingdom, have come through virtually unscathed, bathing in an appearance of moral authority and honesty. France only regained respectability when Nicolas Sarkozy came to power and, with the help of Bernard Kouchner, turned on his predecessors François Mitterrand and Jacques Chirac in a craven attempt to curry favour with Washington.

◆

Like all countries Rwanda has a complex and hotly debated history. Summaries of Rwandan history in recently published books are inevitably coloured by the authors' positions on the 1994 tragedy. Very few references will be made to Rwandan history in this book. This choice has been made not because Rwandan history is uninteresting or unimportant, but rather because the authors of the official narrative of the recent tragedy use Rwandan history, or their version of it, to hide the real causes and thereby protect the criminals. These authors invariably explain the events of 1994 by referring selectively to aspects of Rwanda history that they intentionally present as sinister and foreboding of sad events to come. It is as though the route towards "genocide" could be retraced in Rwandan history alone, and no other forces came into play.

A neutral overview of Rwandan history, geography, and demography is nonetheless very helpful. Books recognized for their objectivity include René Lemarchand's authoritative work published in 1970 *Rwanda and Burundi* (Pall Mall Press, London).

Well before Europeans arrived, Rwanda was a feudal kingdom controlled by the Tutsi minority (Batutsi). The Tutsis were mainly cattle herders. Devotion to the king and poetry were highly regarded by the Tutsis who held agricultural work in contempt. The Hutu majority (Bahutu) were mainly peasants who worked the land and were serfs to the Tutsi aristocracy to whom they owed fealty and fees. Some Rwandan Patriotic Front apologists claim that Rwandans lived happily together until the European colonialists arrival; that notion is widely contested.[2]

After the Berlin Conference of 1885 and the European scramble for Africa, Rwanda and Burundi came under German sovereignty but were ruled indirectly through the kings known as Mwamis. Until the end of the First World War in 1918 Germany also ruled what is now Tanzania but much more directly as a colony. When the victorious powers divided up German possessions Rwanda and Burundi were put under Belgian mandate. Belgium administered Rwanda and Burundi through two kings (Mwamis), both Tutsis, and thereby exacerbated the division between Tutsis and Hutus, the latter representing more than eighty percent of the population. Rwanda and Burundi were economically integrated in the Belgian Congo whose administrative capital was Léopoldville, renamed Kinshasa in 1971.

In 1956 the Belgians took the initiative to organize elections that shook up the feudal and monarchist order. In Rwanda the Hutu majority revolted against the Tutsi aristocracy in November 1959. Many Tutsis fled to neighbouring countries, including Uganda, while others were killed. This social revolution culminated in a referendum conducted by the United Nations in September 1961, the independence of Rwanda on July 1, 1962, and the redistribution of land among Hutu peasants. In an aim to help understand recent events, historian René Lemarchand has pointed out since the 1960s that Rwanda and Zanzibar were the only countries in Africa where revolutionary change occurred.[3]

The Rwandan Mwami (Kigeri V) fled before independence. Rwanda became a republic and Grégoire Kayibanda, leader of the Parmehutu Party, became the first president elected by universal suffrage. Burundi kept the monarchy after independence and the Tutsi minority continued to hold power, especially in the Burundian army.

Between 1960 and 1967 Tutsi exiles calling themselves *Inyenzi*[4] launched many violent attacks against the new Rwandan regime, but were consistently beaten back. Each attack brought about reprisal killings within Rwanda. In 1972 Burundi was shaken by serious troubles. The Tutsi-dominated army of Burundi killed more than 100,000 Hutus, while many more fled to Rwanda as refugees. Shortly thereafter, on July 5, 1973 senior officers of Rwanda's National Guard overthrew President Kayibanda. The leader, Major General Juvénal Habyarimana, became president. The Tutsi elite that had remained in Rwanda after the social revolution and independence supported the new president.

Rwanda lived in relative peace and prosperity between 1973 and 1990. It was considered as a model of economic development and was often cited as an example by the World Bank and the International Monetary Fund. The Tutsi refugee problem had not been resolved to their satisfaction. This then became the pretext for senior officers of the Ugandan army, including many Tutsi exiles born in Uganda or living there since 1959, to invade Rwanda on October 1, 1990. The Government of Rwanda and a vast majority of the Rwandan people saw that invasion as a counter-revolution aimed at catapulting the Tutsi aristocracy back into power. This book deals mainly with events that took place from 1990 on.

Rwanda is one of the most densely populated countries in the world. In April 1994 it had a population of 7.6 million, about 85 to 90 percent Hutu. Rwanda has an area of 26,340 square kilometres, about the same size as the State of Vermont whose population is about 550,000. The estimated population of Rwanda in 2012 was 11.5 million.

◆

A few words are in order to explain where this book comes from. Though Montreal has been my home since 1974, I did not arrive from Ontario where I was born, but rather from Ougadougou, capital of Burkina Faso. More exactly, I was arriving from Koudougou, some one hundred kilometres to the west of Ouagadougou, where I had lived and taught English and History for two years. Before, during, and after my stay in Koudougou, I was lucky enough to visit almost all West African countries, from Mauritania to Cameroon and to pursue my interest in African history that I had studied at the University of Toronto.

Settling in Montreal, Québec, was no accident. Leaving a French-speaking country in a French-speaking region of Africa for another French-speaking country, Québec, was only normal. In addition to language, there were also political affinities. African independence was still fresh in the minds of Africans, as was colonialism, and the very many Quebecers in Africa at that time were talking about independence and Canadian colonialism in Québec.

Bamako, Mali, and not Toronto or Thunder Bay in Canada, was where I first heard music by Québec poet and singer Gilles Vigneault. N'djamena, Chad (formerly Fort-Lamy) and not Vancouver or Ottawa was where I learned who Félix Leclerc was. In Koudougou, I read *Les nègres blancs d'Amérique* (*White Niggers of America*) and found out what June 24 meant for Quebecers. At the same time and with the same enthusiasm I encountered *Une vie de boy* (*Houseboy*) by Ferdinand Oyono, in Yaoundé, Cameroon. In Dakar, I learned who exactly Léopold Sédar Senghor was and read Sembène Ousman's *God's Bits of Wood*, and in Nigeria, I read Chinua Achebe's *Things Fall Apart*.

Interest in Africa and particularly in French-speaking Africa led me to follow the events in Rwanda very closely in the early 1990s. After meeting a number of Rwandans at a demonstration, I published an article in the Montreal daily *La Presse* in September 1994 criticizing the International Centre for Human Rights and Democratic Development (later to become Rights and Democracy, now defunct) then headed by Ed Broadbent.[5] That article started a polemic—it also gave rise to the first accusations of "negationism," as if just weeks after the events the courts of History had already decreed a truth that nobody was allowed to contradict. Essentially, my article accused the organization that became Rights and Democracy and others of doing public relations for the invading army of the Rwandan Patriotic Front in their March 1993 human rights report published following a fifteen-day visit to Rwanda in January 1993. It also pointed out that the report and the media and lobbying campaign that accompanied its publication exacerbated the conflict. (More about this in Chapter 4.)

Following the publication of that article and the creation of the International Criminal Tribunal for Rwanda in November 1994 by the UN Security Council, my brother, John Philpot, a Montreal criminal lawyer, took a serious interest in the Rwandan tragedy and particularly in the people indicted for genocide. He published an important critique of the International Criminal Tribunal for Rwanda in Arusha, Tanzania[6] and was appointed counsel for a Rwandan before the Appeal Court in the Hague. Other well-known lawyers from Québec, Canada, and the United States also became interested and were retained as counsel by Rwandan prisoners in Arusha.

These lawyers and their imprisoned clients have faced a daunting challenge. First and foremost, they have endeavoured to convince the judges that there is a version of the events other than the one Flaubert might have described as "the right and proper tale." As with all tribunals, the Arusha Tribunal, judges and all, has been conditioned by an international public opinion that had already granted the right and proper tale the authority of an adjudicated fact. Yet no facts had been adjudicated, and very few have been adjudicated ever since. Self-appointed authorities have nonetheless continued to repeat that tale.

If this book manages to cast doubt or break the unanimity in favour of that simplistic and simple-minded tale, then it will have been worth the effort.

The first section deals with rarely discussed events that brought Rwanda to the brink of catastrophe before presidents Habyarimana and Ntaryamira were assassinated on April 6, 1994. First came the invasion of Rwanda by part of the Ugandan National Army in October 1990 and the deadly war it waged in that country for the next three and a half years. While that army pursued the war against Rwanda foreign powers imposed a multiparty system that undermined the ability of the Rwandan Government and the country's armed forces to fight off the invader. The same foreign powers led by the United States and calling themselves the international community then imposed a so-called peace process that effectively transferred power to the invader. Non-governmental organizations began slandering Rwanda, its leadership, and its entire recent history. They became the cat's-paw for the invading army and American and British interests in Central Africa.

This section also examines how and why the assassination of two African heads of state has been trivialized by a vast cover-up operation. Who has gained from that cover-up? The section ends with a study of what exactly the United States did and did not do between April 6 and July 19, 1994 when so many Rwandans were killed. It will be shown that the number of dead in Rwanda was of little concern for the world's only superpower. Washington's priority was to see its boys from the Rwandan Patriotic Front win the war decisively—it took much longer than expected—and to bump France out of that part of Africa.

What about the genocide? What about the massacres? Everybody saw those images, the machetes, the bodies, the skeletons. Nobody can claim that it did not happen. Of course not! However, the simplification of the Rwandan tragedy to a tale of "horrible Hutu *génocidaires*" massacring "innocent Tutsis" aided and abetted by France has hidden the causes and protected the real criminals. Rwanda suffered a major human disaster. Like other such disasters, it had political causes. Any serious analysis will show unequivocally that that Manichean good guy-bad guy tale was developed by Western imaginations for Western public opinion. The fact that that tale has so easily taken root is evidence of our blind subservience to real power and historic contempt for Africa.

Names must be named. Each Western country boasts its own journalist, its writer of fiction or nonfiction, its human rights activist or anthropologist who sprang forth to tell the right and proper tale. Pablo Neruda described him—or her—very well: "He's the skulking coward hired to praise dirty hands. He's an orator or journalist. Suddenly he surfaces in the palace enthusiastically masticating the sovereign's dejections."[7] His name is Philip Gourevitch or Alison Des Forges in the United States, William Schabas, Carol Off or Gerald Caplan in Canada, Gil Courtemanche in Québec, Linda Melvern in the United Kingdom, Colette Braeckman or Alain Destexhe in Belgium, Jean-Pierre Chrétien, Gérard Prunier or Jean Hatzfeld in France. Though each has his or her national subtleties, their message remains the same: steer clear of the sovereign and his allies.

The second part of the book looks at how the tale has taken root in books and other publications. Writers of fiction and nonfiction about Rwanda have wittingly or not drawn their material from a popular literary tradition about Africa. That tradition abounds with metaphors, images, and conventions developed at a time when Europe was enslaving Africans and trading African slaves or colonizing the continent. These metaphors, images, and conventions have everything to do with European and North American imaginations and almost nothing to do with African reality. They were developed to legitimate what was totally illegitimate, namely slavery, the slave trade, and Europe's domination and colonization of Africa. The more they were repeated the more they themselves became the message of the works they appeared in.

Four books on Rwanda by four different authors are examined to show not only that *That's not how it happened in Rwanda* but also and above all that *It never could have happened like that in Rwanda*. The authors are the American Philip Gouvevitch, the Canadian Carol Off, the Quebecer Gil Courtemanche, and the Belgian Colette Braeckman. All four helped draft the "right and proper tale," and all four are products—and perpetrators—of a colonial mentality that has unfortunately made a comeback.

The final section examines the work of the International Criminal Tribunal for Rwanda and how international criminal justice has been used as a tool of foreign policy. Former United States Ambassador-at-Large for War Crimes Issues David Scheffer has boasted that they manoeuvred so as to be able "to wield it [the tribunal] like a battering ram in the execution of U.S. and NATO policy." The case of Jean-Paul Akayesu, the first person to be found guilty of genocide and rape as a war crime, is also examined. Jean-Paul Akayesu has always proclaimed his innocence. What's more, he has solid proof of fabrication of evidence presented to the tribunal by the prosecutor's office under the aegis of former Chief Prosecutor Louise Arbour.

This section also investigates the 1996 refugee crisis in Eastern Zaire, now the Democratic Republic of the Congo. It shows how the same Rwandan Patriotic Army that the United States helped put in power in 1994 used the narrative about the Rwandan tragedy, elevated to official status by the International Criminal Tribunal for Rwanda, to justify the invasion of the Congo. Washington took advantage of that refugee crisis to push France out of the Congo, a country coveted for its natural resources. In doing so, the United States got help from trustworthy aides in Ottawa. The Chrétien government was more than glad to play the role of the anti-France, pro-American, French-speaking country.

Interviewed in Paris, Raymond Chrétien, Jean Chrétien's nephew and Ambassador to France, admitted that the November 1996 operation he had been involved in as special envoy of the UN Secretary General resulted in at least one million deaths!

The never-ending war in the Congo began with that operation. It has led to the implosion of that country and the most deadly war since 1945.

◆

A book is never finished. A version of this book first appeared in French in 2003 in both Québec and Europe and is entitled *Ça ne s'est pas passé comme ça à Kigali* (literally, *That's Not What Happened in Kigali*). It has been widely debated in the French-speaking world, having been both heartily commended and bitterly attacked. Within a year, I had translated it into English and submitted it to at least twenty English-language publishers in Canada and the United States. Though some showed interest, none took it on. Perhaps the "official story" was overwhelming. Phil Taylor of the Taylor Report in Toronto then graciously agreed to post the book on the Taylor Report website where it has been since 2006 and was titled *Rwanda 1994: Colonialism Dies Hard.* A young German translator, Klaus Madersbacher, found it on that website, translated it into German, and that version is also on the Taylor Report site with a preface by Helmut Strizek, who has been an expert witness before the International Criminal Tribunal for Rwanda. No printed version of the English book was published until this one.

Much has happened since 2003 and even more has been discovered or revealed by researchers and more importantly by major players in the events that took place starting in 1990. It is hard to keep up with all the statements, books, and sworn testimony that have accumulated in the past ten years and that show just how terrible a lie the "official story" of the Rwandan tragedy is. This means that anybody of good will who takes the time—and hopefully reads French—can get beyond the "official story" even though the anointed experts, like parrots, keep on repeating it. This edition of the book provides extensive notes and references for readers who wish to know more.

April 6, 2014 marks the twentieth anniversary of the shooting down of the Rwandan president's plane which triggered war, destruction, and massacres in Central Africa that have never ceased. At the same time political leaders, diplomats, pundits, intellectuals, retired generals in North America have never ceased to invoke "Rwanda" as though the word alone confers some supposed truth and moral authority on the political, military or imperial positions they defend. "Rwanda" has been used specifically to justify violent military "humanitarian" intervention in countries such as Libya, Sudan, Mali, and Syria. Time has come to determine how a terrible tragedy has been cynically transformed into a useful imperial fiction that has nothing to do with the truth.

PART 1

CHAPTER 1

◆

Invasion? What Invasion?

The vanquished always has a better memory than the victor, who tries to make us forget.

René Lévesque

The official narrative would have it that the Rwandan Patriotic Front under the brilliant military and political leadership of current Rwandan President Paul Kagame, who along with many fellow officers was trained in the best American and British military academies, ended the genocide by taking Kigali on the fourth of July 1994 and by forming a new government on July 19, 1994. A patriotic liberation movement with the right friends puts an end to the worst crime imaginable, similar to the Holocaust, and all that happens on the fourth of July.

The first problem with this part of the tale is that Kigali was not taken on the fourth of July. The decisive battle that allowed the RPF to take the capital city of Rwanda was fought on July 2. Paul Kagame marched into Kigali on July 3. Wasn't Paris liberated when Charles de Gaulle marched in on August 25, 1944? Nobody changed that date to make others happy. But for Rwanda, important people in influential positions preferred the fourth of July. So that day was chosen. It was also important not to be too close to

July 1, which had been Rwandan Independence Day since 1962 and was a powerful symbol of the social revolution that now had to be erased from people's memories. The victors then just had to declare the fourth of July the new Rwandan National Day and then the pipers could play the tune. Everybody knows of course which tune was to be played.

The second problem is that the massacre of civilians did not end with the victory of the Rwandan Patriotic Front. Civilians have been massacred in Rwanda steadily ever since, and massacres have continued even more seriously in the neighbouring Congo where millions have been killed.

The choice of the fourth of July may be a minor point, but in politics nothing is left to chance, especially not symbols. Hopefully, it will be like an alarm bell that might lead people to reread the right and proper tale with an eye out for those optical illusions so often used to distort and misinform.

The army led by Paul Kagame was never a liberation army. Most people knew that from the beginning. The Rwandan Patriotic Front and its leader were more like the paid arsonists masquerading as firemen than patriots who saved the people from the fire, which is what the official story would have us believe.

◆

Until October 1, 1990 the troops that invaded Rwanda were uniformed soldiers in the Ugandan National Army who marched to the orders of Yoweri Museveni, President of Uganda and Commander-in-Chief of the Ugandan Army. The invading troops consisted mainly of Rwandans who had lived in Uganda since the social revolution and independence of Rwanda in 1962. They had been at war in Uganda since 1981 as part of the guerrilla forces known as the National Resistance Army until it took power in Uganda in 1986 and its leader, Yoweri Museveni, became president.

On September 28, 1990 four thousand Ugandan soldiers and officers, including former army Commander and Ugandan

Defence Minister Fred Rwigyema, left their barracks fully equipped with weapons and vehicles. They travelled hundreds of kilometres in Uganda to the Rwandan border and attacked the few Rwandan guards stationed there on October 1. They then advanced some seventy kilometres into Rwanda and by October 4 the invading troops were within seventy kilometres of the Rwandan capital Kigali.

Everywhere in the world, that attack on October 1 would be described as an invasion of one country by another. It was not an incursion, nor a civil war, nor an increase in ethnic tension. The right word is invasion. In legal terms and according to principles established at the Nuremberg trials, so often referred to in the Rwandan tragedy, that invasion was no less than the worst war crime because it was a crime against peace. Yet that invasion has been, at best, trivialized ever since it happened and, at worst, omitted altogether from the tale of events. One of the worst examples was a long article in the *New York Times Magazine* on September 15, 2002, entitled "The Minister of Rape." Not a word is mentioned about the invasion. We only learn that "tensions increased in 1990."[1]

A crime of that magnitude should normally have provoked a sharp international reaction, especially considering that when Ugandan troops invaded Rwandan President Habyarimana and Ugandan President Museveni were both attending a UNICEF meeting in New York. Moreover, two days earlier, on September 28, 1990 President Habyarimana told the United Nations General Assembly that his government would offer citizenship and travel documents to all Rwandan refugees wherever they were and that it would repatriate all those who wanted to return to Rwanda.

International reports on the invasion hinted that the invading army had taken or was about to take Kigali. American authorities jumped suspiciously quickly to offer President Habyarimana political asylum in the United States. According to a story that is surely not very right and proper, but stubbornly tenacious, the late Rwandan president met the United States Ambassador in

Kigali before leaving the country and asked him if the United States had any information about an invasion by Uganda. The Ambassador offered to make some intelligence inquiries—the CIA—and then informed President Habyarimana that there was no such information and that he could safely go to New York.

On learning of the invasion, the Rwandan president immediately returned home but stopped off in Belgium where, suspiciously, he received another offer of political asylum. Belgian news reports amplified the invaders' military success. Meanwhile, Ugandan President Museveni remained in the United States even though his army had just suffered the worst mutiny in its history, involving troops, officers, and military materiel. Though he is an army man to the core and the champion of professional and disciplined armies that Africa supposedly needed so badly, the president of Uganda decided to sit back in New York while a whole section of his cherished army revolted and invaded another country wearing their Ugandan uniforms.

The same Yoweri Museveni had become the darling of the International Monetary Fund, the World Bank, and United States diplomacy since the middle of the 1980s. He was another of the former leftist guerrilla leaders who came over to the gospel of good governance, structural adjustment, privatization and, judging by the turn of events, the remodelling of African geography. The United States saw Uganda as a rampart against Islamic fundamentalism in Sudan, and its president, Yoweri Museveni, as a trustworthy ally to aid United States covert operations in Southern Sudan. Former President Jimmy Carter described Museveni as "one of Africa's most important leaders." Madeleine Albright spoke of him as "a beacon of hope for Africa," whereas Philip Gourevitch of the *New Yorker,* promoted him for years as the "*éminence grise* of the new leadership in central Africa."

President Museveni unconvincingly distanced himself from the invasion by pleading ignorance and surprise and by complaining about how his officers and comrades-in-arms, who became the commanders of the Rwandan Patriotic Front, had tricked him in October 1990. Though totally disingenuous, Museveni's excuses satisfied his friends in the "international community." "The truth of the matter is," he declared in a 1991 address, "that these people conspired, took us by surprise, and went to Rwanda, which was not particularly difficult.... We had some information that the Banyarwanda in Uganda were up to something, but we shared it with the Rwandan government. They actually had, or should have had, more information because, after all, it was their business, not ours, to follow up who was plotting what." [2]

The eminent President Museveni would like us to believe that the intelligence agency of one country—Rwanda in this case—should spy and monitor all the movements and actions of entire regiments of another country's army—Uganda—and take the necessary action to prevent mutiny, revolt, and aggression against neighbours. Let's apply his infallible logic to other countries on other continents. What would happen if Cuba or Mexico did to the United States what Museveni said Rwanda should have done to Uganda? And what if they took action to protect against U.S. interference? What if Ireland did the same in the United Kingdom? Or Algeria in France? France in Canada? India in Pakistan? China in Vietnam? It is obviously ridiculous. Are we expected to believe him just because it is in Africa?

Countries that spy on each other, as Museveni suggested Rwanda should have done, are asking for war. Yet we are invited to believe that the Rwandan government made a serious mistake by not spying on the Ugandan army and by not intervening to prevent it from invading Rwanda. That error was so serious that the "new *éminence grise* of Africa," Yoweri Museveni, was justified in not punishing the mutineers in his army.

The man who refused to punish the senior officers who mutinied in his own army is the same man that United States diplomacy, the World Bank, and the International Monetary Fund adored, particularly because of his unbending leadership and his vision of a professional and disciplined army in Africa. All of Museveni's speeches convey the message of a professional and disciplined army. He talked that way before and after he took power in Uganda, before and after the invasion of Rwanda in 1990, before and after the Rwandan Patriotic Front took power in Kigali. Museveni knew what he was talking about. He took power in 1986 after a long guerrilla war, and then, between 1986 and 1990, he mercilessly suppressed revolt in his army.

In his address five years after taking power and four months after the invasion of Rwanda Museveni left no doubt about his views on military discipline. "As you know, we have dealt very harshly with discipline. There is a very strict code of conduct for the National Resistance Army and a mechanism for dealing with wayward soldiers. No soldier is spared, whatever his rank may be."[3]

One month before the invasion of Rwanda, in August 1990, President Museveni addressed Ugandan army officers who undoubtedly included those who were preparing to invade Rwanda. His subject was combating counterrevolutionary insurgency and his main message was the importance of discipline, loyalty, military training, unity, and the size of the army. He also made a plea in favour of using military intelligence however it may be obtained. All these elements converge in the fight against insurgency.[4]

A month after making this speech the strict disciplinarian, raised and trained in a world of conspiracies and rebellion, sat passively watching his own troops mutiny and invade Rwanda, thereby threatening peace and security throughout Central Africa. These were not a few low-ranking officers; entire regiments invaded, led first by Uganda's former Defence Minister Fred Rwigyema, killed in the invasion, and then by the Ugandan Chief of Military Intelligence, Paul Kagame, who quickly returned from the United States where Museveni had sent him for military training. The invading Ugandan troops that would soon be known as the Rwandan Patriotic Army comprised many senior officers, one hundred and fifty middle level officers, and even some of President Museveni's own bodyguards.

In the next three and half years, Museveni continued to watch "passively" as his former troops went in and out of Uganda as they liked. Uganda became the conveyor of men, munitions, and materiel to an army dedicated to overthrowing the Rwandan government. Despite Uganda's obvious implication in this war, no imperial power ever once threatened to punish President Museveni or cut off support to his country and every power has studiously avoided calling the invasion by its real name ever since.

Yoweri Museveni's August 1990 address to the officers of the Ugandan National Resistance Army on "How to fight a Counter-revolutionary Insurgency" reads like a blueprint for the invasion and war that some of his officers were soon to conduct in Rwanda against President Habyarimana. The difference is that Museveni's officers would soon be calling themselves Rwandan "insurgents" or "rebels."[5]

"We had to reject the concept of 'a small but efficient' army..." he told his officers on August 17, 1990. "This notion is nothing but suicidal. Insurgents do not have to do much, but they will have succeeded in their devices if they simply terrorize the population, stop them from producing wealth for the country, dismantle the network of civil administration and block communications. Once the state does not stop insurgents from doing this on a large scale, the country will rapidly lose income and find it impossible to support the army ... Insurgents will be in a position to create a situation of strategic stalemate or even to launch a strategic counteroffensive to seize state power."

That is exactly what happened between 1990 and 1994 in Rwanda. Moreover, shortly after the Ugandan officers led the October invasion of that country, President Museveni demanded that Rwanda agree to a cease-fire and negotiate with the insurgents, now called the Rwandan Patriotic Front. That was the "strategic stalemate" he had talked about in his August 1990 address. If we move forward to the many "insurgencies" in the Democratic Republic of the Congo since 1994 (i.e., 1996, 1998-2003, and the many other so-called rebellions that followed until the M23), we see exactly the same pattern described by Yoweri Museveni in August 1990.

◆

Rwanda is so tiny. What in the world would the United States want in such an insignificant remote place?

The notion that Africa is, at best, on the fringe of the international community, at worst, completely cut off from it, has been common currency for centuries. Africa is supposedly of no interest to major powers, except as a means to soothe guilty consciences or receive charity and benefit from those altruistic powers. That idea is deep-rooted. Former Canadian Prime Minister Jean Chrétien echoed it in April 2002 shortly before the G8 Summit at Kananaskis when he announced that Africa would become part of the international community in the twenty-first century. It appears to have escaped Mr. Chrétien that most African countries have belonged to the United Nations since the 1960s.

In 1885, when Europe was set to pounce on Africa, the official British position was that of the "reluctant empire" compelled to leave its hallowed isles to look after Africa. Historians consolidated this idea. In a famous address first published in 1883, J.R. Seeley observed that the expansion of England in America and Asia was perceived to be almost accidental. It was "an empire acquired in a fit of absence of mind."[6] Historians subsequently showed that England was not as selfless as it let on and that expansion of the empire closely followed British commercial expansion—the flag followed commerce.

The same image of the "reluctant empire" prevails in all descriptions of the United States in Central Africa at the end of the twentieth century, and now in the twenty-first. Did not the United States claim that it led the invasion of Libya from behind?[7] The reluctant empire. Moreover, the United States State Department carefully and successfully cultivated that image, which could be summed up as follows: We don't want to be there, we don't want to be forced to intervene, we have no interests there, we are only the honest broker working for the good of humanity.

The proof that the United States succeeded in imposing that image was the virtual absence for many years of publications dealing critically with the United States' strategic goals in Africa. Except for a limited number of left-wing publications, discussion of the American role has been couched in talk of democracy, human rights, good governance, trade, and the American determination not to repeat the Somalia fiasco when eighteen U.S. soldiers were killed. Moreover, it would seem now that the mere mention of "another Rwanda" can justify military intervention in Africa or elsewhere and bring on board most of the Western human rights organizations. As Max Forte wrote in *Slouching Towards Sirte,* "Everywhere is Rwanda for the humanitarian imperialist, which makes one want to know what really happened there in 1994."[8]

Although former UN Secretary General Boutros Boutros-Ghali was not convinced of the United States' strategic interest in Rwanda—"I have no real information to that effect," he said in an interview in November 2002—he has no doubt about the Congo. "In the Congo, yes, absolutely! There's tremendous wealth there." Boutros-Ghali added that British intelligence services were very active in the region through Ugandan President Museveni. He also pointed out that the 1898 Fashoda incident, which is seen as a French defeat in Africa, "still dominates people's minds."[9]

Facts contradict the reluctant empire story. For the United States, Uganda as well as Rwanda and Burundi became increasingly important for both economic and strategic reasons in the late 1980s and early 1990s.

The importance of building a front to counter the expansion of Islam in Africa through the Sudan cannot be underestimated. Uganda had a strong, experienced army and was led by a president willing to work for the Americans. U.S. support for the Christian rebellion in southern Sudan was funnelled through Kampala with the help of Museveni's army.[10] South Africa at that time was also unpredictable. Despite an official but belated American anti-apartheid position, South Africa remained an important ally and Washington was worried about what might happen should that country be lost as an ally.

When Ugandan troops invaded Rwanda, the future leader, Paul Kagame, who had been Uganda's Chief of Military Intelligence, was training at Fort Leavenworth, Kansas, under the International Military Education and Training program known as IMET. In fact, the majority of Ugandan military personnel sent to the United States through the IMET program would soon become commanders of the Rwanda Patriotic Front.

IMET was established in the mid 1970s. It is described as an "instrument of influence" by which the United States is able to affect the internal and external policy behaviour of recipient military institutions and governments in a manner congenial with U.S. foreign policy interests.[11] The IMET program, and a modern version known as Enhanced-IMET, was also used to prepare Rwandan troops for the invasion of Zaire starting in 1996.

The United States placed much hope in Yoweri Museveni's Uganda. In addition to the military links, American non-military aid to Uganda between 1989 and 1992 totalled $183 million, twice what the United States granted to Rwanda during the same period.

It has been said that the invasion of Rwanda by Ugandan troops in 1990 was aimed at Kinshasa not Kigali. The wars that followed in the Congo and the scramble by Western corporations for control of the vast Congolese natural resources makes that interpretation very plausible. The British and the Americans have coveted resources in eastern Congo since the end of the nineteenth century. With President Mobutu's health failing and his grip on power weakening, the void foreseen whet the appetite of an American empire giddy after the fall of the Soviet Union.

Since the war began in the Congo in 1996, the rush of American, Belgian, Canadian, British, and French corporations for diamonds, gold, coltan, and other natural resources in the region has been widely documented and denounced. Before the war, these resources belonged to Zaire and were a major source of income. Now they are under the direct control of foreign corporations protected by proxy armies set up since the 1996 invasion and are often exported through Kigali.

Two weaknesses pervade documentation on the exploitation of the Congo's natural resources. First, they fail to deal directly with the Rwandan tragedy and usually fall back on the official narrative. It would appear that accusations of "genocide-denier" or "negationist" have had a powerful silencing effect. Their second weakness is their economic determinism. The eloquent and detailed descriptions of how American and European interests have taken over African wealth are undermined by credence given to the imperial cant that allowed it all to happen. That cant would have it that Western powers led by the United States are involved in Africa to defend human rights and democracy, to combat the evils of corruption, dictatorship, impunity, and genocide, and to foster development. There is not much new under the sun. When England colonized Africa, people were supposed to believe the goal was to stamp out the Arab slave trade and uplift Africans through Christian civilization.

In spring 1993 United States Secretary of State Warren Christopher declared to the African-American Institute that "The people of Africa know where their future lies: not with corrupt dictators like Mobutu, but with courageous democrats in every part of the continent. From Senegal to Benin, from Madagascar to Mali, African nations are building strong democratic institutions."

What was Warren Christopher's real message? First, the United States was staking out the areas it targeted. These just happened to be all countries with close ties to France—note that every country mentioned is a member of the Francophone Summit. Secondly, Washington had decided that Mobutu, who had faithfully served the United States for thirty years as an anti-Communist strongman, was now on his way out and that the Africans' desire for change and their revolt against Mobutu would be used to advance American pawns in Africa.

The anointed strongman in Africa would be Yoweri Museveni even though the Ugandan president thumbed his nose at sacrosanct notions like human rights, democracy, multiparty systems, and economic transparency. Though a large number of Congolese wanted to get rid of Mobutu, in hindsight, were they to have had a choice after, even the most militant among them would prefer Mobutu's Zaire to the Congo killing fields that the wars launched in 1996 foisted upon their country and their people.

The official position of the United States and most European countries regarding Africa remained that of reluctance and disinterest. Nonetheless, their diplomatic, economic, political, legal and military involvement increased exponentially between 1990 and 2003. That involvement became much more direct, very often bypassing the official channels that govern international relations.

◆

The Rwandan government reacted sharply to the October 1 invasion and was supported by France, Zaire, and Belgium; however, the Belgians soon turned on the Rwandan government. The invasion pitted Ugandan troops that had been at war for years in Uganda against a small Rwandan army that had not seen combat since 1969. President Habyarimana's government also took action internally and, not surprisingly, arrested some eight thousand Rwandan citizens, mainly Tutsis, holding them for periods varying from a few days to six months.

The intrepid representatives of the New York based Africa Watch (later Human Rights Watch/Africa) immediately claimed that the arrests provided verifiable proof of serious human rights violations. Later, with their 20/20 hindsight, the arrests became the proof of the genocidal intentions of the Rwandan government leaders. Africa Watch rang the alarm and it has never stopped ringing.

Foreign diplomats from Belgium, the United States, Switzerland, and Canada deplored the action of the government of Rwanda. The Belgian Ambassador Johann Swinnen rushed to the stadium in Kigali where the prisoners were held and, to the joy of those arrested, he condemned the Rwandan government for its human rights violations—would that they had been so prompt when Pinochet locked up thousands in a stadium in Santiago, Chile. Those Western powers obviously wanted to warn President Habyarimana that the going would be tough and that his days were probably numbered.

A few questions must be raised before we delve deeper into this story.

Is it normal in the search for justice during war to condemn one side for human rights violations and not even question the morality of the aggressors, those who violated the principles of all the charters of rights humanity has ever drafted? Is it right to shout about how a government violates rights and yet turn a blind eye to the launching of an aggressive war?

The vast majority of Western human rights organizations and their representatives appeared to consider it perfectly normal to whitewash the invaders and denounce the invaded country, its leaders, and its people. At the top of the list was the late Alison Des Forges, an ubiquitous American Rwanda activist who wrote reams of reports including the Africa Watch report on the arrests and who was the main prosecution witness at the International Criminal Tribunal for Rwanda. In a statement made under oath in a 1995 Montreal hearing, Ms Des Forges declared that human rights activists "do not examine the issue of who makes war. We see war as an evil and we try to prevent the existence of war from being an excuse for massive human rights violations." It is like an armed break and entry during which the homeowner defends himself. The Justice Department arrests the homeowner for possession of arms and lets the armed robber off scot-free.

The refusal of human rights organizations to condemn the worst human rights violation, the invasion, invalidates all the reports they have published and weakens the foundations on which the "right and proper" tale has been built. It bears sad witness to the lightness with which many of these groups undertake their work, and also reveals the tacit agreement between them and the big Western powers who wield much more influence than the Rwandan government could dream of having. Worst of all, however, is their blatant double standard in respect to Africa. The same groups would never dare apply the same criteria in cases of war in or by their own countries.

In his *Discourse on colonialism* published in 1955, Aimé Césaire denounced a similar double standard observed among European humanists. Though many humanists were anti-Nazis in the Second World War, they avoided taking up the fight against colonialism. "And that is the great thing I hold against pseudo-humanism," wrote Césaire. "For too long it has diminished the rights of man, that its concept of those rights has been—and still is—narrow and fragmentary, incomplete and biased and, all things considered, sordidly racist."[12]

The Habyarimana government arrested eight thousand Rwandans but released them all within six months. For a country that has been invaded, neither the number of arrests nor their duration is excessive, especially considering the revelations of former leaders and collaborators of the Rwandan Patriotic Front. One such leader is Valens Kajeguhakwa, a businessman and formerly one of the RPF's main financial backers. In 2001 his erstwhile comrade-in-arms, Paul Kagamé, forced him to leave the country. Kajeguhakwa, who had also been close to President Habyarimana before he joined the RPF in 1990, published a book in which he described himself as the "bridge that clandestinely united the action of patriots outside and within Rwanda."[13] He boasts of the invaluable role of his vast network of civilian and military informers that he had carefully developed and who were infiltrated throughout Rwanda up to the highest echelons of the Government of Rwanda.

"They were placed in the army, in the Gendarmerie, in government ministries, in all the main public and private companies, in the National Bank of Rwanda, in parishes, in markets in Kigali, Butare, Ruhengeri, and Gisenyi, in the University in Butare and Nyakinama, in the prisons in Gisenyi and Ruhengeri." Valens Kajeguhakwa left Rwanda for Uganda just before the invasion in October 1990. He points out in his book that he ensured his network would continue working for him and the Rwandan Patriotic Front in his absence.

Leaders of the Rwandan Patriotic Front claim that they had thirty-six clandestine cells operating inside Rwanda on October 1, 1990. The number of cells grew steadily as the invaders gained ground and especially as they gained international recognition and support. The same sources boast that by 1993 the RPF could activate 146 clandestine cells in Kigali alone.[14] Ever since the Spanish Civil War, an expression accurately describes such cells: a fifth column. In Rwanda, however, that fifth column was and still is conveniently qualified as innocent human rights activists.

The number of arrests and their duration were limited. Since memory is always selective and always very poor in powerful dominating countries, a few comparisons would be helpful.

According to Professor Panikos Panayi who studied the question of minorities in wartime, "Some of the most systematic persecution of racial and ethnic minorities in recent history has taken place during the two World Wars. Anyone studying the twentieth century cannot avoid this conclusion. In fact, the historian dealing with any period of human development would find that the years 1914-18 and 1939-45 witnessed unprecedented heights of intolerance towards outgroups."[15] Professor Panayi also deplores the lack of research conducted about minorities in wartime.

Take Canada as an example. In 1914 Canada was automatically drawn into the First World War by England when it declared war on August 4, 1914, but the country was not invaded. In fact, it has not been invaded since 1812. Nevertheless, two weeks after the war began in Europe, the Parliament of Canada adopted the War Measures Act granting the government power to arrest, detain, exclude, and deport individuals. Under the Act, the government could refuse release on bail and suspend habeas corpus for any person suspected of being an enemy alien. Canada interned 8579 people in "concentration camps"—the term coined in the Boer War was still fashionable. Most were Ukrainians that Canadian officials mistook for Austrians.

As war progressed, naturalized German Canadians including many born in Canada soon went from being "among our best immigrants, white people like ourselves," as J.S. Woodsworth noted, to "sub-human" or "blood-crazed madmen."[16] In 1917, to the applause of much of English Canada, the Parliament adopted the War-time Elections Act that took away voting rights from tens of thousands of naturalized Canadians, most of whom were Ukrainian.

During the Second World War Canada interned 21,000 of the country's 22,086 residents of Japanese origin. Ninety-one percent of those interned were Canadian citizens. Officially, Canada "evacuated" the Japanese Canadians, who were dispersed throughout Canada, sometimes up to five thousand kilometres from their homes. All their property was confiscated, farms, homes, and fishing boats, never to be returned. When the war was over, none was allowed to return to British Columbia, and three thousand Japanese Canadians were deported to Japan.

The United States interned all Japanese Americans after the attack on Pearl Harbour. Pearl Harbour, it should be noted, was not an invasion and did not touch continental United States. The 1940 U.S. census established that 116,947 American residents were of Japanese origin. Sixty percent were born in the United States. In 1942, that country interned—evacuated according to the official euphemism—all the 119,803 men, women, and children of Japanese origin.[17]

Countries are obsessed with the loyalty of their citizens in wartime. Every minority and every internal nation becomes suspicious. In 1917 Londoners rioted against Jews who were accused of being opposed to compulsory military service or conscription. In the United States, suspicious minorities were tarred and feathered or even lynched. In Canada, the loyalty of French Canadians was immediately questioned in both World Wars, as it was during the Boer War. French Canadians were called Zombies during the Second World War because of their opposition to conscription.

Former colonial possessions are inevitably among the first suspects of countries at war. Ireland, for instance, was independent from England since 1922 and remained neutral during the Second World War. When Winston Churchill suspected these former subjects of Her Majesty to be sympathetic to the Germans, he threatened to bomb all the ports in Ireland.

The treatment of minorities in wartime requires much further study. Suffice it to say that self-righteous human rights activists in Europe and North America would have been well advised to look closely at their own countries' records before pouncing on Rwanda.

◆

The invading army, known by the right thinking as a liberation army, settled in for a prolonged guerrilla war when they realized that the Rwandan army was tougher than had been expected. At the end of October 1990, the RPF pulled partly back into Uganda which it used as a base to launch guerrilla attacks. In November, however, Belgium joined Uganda in calling on Rwanda to negotiate with the invading army. Here was the "strategic stalemate" Ugandan President Museveni had talked about in August 1990. The United States and Britain soon joined the chorus of calls for negotiations.

Though the RPF was talking liberation and human rights to the international press in English and French, its writings in Kinyarwanda left no doubt as to its desire to return Rwanda to a pre-independence situation in which the Tutsi minority would dominate.[18] This was confirmed as the RPF behaved like all occupation armies do. They attacked and terrorized civilians, forcing them to flee in large numbers, and targeted the Hutu peasants rather than the Rwandan troops.

What liberation army can boast that it emptied one of the country's, and the world's, most densely populated areas? Two and a half years after the invasion, only 1800 people lived in an area of northern Rwanda that previously had a population of 800,000. As the "liberators" advanced, the Hutu peasants fled. By April 1993 Rwanda had more than one million internal refugees. That means one million farmers (one seventh of the total population) who are no longer producing on the most fertile lands in the country. It also means one million people to house and feed, and hundreds of thousands of young adults and children absent from school, which was a source of great anxiety.

The Rwandan Minister of Agriculture, Husbandry, and Forests in 1992, James Gasana, described the situation in the war torn Byumba prefecture north of Kigali in a book published in 2002. "A prefecture that had been the country's breadbasket now had the largest population in need of welfare and the highest mortality rate due to malnutrition."[19]

When have we seen a people flee from its liberators? It didn't happen in France (1940-1945), nor in Cuba (1951-1959), nor in Algeria (1954-1962). The "right and proper tale" would have us believe, however, that the invading RPF army were "liberators."

These "liberators" were also able to count on a powerful ally. That ally, known as the Structural Adjustment Program or SAP, was being imposed in unison by the World Bank, the International Monetary Fund, and USAID. Acronyms have a canny way of transmitting messages, and in this case it is particularly eloquent, both in English, SAP, and in French, PAS (*Programme d'ajustement structurel*). The message could not be clearer: *PAS d'argent* (no money) unless you SAP the very foundations of the society you built since 1960. That means deregulating the economy, devaluating currency, eliminating agricultural subsidies, privatizing utilities and state-owned corporations, laying off civil servants, and more. The result is what imperial powers are looking for, a failed African state.

Rwanda felt the impact immediately. Inflation increased from one percent in 1989 to twenty percent in 1991. Devaluation of the currency was even more brutal. In 1990, one U.S. dollar was worth 82 Rwandan Francs. In 1993, it was worth 183 Francs.

The taskmasters at the World Bank, the FMI, and USAID knew exactly what was happening. They could see an offshoot of the army led by their friend Ugandan president Yoweri Museveni pitted against a government led by Juvénal Habyarimana. Whereas Museveni was calling on Africa to abandon its anti neo-colonial rhetoric and declare loud and clear that Africa's problems were of its own making, Rwandan President Habyarimana had a relatively prosperous and stable economy but was not as favourably disposed to the new dogma brought down by the Bretton Woods institutions.

Privatization and a totally free-market economy presented specific problems for Rwanda. The social revolution of 1959 and independence combined with the growth of a public sector and educational institutions had enabled Rwandan Hutus to gain some economic power and prestige. The private sector, where incomes were much higher, remained largely dominated by Tutsis. The aggressive privatization and deregulation imposed by the Structural Adjustment Program meant an inevitable return towards what had been rejected since the 1960s and a reinforcement of the Tutsis' power in the economy.

Structural adjustment had another perverse effect on Rwanda. Funds would be granted to countries that downsized their armies. When Ugandan troops invaded Rwanda, the country officially reduced the size of its army. On paper all those Ugandan troops at war in Rwanda were no longer part of Museveni's army. Funding to Uganda therefore increased proportionally. Under the same policy, funding to Rwanda was cut since the Habyarimana government increased the size of its army threefold in order to fight the invaders. These were the funds used by Uganda to finance the war in Rwanda. James Gasana, who became Rwandan Defence Minister until he left the country in 1993, wrote a scathing criticism of that policy. "It is no secret that funds granted to two poor countries at war are used to procure weapons. That undercover funding by international development banks prevented international public opinion from understanding the international nature of the war."[20]

Each time the government of Rwanda hesitated to negotiate with the invader or showed reluctance during negotiations, the bankers in New York and Washington would put pressure on Kigali by refusing to provide the funds the government needed and counted on. Each time the RPF would gain new international recognition, the morale of the Rwandan armed forces would plummet as they increasingly got the impression they were fighting against the whole world. The war quite predictably aggravated latent hostility between the Hutu majority and the Tutsi minority.

The expression "peace process" then quietly and unsurprisingly crept into the vocabulary of the "international community" led by the United States and Britain. The "peace process" was to be initiated at Arusha, Tanzania. Peace process essentially means war, a war in which the sponsors of the process choose the winner before the meeting they call takes place. They then pretend to be neutral during negotiations. Having bought time, they tighten the noose around the designated loser's neck and prepare the ground to install a government that is totally subjected to their will. Peace process was on the lips of all the right thinking people, as was multiparty democracy.

CHAPTER 2

In the Name of Peace and Democracy

...a British Governor of Rhodesia in the 1950s
defined partnership between black and white
in his territory, apparently without any sarcasm,
as the partnership between the horse and its rider.

Chinua Achebe, *Hopes and Impediments*

In July 1990 President Juvénal Habyarimana announced his intention to introduce multiparty politics to Rwanda. This was two months before Ugandan troops invaded Rwanda. Habyarimana had been answering François Mitterrand's call made in June during a speech at La Baule, France. With the end of the Cold War that saw rich countries in Europe and America marching in lockstep with military leaders they had often put into power and who ran one-party systems, it was now decreed that time had come to adopt a new model touted to be the pinnacle of democracy.

Pushed by her friends and rivals, France invited African countries to commit to applying that model posthaste. In polite terms, French foreign minister Roland Dumas declared lyrically, "the winds of freedom blowing East must inevitably blow South too."

Diligently, Pope John Paul too bore that message when he visited Rwanda in 1990. The fact is that when invitations like that are sent from North to South they are the carrots; the stick follows closely. The real message was: "Do what you're told or we'll get together and cut you off, whether you are at war or not!"

Rwanda obeyed even though the country was at war. On June 10, 1991 the Rwandan Constitution was amended to allow for multiparty politics. Rwandan leaders were nonetheless told continually that it was too little, too late, and altogether too slow. Each of these warnings was accompanied directly or indirectly by reduced aid and stiffer funding and borrowing criteria. Adding insult to injury, the powers that be applied their new creed of multiparty politics selectively. During the same period in neighbouring Uganda, Yoweri Museveni, who shot his way to power between 1981 and 1986, held no elections and announced the creation of his specious *no party democracy*—a dictatorship by any other name is a dictatorship. Uganda and President Museveni just sailed along untroubled even though they blatantly bucked the "winds of freedom and democracy," which were supposedly blowing from North to South. What's more, the same matrix was never applied to the invading army, the Rwandan Patriotic Front. Paul Kagame's former comrade-in-arms and the RPF's head of Foreign Intelligence, Patrick Karegeya, was asked in 2013 how Paul Kagame rose to total power from before the beginning of the war in 1990 and why he was never challenged. His reply: "There were no challenges. It would be difficult for military people to challenge that type of decision. It's not like politics. And don't forget, we were at war, there was no place for politics and considerations about democracy."[1]

But "politics and considerations for democracy" were made mandatory for Rwanda under Habyarimana and he obeyed. Opposition parties formed and under intense international pressure Rwanda's first multiparty government was sworn in in April 1992. The government included members of all the major parties: President Habyarimana's party, Le Mouvement républicain national pour le développement et la démocratie (MRND), Le Mouvement démocratique républicain (MDR), Le Parti social démocrate (PSD), Le Parti démocrate chrétien (PDC) and Le Parti libéral (PL).

These new parties were obviously seeking power. They had to define their positions with regards to President Habyarimana, but also define themselves in relation to the occupying RPF army and its supporters throughout the world. Each of the new parties knew that it had to appeal to Belgian, American, French, and British diplomats, who proved to be the most important stakeholders, much more so than Rwandan citizens. The foreign powers appeared to side with the invading RPF army and were prepared to jettison President Habyarimana. Seeing the way the wind was blowing, the new opposition parties began to establish direct ties with the Rwandan Patriotic Front in the hope of gaining similar international support for themselves. Opposition party leaders thus met with the Rwandan Patriotic Front in Brussels from May 29 through June 3, 1992, and issued a joint press release. In fact, the opposition parties attended that meeting because the U.S. Assistant Secretary of State Herman Cohen demanded it.[2] In short, Rwandan opposition forces, instead of building a national coalition to fight the invading army, formed a coalition that included and protected the invader with the irresistible blessings of major Western powers.

Linking up with the enemy to obtain concessions from one's main opponent—in this case a weakened President Habyarimana—is a time-warn though dubious political strategy. The reasoning is limpid considering that real power was backing the RPF troops, yet in any other country at war meeting with invading troops is considered treason.

The army of the Rwandan Patriotic Front would have lost the war in December 1990 if Western powers had not been on its side. Many observers have reached this conclusion.[3] By the end of 1990 the invading army could count on the solid support of the United States, Britain, Uganda, and, increasingly, Belgium, while France was hedging its bets on Rwanda. The Socialist Party under

François Mitterrand was in power and had many RPF supporters in its midst. The invaders were therefore able to prolong the war for three and a half years and provoke dissension, demoralization, and division in all parts of Rwandan society.

None of the countries that forced Rwanda to negotiate during the war would have allowed such conditions to be imposed on them. They take, and have always taken, the necessary measures to rally the population against the enemy and eliminate obstacles to full mobilization. They do so whether they are directly attacked or invaded or not. Countries at war take a vast array of actions that include restrictions to freedom of opinion, freedom of the press, freedom of political activities, as well as special laws and constitutional amendments. The latter may be touted as temporary but they often remain after the war is over. Some governments at war or threatened by war are known to outlaw political movements and parties. Generally speaking, the people of the country and the country's allies understand and support these actions that are seen to be wartime measures only.

Nothing would be easier than to list the violations to basic standards of freedom and democracy in each of the countries that criticized Rwanda during the war from 1990 to 1994. Historical amnesia has conveniently erased these violations from the active memories of most people in Europe and America. They have become footnotes to a self-congratulatory narrative of valour and bravery.

Modern-day violations of these basic standards are attributed primarily to terrorism. They generally earn some support among the people because of the siege mentality that has been created and because of the prevailing cultural superiority with respect to non-Western countries who are blamed for the terrorism. The victims of modern-day violations (i.e., people locked up in the wake of September 11, 2001, prisoners in Guantanamo, Rwandan Hutu refugees) are often presented as people devoid of the culture of democracy and rights, which we are led to believe we have. They are thus undeserving of basic democratic rights.

How many young people in Canada or elsewhere know what was done during the Second World War to Camilien Houde, Mayor of Montreal, Canada's largest city? Under the War Measures Act the Royal Canadian Mounted Police arrested the very popular mayor and member of Québec's Legislative Assembly on August 9, 1940. Mayor Houde was interned near Ottawa for almost four years. He was never charged nor brought to trial. For sixteen months his wife and children were not allowed to visit him. The Canadian Government arbitrarily interned Mayor Houde because he had stated in a conversation with newspaper reporters that he was opposed to the army registering all men over sixteen years old. The next day *The Montreal Gazette* made that statement its headline and Camilien Houde was immediately arrested. Montreal's mayor was also interned because he had a number of Italians in his organisation. To this day people avoid talking about Camilien Houde for fear that they will be associated with the enemy.

During the Second World War, as in the First World War, if any Canadian political party was suspected of developing ties with political parties in any enemy country (i.e., Germany, Japan, Italy, Austria), Canada would have outlawed the local party and interned its leaders for the duration of the war and after. In comparison, Rwandan opposition parties were making it a point of honour and distinction to link up with the enemy. By 1993 and 1994 the pro-RPF circles within Rwanda were no longer hiding their political opinions. They boasted to anybody listening that a party so strongly supported by the United States could never lose.

In the same vein, how many young Canadians, or Quebecers, denounce the War Measures imposed in Canada in October 1970? What do they say about the five hundred middle-of-the-night arrests of journalists, poets, singers, and trade unionists, their detainment incommunicado, the ten thousand homes entered and searched, and the occupation of Québec by some 13,000 troops? More than forty years later, educators, political parties, and politicians rarely dare criticize Pierre Trudeau and the

Government of Canada openly for what they did in 1970. The reason is that they all fear that they will be associated with the enemy, in this case the *Front de libération du Québec* (FLQ).[4]

Countries in North America and Europe have passed draconian legislation to combat some illusory terrorist enemy both inside the countries and beyond their borders. People are spied on and arrested while political parties and movements are prohibited. Dirty campaigns of informing on suspicious neighbours have been deployed. Solidarity organizations are forced to disband in many countries that may never even have been targeted by the terrorists. Few people dare contest these measures however since they fear that they will be associated with the enemy.

The truth and the details in the cases mentioned have been quietly and conveniently forgotten because of the fear of guilt by association.

In 1940 Canada had not even been attacked when the War Measures were invoked. In 1970 the FLQ had only a few active cells that had kidnapped two people. In 2002 many countries that adopted strict anti-terrorist laws were not even hit by terrorists.

In contrast the invading RPF army that occupied a large swathe of Rwandan territory was operating 146 active clandestine cells in Kigali alone in 1993. Each time President Habyarimana and others tried to mobilize the population against the enemy, they were immediately accused of being Hutu extremists with genocidal intentions. We are supposed to believe that their actions are proof that they were on the "path of a genocide," as some "scholars" have written.

In Rwanda between 1990 and 1994 RPF terror was the rule, not the exception. The so-called donor countries nonetheless continued to force the Rwandan president to negotiate with the terrorists and to include in the government newly formed parties that were openly allied with the invader. In addition to the RPF's brutality, violence, and political assassinations, which caused hundreds of thousands of peasants in northern Rwanda to flee southwards, RPF agents carried out terrorist activities throughout

Internal Refugees, 1993
The Ugandan/RPF invasion forced more than one million Rwandans off their land and into makeshift camps north of Kigali.

Rwanda in an aim to divide the newly formed political parties. By targeting civilians rather than the military, the RPF became an organization that more resembled the European fascist parties of the 1930s that targeted crowded popular places than it did a liberation army.

When I visited Jean-Paul Akayesu in his prison cell in Mali where he is serving a life sentence he recounted an event that took place in the town of Taba just west of Kigali where he was burgomaster in 1993 and 1994.[5] "RPF agents put a bomb near a school. Seventeen school children were killed. Others were injured. They wanted to provoke a confrontation between my party (the opposition MDR) and the President's party (the MRND)." How does Jean-Paul Akayesu know that the RPF was responsible for those deaths? "After the RPF victory the criminals started talking openly about what they had done," says Akayesu. "The person responsible was prosecution Witness D who appeared before the International Criminal Tribunal in Arusha. His name is Ephrem Karengwa."

War, combined with the new multiparty system, had a devastating effect on Rwanda's civil service. Parties wishing to take power in Rwanda were more interested in their relations with the invader and with Western diplomats, who openly expressed sympathy with the RPF, than they were in the opinions of the Rwandan people.

Rwanda's Defence Minister James K. Gasana candidly described the situation in July 1993 just before the Arusha Peace Accord was signed. "This transition period [starting in April 1992] was characterized by the disintegration of the civil service illustrated by the paralysis of government services. This was due to the excessive polarisation in the civil service. Most civil servants were looking out for their own parties' interests instead of national interests ... This all contributed to decimate the cohesion that should be a feature of public administration whose only *raison d'être* is the interest of Rwandan citizens."[6]

Such an admission by a government minister is troubling, but it is not surprising considering the pressure exerted on the political parties. If taking power depends on the people's will as expressed in free elections, political parties wherever they are will make the good management of government affairs their top priority. On the other hand, if taking power depends on obtaining the blessing of diplomats from rich and powerful countries and from bankers in those same countries, and if that blessing is conferred in private meetings or during secret negotiations, political parties will do their utmost to show foreign diplomats and bankers that they already control the administration. By the same token, they will pay little attention to the needs and opinions of their fellow citizens who are clearly not the source of power in the country.

Should the invading army during negotiations sponsored by the same Western powers obtain much more power than the people would ever give it in free elections, namely the required political power to control government, then not only will the civil service likely disintegrate, but so will the country's entire social fabric. That is what happened in Rwanda between September 1993 and April 1994.

President Habyarimana and the leader of the Rwandan Patriotic Front signed the Arusha Peace Accord on August 4, 1993. According to Faustin Twagiramungu, who was designated to be prime minister of the broad-based transitional government established by the Accords, the parties would never have reached an agreement if the American, British, and Ugandan sponsors had not applied enormous pressure. "Neither the opposition parties nor President Habyarimana wanted an agreement like that," said Twagiramungu.[7] Only the RPF and its army came away happy because they had "stripped President Habyarimana of all his power." Former Prime Minister Twagirmungu was particularly angry about British participation in the Arusha negotiations. The British did not even have a consulate in Rwanda at that time. He also pointed out that the RPF army relied on the British intelligence network used by Ugandan President Yoweri Museveni.

The Arusha Peace Accord was supposed to solve many problems. It included provisions for power sharing in a broad-based transitional government, return of refugees to Rwanda, and return of the people displaced by the war in Rwanda. It also called for the deployment of a neutral international force, the integration of the RPF in Rwanda's national army, and the deployment of an RPF battalion in Kigali. In fact, the Arusha Peace Accord sealed the president's loss of power and effectively handed power over to the invading army.

The transitional government was to have twenty ministers and secretaries of state. The invading RPF and the president's party (the MRND) would each have five ministers, an unbelievable and incomprehensible parity. The other opposition parties shared the other ten ministries. It should be noted that all but one of the parties had signed the joint press release with the Rwandan Patriotic Front at the U.S.-sponsored meeting in Brussels in June 1992. The RPF was thus in a position to control the government of Rwanda.

The most surprising provision of the Arusha Accord concerns the integration of the RPF army in the Rwandan National Army. The crucial clauses in Article 74 of the Peace Accord is:

> During the establishment of the National Army, the proportions and distribution of Command posts between the two parties shall abide by the following principles:
>
> 1. The Government forces shall contribute 60% of the forces and the RPF 40% of the forces for all levels apart from the posts of Command described below.
> 2. In the chain of command, from the Army Headquarters to the Battalion, each party shall have a 50% representation for the following posts.[8]

An exhaustive list of military positions down to army school trainers follows. In addition to this formal division of power, the existing political allegiance of the Rwandan military must be factored in. According to Rwanda's former Defence Minister, James Gasana, the opposition parties close to the RPF and the RPF itself enjoyed the support of thirty-five percent and five percent of military personnel respectively.

In other words, if the Arusha Peace Accord had been applied, the RPF would have controlled the government of Rwanda and the army without ever having run in an election. Yet all it could boast was its army, the murderous war it had launched, and the steadfast support of the Americans and the British. People would like us to believe that this was accomplished in the name of the "winds of freedom and democracy" blowing from the North. Twenty years later, some people would have us go one step further and call that murderous war between 1990 and 1994 the 'Rwanda Liberation War.' As we go to press Hollywood is said to be preparing a big film titled *Before and After* with "liberation" being the central theme.

It is now known that the Rwandan Patriotic Army in alliance with the armies of Burundi and Uganda spearheaded the wars in the Democratic Republic of the Congo beginning in 1996. The precursor to those wars can be found in the military provisions of the 1993 Arusha Peace Accord. It is clear that the United States and Britain who oversaw that process were working on a roadmap that would lead to the installation of a regime and an army in Rwanda loyal to them during the post-Mobutu era in the Congo. Rwandan peace and national reconciliation were nowhere to be found on that roadmap. In a nutshell, if President Habyarimana, an ally of France and Mobutu, were to remain, it would be as a figurehead only. The Rwandan army would be controlled by the RPF who was allied unconditionally with Washington and London.

Recent testimony converges on this point. From the moment the first multiparty government was established in April 1992, no important minister in Rwanda was appointed without prior consultation with the United States Embassy. "With the breakdown of the Rwandan state," wrote James Gasana, "the country was in fact administered from beyond its borders." The prime minister designated for the transitional government, Faustin Twagiramungu, said essentially the same in an interview: "There was no longer any decision-making power in Rwanda." In fact, the Arusha Peace Accord only consolidated the transfer of decision-making power from Rwandans to foreign diplomats, mainly from the United States. The RPF was the dirty-handed go-between in this transfer.

A month after the Arusha Peace Accord was signed the Rwandan Patriotic Front received a democratic kick in the face from the Rwandan people. Serious people of good will should have taken note. In September 1993 the RPF ran candidates in municipal elections in the demilitarized zone of northern Rwanda. Voters flatly rejected them. Though the Rwandan voters' behaviour was predictable—the RPF, despite a few token Hutus, represented only the Tutsi minority and could never win an election based on 'one person one vote'—Western support for the RPF did not flinch.

◆

Heavy international pressure was applied to bring Rwanda to sign the Arusha Peace Accord even though it ran contrary to the interests of the Rwandan Government and the Rwandan people. Pressure dropped, however, when time came to provide troops for the neutral international force called for in the Accord which became the United Nations Aid Mission for Rwanda or UNAMIR. Neither the date of deployment nor the number of troops the parties had agreed upon was respected. The force was supposed to be in place thirty-seven days after the Accord was signed. In fact, it took four months to be deployed. The parties had agreed on 4500 troops; UNAMIR troops never exceeded 2500.

Many have blamed that delay on UN bureaucracy and its traditional lack of sensitivity. Similar reasons are advanced to explain the slow UN reaction during the killing that followed the shooting down of the presidential plane on April 6, 1994. It is much more likely that the Americans and the British paralysed the UN Security Council as they vied to take control of the African Great Lakes region from France. The delay foreshadowed others to come.

The UNAMIR force resulting from this Security Council skirmish also represented a victory for the two English-speaking powers. The Habyarimana government wanted French troops in the force whereas the Rwandan Patriotic Front strongly objected, accusing France of the worst crimes. The RPF succeeded in having Belgium provide the largest contingent followed by Bangladesh. The RPF and its sponsors in Washington and London scored another victory when the UN office in New York imposed English as the language of the mission. Imagine: an English-speaking army invades a French-speaking country and the so-called neutral UN forces are obliged to operate in the language of the invader. The use of English thus greatly undermined UNAMIR's credibility in the eyes of Rwandans. Moreover, UNAMIR interpreters who knew English, French, and Kinyarwanda were inevitably Tutsis.

Canada chose not to participate in UNAMIR. The Security Council however appointed a Canadian as force commander,

Lieutenant General Roméo Dallaire, because the United States wanted a French Canadian.[9] General Dallaire was one of the first Canadians appointed to a senior position in the Rwandan crisis. Others would follow. The key to such nominations was for the appointee to speak French fluently without being a French national and to have no political or emotional attachment to France. Roméo Dallaire fit the bill perfectly and never did he let his superiors down. Throughout the mission, Dallaire provoked and baited the French to the point that Paris pressured Canada to have Roméo Dallaire removed as commander.[10]

Rwanda had been paralysed by a Western-sponsored, two-pronged attack aimed to consolidate the RPF army's military gains and transfer power from Kigali to that proxy army's headquarters in Mulindi. Catchy phrases like "peace process" and "multiparty democracy" were invoked to justify the two-pronged attack on Rwanda, but as usual those phrases only served to camouflage reality, which was the exact opposite: war and dictatorship. The same Western powers that invented those catchy but deceitful phrases never miss a chance to claim that Africa lacks a culture of democracy and needs Western help to learn it.

CHAPTER 3

The Power of a Word

There is nothing like belling the cat.

Victor Hugo

In the current situation in Africa and the world, when you play with words you play with lives.

Aminata Traore, *Le viol de l'imaginaire*

Twenty years after the assassination on April 6, 1994 that escalated the Rwandan tragedy beyond imagination, the relentless hunt for those who have been tagged as *génocidaires* goes on. In the name of that hunt, sanctified by the United States, Canada, the United Kingdom, Belgium, and other Western nations, we sat back and watched the army of the Rwandan Patriotic Front bomb refugee camps in the eastern Congo; we applauded as hundreds of thousands of refugees were forced to return to Rwanda in flagrant violation of the 1951 Refugee Convention. We then watched passively or simply turned the other way while the same army accompanied by the Ugandan and Burundian armies invaded the Congo and inflicted a merciless war that has left millions dead. The countries of Central Africa have been turned upside down in the name of hunt for *génocidaires*.

Rwandan prisons are overflowing with "*génocidaires*" waiting to be tried: in 2003 there were more than 140,000 according to

Paul Kagame; in 2013, upwards of 60,000 prisoners remained in squalid Rwandan prison. Some observers have remarked that prison and the traditional "Gacaca" national justice system restored in 2003 have been used to bring back a form of serfdom for the Hutu majority which had been abolished following the social revolution and Rwandan independence in 1962. Prisoners earn their "freedom" essentially by admitting to crimes, but their punishment is to work as serfs for the new Rwandan ruling minority.

An entire book could and should be written about Victoire Ingaribe. Ms Ingaribe, who dared to form an opposition party in Rwanda and run for president in 2010, was put under house arrest during the election, was arrested shortly after and was sentenced in 2012 to eight years in prison for ... "genocide denial" and other charges.

Whatever their political stripe or background, Rwandan Hutus—and Tutsis—have been living and continue to live in fear of being accused of genocide, arrested, and brought to court in Arusha, in Kigali or in countries such as Canada that have adopted the principle of universal jurisdiction. Many fear assassination. Though Rwandans are now dispersed throughout the world, nowhere do they feel safe. Most astounding, and ridiculous, is the fact that between 1994 and 2000 following the takeover by the Rwandan Patriotic Front, the two Prime Ministers who led the RPF governments, both Hutus, were accused of being involved in genocide.

The first was Faustin Twagiramungu, leader of the Mouvement démocratique républicain (MDR), the main political party opposed to President Habyarimana. Faustin Twagiramungu was sworn in as Prime Minister of Rwanda on July 19, 1994 when the Rwandan Patriotic Front took over. He remained in power until August 28, 1995 when he fled to Belgium where he now lives. He returned to Rwanda in 2003 as the opposition presidential candidate and now leads the Rwanda Dream Initiative.

In 2002 Mr. Twagiramungu applied for a visa at the Canadian Embassay in Paris in order to speak at a conference at the Université du Québec à Montréal where he had studied in the

1970s. After being interrogated at length at the Canadian Embassy, to his surprise he received a short letter from the Embassy denying him a visa. A few weeks later, the Canadian daily *The National Post* ran an article about war criminals in Canada and referred to the Canadian Embassy's refusal to grant a visa to the former Rwandan leader who, according to *The National Post*, had been involved in the genocide.[1] In short, the Prime Minister of the government that supposedly ended the genocide had now become a *génocidaire*. Canada had already received Prime Minister Faustin Twagiramngu with all honours in December 1994 when he was looking for funding to rebuild Rwanda under the RPF. Either Canada's institutional memory is short and selective or, more likely, the country has a policy of supporting the RPF government at all costs. Canada's ambassador to France, Raymond Chrétien, refused to take responsibility for the Embassy's actions: "The people responsible for visas here at the Embassy must have reasons that I am unaware of," he said in an interview.[2]

The second Rwandan prime minister targeted was Pierre-Célestin Rwigema. Mr. Rwigema was sworn in immediately after Faustin Twagiramungu's departure in 1995. He was a leader of the same party, the Mouvement démocratique républicain (MDR). Prime Minister Rwigema held office until February 2000 and diligently sought to bring the *génocidaires* to justice. Quite ironically, he represented the Rwandan Government at the solemn ceremony inaugurating the International Criminal Tribunal in Arusha on January 8, 1996. His speech on the importance of capturing and judging thc *génocidaires* was particularly eloquent.[3]

When relations soured between Prime Minister Pierre-Célestin Rwigema and the Rwandan Patriotic Front at the end of the 1990s, Mr. Rwigema decided to emigrate to the United States. Shortly after leaving he learned that Rwanda had issued an international arrest warrant for him and that he was being charged with the crime of ... genocide. Rwigema pointed out how former Rwandan President Pasteur Bizimungu, a loyal RPF leader from 1990 on, was imprisoned in Rwanda for founding an opposition movement, the Party for

Democratic Renewal. Bizimungu had been president from 1994 until March 2000. The former president was accused of "embracing a genocidal ideology." According to Rwigema, "If you are Hutu and you dare criticize the RPF regime, you are treated as a genocide perpetrator with the consequences of being jailed or killed. If you are a Tutsi and you talk against the system, you are treated as a negative element and sidelined. The RPF uses the accusation of 'genocide' to silence influential Hutus."[4] The list of former RPF dignitaries who have fallen out of grace only to be accused of genocide has burgeoned and includes some of Paul Kagame's closest collaborators.

As long as the word "genocide" and all its derivatives dominate the description of events in Rwanda in 1994 and thereafter, peace in Central Africa and national reconciliation in Rwanda will be unattainable. Who would ever want to sit down and negotiate with people suspected of having taken part in such a horrible crime? What international power could ever agree to broker a regional peace conference with African leaders accused of harbouring *génocidaires*? How can serious and credible representatives of the vast majority of Rwandans come forward and take their rightful place when every one of them could be accused anytime and anywhere of having been involved in genocide or of embracing the ideology of genocide?

The term is a gag order, which obviously pleases Kigali. But it is also very useful for Western powers, and particularly the United States, who brandish it like a weapon of mass destruction aimed at any African leader or regime that bucks the current. "You see what happened to Habyarimana and to Rwanda? Be careful! It could happen to you too." Though the official reason for launching the never-ending war in the Congo was the refugee crisis and the hunt for Rwandan *génocidaires*, it is obvious that war in the Congo has nothing to do with *génocidaires* and everything to do with domination of the post-Mobutu Democratic Republic of the Congo and a scramble for its riches.

Other countries that have lived through crises like the one that shook Rwanda from 1990 through 1994 have reacted in different ways. International criminal justice has not always been seen as the way to resolve deep-seated problems. In an interview former UN Secretary General Boutros Boutros-Ghali, who presided over the creation of International Criminal Tribunal for Rwanda, hinted in 2002 that he might have done things differently now.

"In some cases, we have created Truth Commissions," noted the former secretary general. "In South Africa, for instance, efforts were made to identify the criminals, but they were not punished. They are prevented from causing harm, but are not sentenced. Truth commissions are based on what is probably the Christian principle that mercy and forgiveness are more important than justice. In fact, it is more important to maintain the unity of a country than to try to impose justice and tear the country up even more. We have to know how to forget and sometimes forgive or else we'll find ourselves with a coup d'État, a prolonged war or a new war ten years later." Are these prophetic words from Boutros Boutros-Ghali? Or is it a simple observation of what has happened in the Great Lakes region of Central Africa?

Boutros-Ghali also recalled that following the Second World War General de Gaulle turned a blind eye to a lot of collaboration with the Nazis. He probably knew that justice at any cost would have obstructed any real national reconciliation in France. The former Secretary General also considered that the Maurice Papon trial fifty years after the events took place was an error. In both cases cited by Boutros-Ghali, Apartheid South Africa and Vichy France, the systematic planning of discrimination, oppression, and massacres based on race and religion are easier to identify and adjudicate than in the case of Rwanda under the Habyarimana government and after his assassination.

Why then did the United Nations not establish a Truth Commission in Rwanda as it did in South Africa, El Salvador, and Guatemala? Boutros-Ghali's answer to the question was curt and categorical: "Because the Tutsis wanted revenge."

Though justice is the antithesis of revenge, by creating the International Criminal Tribunal for Rwanda in November 1994 the United Nations astonishingly gave all the trappings of justice to what Secretary General Boutros Boutros-Ghali says was the Rwandan Patriotic Front's desire for revenge. Moreover, the Security Council resolution creating the Tribunal and subsequent actions by the United Nations have led international public opinion to consider the genocide itself to be like an "adjudicated fact" not to be contested. This of course jibed perfectly with the political strategy adopted by the Rwandan Patriotic Front well before 1994. The RPF's desire for revenge muted into a lofty and honourable justification for every military action taken since July 1994. As we shall see in Chapter 13, adjudicated facts about Rwanda are few and far between.

Two specific events that often go unnoticed contributed to the official sanctioning of the use of the word "genocide" to describe the entire Rwandan tragedy. The first was a conference held in Kigali organized by the Office of the President of Rwanda attended by Efraim Zuroff of the Simon Wiesenthal Center and Michael Berenbaum of the US Holocaust Memorial Museum, among others. Both were invited to make proposals on the memorialization of genocide. Efraim Zuroff then became an advisor to the Rwandan government in its hunt for *génocidaires.*[5] From that point on Zionists throughout the world were prepared to share the use of the term with Rwandan Tutsis, which has never been the case for the Armenians, largely because of Israel's strategic alliance with Turkey. The second event less than a year later was Paul Kagame's official visit to Israel where he received all the honours from Israeli Prime Minister Benjamin Netanyahu.

The Western powers backing the RPF claim that they are only seeking to bring justice to that part of Africa and economic development. Our knowledge of the history of European—and American—colonization and exploitation of Africa should have protected us from believing such fairy tales.

◆

Paul Kagame in Israel, October 1996.
Paul Kagame was received in Israel by Prime Minister Benjamin Netanyahu in October 1996; the meeting sealed their alliance and provided Israel's blessing to the RPF for the use of the phrase "genocide against the Tutsis." Shortly after that meeting, Rwandan troops invaded the Congo and attacked the refugee camps. (Photo credit: *Africa International*)

Was there genocide in Rwanda in 1994?

On September 14, 1994 on CBC's French language television magazine *Le Point*, General Roméo Dallaire answered a question from a Rwandan who lived in Québec City: "In your opinion, was there a genocide in Rwanda, that is the carrying out of a plan to eliminate ethnic Tutsis in Rwanda?"

"The plan was more political. The aim was to eliminate the coalition of moderates ... I think that the excesses that we saw were beyond people's ability to plan and organize. There was a process to destroy the political elements in the moderate camp. There was a breakdown and hysteria absolutely ... But nobody could have foreseen or planned the magnitude of the destruction we saw ... I would say there was a national genocide, a genocide based on a political basis, not only ethnic," replied Roméo Dallaire. "Many Hutus and many Tutsis were killed... I think that the explosion we saw could not have been planned. I don't think that anybody could ever have planned an explosion of that magnitude." Note that if Dallaire said that in 2014, he would be lumped in with the genocide deniers and negationists. Yet that was his description upon returning from Rwanda.[6]

Roméo Dallaire refused all my requests for an interview. Since his declarations after 1994 have been incoherent to say the least, I hoped to ask him if he maintained his September 1994 position.[7] General Dallaire's interpretation of the events in Rwanda has changed over the years, which is not surprising considering the enormous pressure put on him.

Dallaire was military commander of the United Nations multinational force UNAMIR in April 1994. Jacques-Roger Booh-Booh was the UN Secretary General's special envoy responsible for political relations, and thus Dallaire's superior. His political attaché during the crisis was Gilbert Ngijol from Cameroon. Ngijol's view of events in Rwanda resembles Roméo Dallaire's September 1994 position. Unlike General Dallaire however, Gilbert Ngijol did not alter his position.

"There was no genocide against Tutsis in Rwanda," Ngijol insisted in an interview in Paris in November 2002. "Among the rank and file population, there was little animosity between Hutus and Tutsis before the assassination of President Habyarimana on April 6. But after, it was another story," he said shaking his head. "I remember one day just after the president was assassinated. I was on the third floor of the Meridien Hotel in Kigali. In one direction, I saw RPF soldiers killing women and children. On the other side, I saw militias doing the same thing. There's no way that could have been planned."[8]

Former Prime Minister Faustin Twagiramungu categorically rejects the idea that the killings were planned. "The RPF army may have killed more people than the Interahamwe militias did," he declared. Under oath at the Tribunal in Arusha Twagiramungu testified that probably more Hutus than Tutsis were killed. He pointed out that RPF soldiers took pictures of bodies of people in President Habyarimana's party, the MRND. The RPF had killed those people. Obviously most were Hutus. They then used the pictures of Hutus as proof of the genocide against Tutsis. "We know they did it because some of the victims in the pictures were wearing hats belonging to the president's party."

Even Justice Louise Arbour, Chief Prosecutor at the International Criminal Tribunal for Rwanda from 1996 to 1999, inferred that things were not as clear as some terrible simplifiers would have us believe. Following a speech in Paris on the International Criminal Court in November 2002, the Kenyan journalist Ruth Nabakwe asked the former Chief Prosecutor why the Tribunal only indicted Hutus and no Tutsis.[9] "Do you foresee the Tribunal indicting Tutsis in the future?" Though Louise Arbour made a career for herself as a renowned hunter of *génocidaires*, her answer was troubling. "We must avoid seeing the world purely in ethnic terms," she said. "It is not only a question of Tutsis and Hutus, but a question of political formations and alliances."

After all those years, former Chief Prosecutor Louise Arbour admitted that the massacres were political in nature, and not only ethnic. Yet the *sine qua non* of genocide is that the victims have a common ethnic, religious, racial or national identity. That is the fundamental characteristic of the only genocide that is fully agreed upon internationally, the genocide of Jews by the Nazis. If people who were so close to events or who were mandated to investigate them consider that the massacres were political, why are Rwandan Hutus still being burdened by this overwhelming and imprescriptible charge?[10]

Ramsey Clark was United States Attorney General and Assistant Attorney General under John F. Kennedy and Lyndon B. Johnson. He drafted and supervised the adoption and application of Civil Rights legislation in the mid 1960s. Beginning in 1995, he was counsel to the late Élisaphan Nkatirutimana, the Seventh-day Adventist pastor who was indicted by the ICTR for crimes of genocide at the age of seventy, extradited from the United States to Arusha, found guilty in February 2003, and sentenced to ten years in prison. Mr. Nkatirutimana died in 2007. For Clark, crying genocide is like crying murder: it does not mean that a murder was committed.

"The use of the word genocide in such a pervasive undefined way as it is used in public discussion and media discussion about Rwanda is an attempt to demonize and dehumanize the Hutu peoples," insists Ramsey Clark. "The insistence that there is only one ethnic group that is in conspiracy to destroy all the members of another group is contrary to possibility and to all experience. It's an effort to simply manufacture consent of public opinion to condemn the great majority of the people of Rwanda. They talk of Tutsis and this thing called moderate Hutus, which probably means Hutus who supported the RPF. They don't want to put it in a political basis, they want to put it strictly on an ethnic basis, which is a terrible falsehood.

"It's a political struggle, a political struggle that has been going on for years. Everybody knew that it was a political struggle since the colonial period. The exiled groups that had been colonial surrogates, the dominant Tutsi, had been trying to overthrow the government of post-colonial Rwanda. They invaded seven times between 1960 and 1967. Pretty dangerous too." What Ramsey Clark considered "pretty dangerous too" were what is known as the Inyenzi wars.

◆

It is particularly interesting to observe how the charge of "genocide against ethnic Tutsis" became part of the official narrative about Rwanda. Following the RPF victory in 1994, some people with fertile, elastic imaginations and hidden political agendas tried to prove that the genocide began in 1959 with Rwanda's social revolution that resulted in the abolition of the monarchy and Rwandan independence in 1962. The accusation is about as subtle as a George W. Bush speech; but it is not without method. It is essentially a convenient blanket rejection of everything Rwandans achieved since independence and it sullies or compromises the reputation of everybody who participated in any way in the development of Rwanda since then.

One striking example is the late Georges-Henri Lévesque, the Dominican priest from Québec City who founded the National

University of Rwanda. Father Lévesque was also known as the mentor for those who led Québec's Quiet Revolution. Articles on Father Lévesque and his contribution to Rwanda unfailingly draw a causal relationship between his work and the "genocide," even though he left Rwanda at the end of the 1960s. Shortly before he died, Father Lévesque wrote an article in the Montreal daily *Le Devoir* denouncing attempts to link him and his work to the people who were being blamed for the massacres.

If we stick to facts and leave imagination to poets and novelists, the first use of the "genocide" charge in the international narrative dates to January 28, 1993. It was used at a meeting with the press organized by William Schabas who was a member of an International Commission of Inquiry that had just returned from a two-week mission to Rwanda to investigate human rights violations.[11] Schabas was aware that members of the Commission had not reached a consensus on the use of the term, but he jumped the gun and made the accusation immediately after he returned from Rwanda. Schabas repeated the charge in an international press release he drafted to accompany the final report issued on March 8, 1993.[12] The press release was entitled "Genocide and War Crimes in Rwanda." The charge is absent from the final report because Kenneth Roth, executive director of New York-based Human Rights Watch, threatened to withdraw his organization's sponsorship and signature from the report if it contained the charge.[13]

Eleven days after the Commission left Rwanda, on February 8, 1993 RPF troops launched a massive attack in northern Rwanda supposedly in reaction to the revelations. This "punitive" attack, as they called it, resulted in thousands of civilian casualties and brought the number of internal refugees camped in and around Kigali to more than one million. The Rwandan Patriotic Front released a press statement explaining that it had broken the cease-fire in order to stop the "genocide" and counter the presence of French troops.[14] The "punitive" attack doubled the territory occupied by the invading RPF army and put it within thirty kilometres of Kigali. The RPF withdrew only after a cease-fire was reached, but the territory it had taken was declared to be a neutral and demilitarized zone, thus effectively removed from control of the Rwandan Government.

Aminata Traore, a former Malian Minister of Culture in the 1990s, has written, "In the current situation in Africa and the world, when you play with words you also play with lives."[15] Westerners who play and have played with the word "genocide" have also played dangerously with Rwandan lives. Béatrice Umutesi, for example, described how the RPF "punished" the population of the Byumba region north of Kigali after the charge of genocide was released internationally. This was in February 1993.

> Thursday morning the rebels began a clean-up operation in the area. Everyone—men, women, and children—was summoned, supposedly for an informational meeting. People were confident. The rebels were courteous and the peasants had nothing against them. It seems that things began to sour when they got to where this meeting was to take place. The rebels forced the peasants into houses, locked them from the outside, and then attacked them with grenades. The survivors were finished off with knives. The person who told me this story had himself miraculously survived the massacre. Finding himself alive under the bodies of his dead companions, he took advantage of the nighttime to escape and was able to join the other displaced persons in the camp at Rusine, where I met him a few days later.[16]

According to the "right and proper tale," the RPF "rebels" referred to by Beatrice Umutesi were the saviours and liberators who put an end to genocide. The methods and the cold-blooded nature of the massacre described by Ms Umutesi would become a recognizable pattern wherever the Rwandan Patriotic Front would go, be it Kigali, Kibeho or the entire Democratic Republic of the Congo. The perpetrators would always be conveniently qualified as "rebels" since "rebels" usually fight the good fight.

After January 28, 1993 the charge of genocide appeared in all RPF documents and was heard in all speeches and interviews made by the RPF, its friends, and its representatives throughout

Marie-Béatrice Umutesi
Author of *Surviving the Slaughter, The Ordeal of a Rwandan Refugee in Zaïre.*

the world. This was fourteen months before the presidential plane was shot down on April 6, 1994, the event that later was alleged to have triggered genocide. For strategic reasons, the Anglo-American alliance did not support the charge immediately, but most of the so-called human rights and humanitarian workers from Europe and North America began using the term with the ardour of a nineteenth-century Christian missionaries or modern born-again Christian.

CHAPTER 4

Scouts at Her Majesty's Service

It's difficult to understand the Rwandan drama when you depend only on a short stay in the country and on informers who work for specific interests.

Georges-Henri Lévesque, February 1, 1995[1]

"Before October 1990, there was not a single human rights organization in Rwanda. After the invasion they grew like mushrooms," declared Faustin Twagiramungu, prime minister of Rwanda in 1994 and 1995 and presidential candidate in 2003. "As for international NGOs, we really had no idea what they were up to. I met them all because I led a political party opposed to the Habyarimana government."[2]

Victories loosen tongues and make people careless. We now know that the Rwandan Patriotic Front operated thirty-six active clandestine cells in Rwanda when it invaded on October 1, 1990 and that these cells worked through human rights groups.[3] The groups created after 1990 were supported financially and politically by the large European and North American human rights organizations such as Human Rights Watch/Africa in New York the Fédération internationale des droits de l'Homme in Paris, the

International Centre for Human Rights and Democratic Development in Montreal (later Rights and Democracy), African Rights in London, and several others. During the Rwandan war from 1990 to 1994 these groups provided the invading RPF army with the veneer of respectability it needed.

Former Prime Minister Faustin Twagiramungu claims that the international human rights groups were terribly biased before they even arrived in Rwanda. "They were all in close contact with the Tutsi diaspora dominated by the RPF." Gilbert Ngijol is even more emphatic. The political attaché to UN secretary general's special envoy maintains that, "Financial support for the Rwandan human rights groups was a way to launder aid to the RPF army."

Though many human rights declarations and reports were issued during the war, one commission stands out because of its devastating influence on the course of the war, but also because of its dishonesty. The report was published in March 1993 by three of the above human rights groups and one African organization. The very title of the report betrays its bias: "Report of the International Commission of Inquiry into human rights violations in Rwanda since October 1, 1990."[4]

By limiting the investigation into rights violations after October 1, 1990, the commission conveniently avoided investigating the worst crime in international law, namely the crime against peace and national sovereignty perpetrated by the invading RPF army. Such selectivity compromises the whole report. One wonders how so-called international human rights specialists could sign such a report without feeling compelled, if only for their professional reputations, to ask the obvious first question on rights violations: who started the war?

In September 1994 two of the authors, William Schabas and André Paradis, showed how shoddy the commission's work was in a reply to an article criticizing the report in the Montreal daily *La Presse*.[5] "The date was chosen," they wrote, "only because that was the date chosen by the Rwandan human rights organizations who sponsored the commission."[6]

Faustin Twagiramungu
Leader of a political party opposed to President Habyarimana, Faustin Twagiramungu was prime minister of Rwanda after the RPF took power from July 1994 until August 1995 when he fled to Belgium.

It is now known that the groups who sponsored the commission were either founded directly by the RPF or infiltrated by it. One important sponsor, the *Association rwandaise pour la défense des droits de l'Homme*, was founded—quite the coincidence—on September 30, 1990, the day before the RPF invaded Rwanda. Its founding chairman was Alponse-Marie Nkubito, who was seconded to the International Commission of Inquiry during its visit to Rwanda in 1993. Nkubito was appointed minister of justice in the first government set up immediately following the RPF victory in July 1994. There is no doubt now that the RPF, the aggressor in a murderous war in Rwanda, was the driving force behind the 1993 commission.

Even if one disregards the dubious links between the commission and the RPF, the report reeks of collusion since it barely mentions crimes committed by the RPF. Though commission investigators spent two weeks in Rwanda, they only spent two hours in territory occupied by the RPF army. William Schabas, in a self-aggrandizing article, wrote that the commission went there only "to demonstrate our impartiality."[7] Whereas the Habyarimana Government gave the commission full freedom to investigate, the RPF only allowed commission members to meet witnesses in the presence of armed RPF officers and soldiers. Under such restrictions and with so little time to look into RPF rights violations, the commission should have refused to issue the report until it had thoroughly investigated RPF-controlled territory for the same length of time and under the same conditions it had enjoyed in government-controlled territory. The commission chose rather to sanction a selective, limited, and partial inquiry that was inherently unjust.

The report is a sham because of the time period chosen. It is a sham because of the commission's collusion with the RPF. It is also a sham because of self-imposed limits to the commission's mandate. Schabas and Paradis claimed that their "commission was in fact indifferent about the identity of the aggressor, because international humanitarian law is not concerned about that question."[8] Legalists seem to enjoy compartmentalizing international law but common sense demands that the worst crime of all be investigated when that crime puts the lives of millions at stake. Moreover, this convenient distinction between international humanitarian law and international law has proven to be a gold mine for some jurists who proudly hunt down "international criminals" while working for the worst criminals.

Though the authors of the commission's report claim to be learned jurists working in the tradition of Nuremberg, they chose to reduce the scope of their work in a manner that nobody would have dreamed of doing in the first international criminal tribunal established in Nuremberg in 1945. The Nuremberg Tribunal looked first and foremost at the worst crime, namely the crime against peace: the planning, preparation, initiation and waging of war of aggression. It then investigated how the war was conducted.

Schabas and Paradis were also mistaken about the relation between the right to self-determination and other human rights. The World Conference of the United Nations on Human Rights held in Vienna in June 1993 reaffirmed the spirit of Nuremberg. The Vienna Declaration and the Action Program specifies that the denial of the right of self-determination constitutes a human rights violation. Peoples have the right to legitimately engage in self-defence against all forms of foreign domination and occupation. Human rights are not limited to civil and political rights or to economic and social rights considered independently. They include the full right to self-determination, national sovereignty, and independence, which encompasses the right not to be the target of foreign aggression as Rwanda was in October 1990.[9]

To appreciate the importance of the crime that the commission chose to ignore, it is edifying to return to the Nuremberg rulings. Judge Norman Birkett from the Nuremberg Tribunal wrote: "The charges in the Indictment that the defendants planned and waged aggressive wars are the charges of utmost gravity. [...] To initiate a war of aggression, therefore, is not only an international crime; it is the supreme international crime differing only from the other war crimes in that it contains within itself the accumulated evil of the whole."

The commission also erred by ignoring the African Charter on Human and Peoples' Rights when it pompously listed the legal instruments that guided its work. The African Charter compels signatories to protect the national sovereignty of other signatory states and that prohibits the use of one country's territory by subversive elements or by refugees to invade another country. Signatories of the African Charter must prevent subversive or terrorist activities from being launched from their territory. By its very title, the African Charter on Human and Peoples' Rights proclaims that individual and collective rights are inseparable and reflects the concerns of those who devised the Charter, such as Léopold Sédar Senghor, to preserve peace in African countries whose borders had been drawn by European colonialists. If the commission had used the African Charter it would necessarily have investigated the October 1990 invasion of Rwanda by troops from Uganda.

The commission could have published its report but with a formal disclaimer about the numerous and serious shortcomings. On the contrary, it chose to launch the report with a massive media and public relations campaign vaunting the scope, credibility, and prestige of the commission and its authors. A lobbying campaign followed. All the foreign embassies and ministries were targeted, as were the major European and North American funding organizations. The international reaction was swift and devastating. Belgium recalled its ambassador from Kigali. Within months Canada, citing the report, suspended twenty million dollars of aid to Rwanda's national university in Butare. The report became the pretext for an arms embargo on Rwanda while the invading RPF army had easy access to all the weaponry it needed. From March 1993 on the Commission's report was the backdrop to all international meetings about or directly involving the Habyarimana Government.

The collusion between commission members and the RPF has been unambiguously established. As indicated in Chapter 3, the RPF army used the commission's "revelations" to justify its major "punitive" offensive in northern Rwanda in February 1993. An RPF leader however had already written a letter to the pro-RPF newspaper *Isibo* on December 26, 1992 in which he announced that the invading army would wait for the report to be published before launching its offensive and breaking the cease-fire that had held since July 1992.[10] The results of the report were obviously a foregone conclusion for the Rwandan Patriotic Front.

Over and above the report's limited scope and the unacceptable relationship between the RPF and commission members, the whole operation reeks of colonialism.

A commission comprising mainly American, Canadian, and French nationals spends two weeks in an African country and a month later issues a report that becomes the gospel in Western foreign affairs departments. Six of ten commission members admitted that they knew nothing about Rwanda before going there in January 1993. None spoke Kinyarwanda, Rwanda's national language.

In any other situation candidates for an important commission like this one with no experience or knowledge of the country in question would be expected to decline to participate to avoid the disapproval of their peers and the public. This commission's members had no such qualms. Could it be because they were dealing with remote Africa? Some even vaunted their lack of knowledge of Central Africa, saying that they had to look for Rwanda on the map before getting on the plane. As will be shown, the habit of boasting about one's poor grasp of Africa prior to going on a mission to that continent has paradoxically been a constant for centuries in popular literature. It is a way to emphasize the gulf that separates Europe and Africa.

For some commission members the mission appears to have been a lark. For instance, in a macabre description of grave-digging in northern Rwanda, William Schabas has himself identified as "Humphrey Bogart, alias Bill," obviously a reference to the adventurer Bogart played in *The African Queen*, the Oscar-winning film shot in the "Dark Continent," as the film preview boasts, in 1951 when colonialism was still in vogue.

Imagine the outcry if an international commission of African jurists who had never been in Canada and spoke neither English nor French came to investigate the living conditions in First Nations communities such as Attawapiskat. What if the same commission went to the United States to look into prison conditions for African Americans or the treatment of Muslims in that country since September 11, 2001? Chances are that the plane carrying the African commissioners would not even make it on to the runway of an African airport.

The International Commission of Inquiry's report on Rwandan human rights became an important building block on which the official narrative was erected. Every book on Rwanda refers to it. Every film and television report cites it as proof of the genocidal intentions of Rwandan Hutus. Commission members became the main source of information about Rwanda in their respective countries. Media and foreign affairs departments sought them out. Reporters no longer had to find Rwandans to explain what was going on in their country. New resident experts with some two weeks' experience in the country could now explain everything simply... and simplistically.

Some authors of the report dropped all pretence of neutrality immediately after President Habyarimana was assassinated and especially after the Rwandan Patriotic Front took power in July 1994. A serious commission should have demanded that members maintain a certain reserve or neutrality whatever the outcome of the war. One commission member, Jean Carbonare, began working directly for the RPF as early as July 1994.[11] William Schabas has travelled back and forth from Canada to Kigali and basically operated as an RPF flack. He managed to obtain considerable Canadian aid money for the RPF and regularly boasted about being the author of that government's organic genocide law. Rwanda became a staging point for his international career that has included constant defence of that country and its strongman up to and including expert witness testimony for the Crown Prosecution in extradition hearings in the United Kingdom. He claimed that those threatened with extradition would get a fair trial despite vast testimony to the contrary, yet the court concluded that his "reliability as a dispassionate expert" was undermined by the selectivity of his expert report, particularly about extra-judicial killings.[12] Quite unbelievably, despite his verifiably close ties with the Rwandan government, some courts and media continue to consider him a "neutral" expert.

The late Alison Des Forges promoted herself as the expert of experts in all the major trials in Arusha as though she understood

Rwandans better than they understood themselves. The ICTR has treated her as the most expert among expert witnesses. (For more on Alison Des Forges, please see Appendix II). "Alison Des Forges behaves as if she is Rwanda's honorary consul," complained former Prime Minister Faustin Twagiramungu in 2002. "When I met her for the first time in 1992, even though she had done her thesis on Rwanda, it was obvious she knew very little about Rwanda." Supporters of the "right and proper" make much of Ms Des Forges' vast knowledge of Rwanda and of her selfless dedication. They conveniently forget to mention that she was employed by the United States State Department in 1990 and 1992 and that she maintained close relations with the US National Security Council and the Pentagon throughout the 1990s.[13]

With the zeal of a Javert hounding Jean Valjean in *Les Misérables*, Alison Des Forges and William Schabas have pursued Rwandan Hutus throughout the world, appearing regularly as expert witnesses in criminal and extradition hearings.[14] Other commission members, such as Éric Gillet and Philippe Dahinden, also became expert prosecution witnesses in a variety of trials, including those at the ICTR in Arusha.

Twenty years later important lessons can be learned about that commission and its impact on the unfolding events in Rwanda. Human rights are the unofficial religion and uncontested foreign policy of Western countries and particularly the United States. Like the environment, democracy, and motherhood, everybody is obviously in favour of human rights. Who could think of being against them? Such unanimity is always dangerous. When the slightest doubt is raised about someone's commitment to such motherhood issues, the unanimity mutates into intolerance and provokes an almost religious fervour that drowns out the facts. When that happens the normal rules guiding international relations give way to the mentality of the lynch mob or the inquisition. "Aren't we all just nice, reasonable and tolerant people? The problem is those people over there. We'll stone them and everything will be fine!" The 1993 International Commission of Inquiry on Human Rights Violations in Rwanda effectively became the template for Western humanitarian intervention.

The Rwandan Patriotic Front or its advisors understood the nature of Western public opinion, particularly in the United States. They knew that they could easily find craven visibility seekers who would carry the ball for them in Western countries.

Imperial strategists in North America and Europe also undoubtedly looked favourably on the publication of a report that devastated the Habyarimana government and spared the Rwandan Patriotic Front. After all, the same powers condoned the military occupation of part of Rwanda by initiating the euphemistic "peace process" in Arusha. While war raged they imposed a new economic model on the country, the so-called Structural Adjustment Program, as well as a new political model. Then, Bingo! Right-thinking human rights experts from Europe and North America produced this new weapon that rounded out the arsenal at their disposal.

CHAPTER 5

A Coup by Any Other Name...

... all on the basis of a single childish accusation, that idiotic bordereau... since almost all the so-called secrets that had supposedly been turned over to the enemy were of no value.

Émile Zola, *J'accuse*

One fine spring day in 1998 the ring of a fax interrupted Philip Gourevitch, staff writer with *The New Yorker.* Some unknown source surprisingly sent him a copy of a document that reporters and investigators had been trying to track down for years. It was the answer from the New York office of the United Nations Peace Keeping Operations to the fax that General Roméo Dallaire sent on January 11, 1994, which supposedly warned UN authorities of an imminent genocide in Rwanda.

In his much-cited article in *The New Yorker* entitled "The Genocide Fax," and then again in his book,[1] Gourevitch attempted to show that the UN leaders knew there would be a genocide because Dallaire had explicitly warned them after obtaining trustworthy information from a "big fish" by the name of Jean-Pierre. He also tried to prove that the same United Nations leaders chose to do nothing other than inform President Habyarimana and foreign embassies in Kigali. In a nutshell, a "very very important government politician," to use Dallaire's word, had put Dallaire in contact with a senior cadre of the president's MRND party and its militia. Troubled by a guilty conscience, Jean-Pierre apparently decided to spill the beans.

According to Gourevitch's story, Rwandan leaders were planning to provoke a civil war by assassinating selected political leaders and Belgian troops. The informer, Jean-Pierre, apparently suspected that the same leaders were drawing up lists of Tutsis in order to exterminate them. He also said that with his small staff he could kill up to two thousand Tutsis in twenty minutes. Weapons were hidden throughout Kigali and could even be found at the MRND headquarters. In return for this information, the mysterious Jean-Pierre only wanted to obtain UN protection for him and his family.

This was the golden nugget, the first documentary evidence to be found from the period before April 1994. Finally a piece of paper proved the existence of a comprehensive plan to exterminate Rwandan Tutsis, just as the Nazis had left a paper trail of documentary evidence proving their intention to exterminate the Jews. What's more, UN Secretary General Boutros Boutros-Ghali and his successor Kofi Annan, who then headed peacekeeping operations, were fully informed of the imminent genocide. Instead of taking immediate action, as the fax most obviously would have required, both Boutros-Ghali and Kofi Annan preferred typical UN bureaucratic inaction. They did not even inform the Security Council. As a result of their turpitude, the international community was caught unprepared for the apocalypse a few months later.

Thanks to investigations by the intrepid Philip Gourevitch the truth was now out and therefore we should all apologize profusely for our inaction during the genocide that was so clearly foretold. Fortunately, President Clinton and his Secretary of State Madeleine Albright apologized for us when they gracefully visited Central Africa in 1998.

That's how the "right and proper tale" goes, but what really happened?

"Neither General Dallaire nor I ever met that famous Jean-Pierre," said the fax's *very very important government politician* in an interview in Brussels. "I told Dallaire about this story I had heard and about the informer. Dallaire sent one of his assistants to meet him and two days later he came and told me that they had found a few guns. The UN was not about to provide protection for him." That doubly important government politician was Faustin Twagiramungu, leader of the opposition MDR party and prime minister designate.

For Mr. Twagiramungu the tale of Jean-Pierre reveals a terrible contempt for Africa and Africans. "I provided information to the UN Mission in Rwanda, but I never spoke about massacres or extermination of Tutsis. A fax is then sent to New York with reference to the extermination of Tutsis. Nobody talked to me about that. Except for a few words from Dallaire, I heard nothing more about this business for several years."[2] On February 25, 1998 in Arusha General Dallaire confirmed under oath that he had never met Jean-Pierre.

Jean-Pierre's real name was Abubakar Turatsinze. He had been hired by the MRND as a chauffeur mainly because he was Muslim and would not likely drink and drive. Since Jean-Pierre was a good talker and had some success with the youth wing, the MRND gave him certain responsibilities in that area. In November 1993, however, suspecting that Jean-Pierre was peddling information to others, the national secretary of the MRND, Joseph Nzirorera, fired him. He was reengaged by another leader to accomplish small tasks. Soon after Jean-Pierre indirectly informed Faustin Twagiramungu, chairman of the main party opposed to the MRND, that the leaders of the MRND were targeting him for assassination. His authority for such a statement was that he worked for the MRND, yet he had been fired two months earlier and was perceived to be unreliable. Faustin Twagiramungu suspected a trap was being set to provoke confrontation between his own party and President Habyarimana's MRND. He was also aware of the danger of circulating unfounded accusations. This prompted him to inform the UN Mission, which was responsible for investigating these types of reports.

Roméo Dallaire sent Colonel Luc Marchal, the Belgian commander of UNAMIR troops in the Kigali area, to meet Jean-Pierre/Abubakar Turatsinze on January 10 in the evening along with Captain Amadou Deme. They also visited the MRND offices and saw a number of light weapons, which was perfectly normal for security purposes. Luc Marchal believed Jean-Pierre's story and relayed the information to Dallaire who sent the famous fax without counterchecking or investigating the story any further.

The promoters of the "right and proper tale" unfailingly forget to mention that the main reason Dallaire sent an urgent fax to New York was to get advice from his superiors. This was fully understandable. Dallaire had no experience in this area, he had reservations about the informer's credibility and he suspected a trap. Here are the sections of the fax that have been studiously omitted from the "right and proper tale."

> *THIS HQ DOES NOT HAVE PREVIOUS UNITED NATIONS EXPERIENCE IN SUCH MATTERS AND URGENTLY REQUESTS GUIDANCE.*
>
> *FORCE COMMANDER [Dallaire] DOES HAVE CERTAIN RESERVATIONS ON THE SUDDENNESS OF THE CHANGE OF HEART OF THE INFORMANT TO COME CLEAN WITH THE INFORMATION.*
>
> *POSSIBILITY OF A TRAP NOT FULLY EXCLUDED, AS THIS MAY BE A SET-UP AGAINST THIS VERY VERY IMPORTANT POLITICAL PERSON.*

It was normal for Dallaire and Marchal to request guidance from their superiors. Marchal had been in Rwanda since the end of November—one month. Dallaire had arrived at the end of October—two months. How could either determine the veracity of detailed information about the political parties in a country they knew little about and in which everything went on in a language they did not understand?

The following day Dallaire's superiors in New York advised him in a fax to inform President Habyarimana and to warn him of the risk that armed militias represented for the implementation of the Arusha Peace Accord. They also suggested that he communicate the same information to the main foreign embassies in Kigali. Nothing that Jean-Pierre predicted came about. If he had spoken about plans to assassinate President Habyarimana, perhaps his predictions would have warranted greater attention. But no mention is made of the upcoming assassination. The advice of Dallaire's superiors therefore seems simple, reasonable, and wise.

The "very very important" Rwanda politician, Faustin Twagiramungu, thinks that the Jean-Pierre story is totally false and that there was absolutely no planning of a genocide. What's more, he told Philip Gourevitch as much before *The New Yorker* article on "The Genocide Fax" appeared and before Gourevitch published his book on the Rwandan tragedy. *The New Yorker* staff writer did not bother quoting him even though he was at the heart of the whole story. Was Jean-Pierre just trying to obtain favours in return for information? Did he want a visa for the United States or Canada? Whatever the case may be, his story resembles so many others in every country in the world. It is the story of the clerk, driver or telephone operator who works for important and powerful people and glorifies his role and position to win influence, notoriety and, sometimes, financial gain. The possibility that he was an RPF "plant" cannot be eliminated.

◆

The story of Jean-Pierre is at best dubious, but what can be said about the content of Dallaire's fax and the questions it raises? What about the alleged preparations to exterminate Tutsis? What about the alleged armed militias and political assassinations? What about President Habyarimana's loss of control of elements of his own party? And what about the lists? The whole picture would appear very sinister.

Faustin Twagiramungu never heard of any intentions to exterminate the Tutsis as Jean-Pierre described in detail to Colonel Luc Marchal.[3] He also testified to this effect under oath at the ICTR. In other testimony before the ICTR, Belgian Colonel Frank Claeyes, who also met Jean-Pierre, stated that he had never seen any lists and that after January 11 Abubakar Turatsinze/Jean-Pierre refused to produce the lists he had talked about even though Claeyes asked specifically for them or for samples every time they met. Other prosecution witnesses testified under oath that Turatsinze was active in the flourishing black market arms trade in Kigali.

Turatsinze undoubtedly knew that a Rwandan politician like Prime Minister designate Faustin Twagiramungu was familiar with the RPF and its tactics, just as he was with the other Rwandan political formations. He could not be easily fooled into believing such a story. On the other hand, Luc Marchal and Roméo Dallaire who had just arrived and knew virtually nothing about Rwanda were much more gullible. The Belgian peacekeeper later wrote about how he had been "taken in by the RPF's formidable propaganda" ever since the Arusha negotiations.[4]

Pro-RPF publications abounded with accusations similar to those made by Jean-Pierre. The Rwandan Patriotic Front's goal was to prepare Western public opinion to accept and support the resumption of war since it knew very well that it could never win power in democratic elections. During the period prior to Jean-Pierre's meeting with Luc Marchal, pro-RPF publications such as *Isibo*[5] ran articles closely resembling descriptions made by Jean-Pierre. Nearly twenty years after the events and despite long and detailed trials of alleged *génocidaires* in Arusha and elsewhere, absolutely no evidence of the planning or intention of exterminating Rwandan Tutsis has been found or presented. Philip Gourevitch, who has been one of the RPF's main cheerleaders, explicitly recognized this when he insisted that his "genocide fax" from Dallaire was the most important documentary evidence of an extermination plan.

What about the weapons and the armed paramilitary militias in Kigali and elsewhere? It was widely known that youth groups, made up mostly of young armed thugs, often paraded as members of political parties or militias. These light weapons including grenades were available in public markets. Although the idea of arming the population in the areas near the territories occupied by the RPF and used to launch incursions was debated, no decision was made to implement such a policy.

RPF combatants had also infiltrated Kigali and other important centres in Rwanda. These brigades had weapons and were not afraid to show them and use them. As the number of weapons in urban areas increased, so did rumours about weapons and ammunition. People inevitably felt increasingly obliged to take all necessary means to ensure their own security. Weapons of all kinds proliferated in Kigali and throughout Rwanda. This proliferation was in fact another symptom, albeit more visible and threatening, of the breakdown of Rwandan society, which had been provoked by the cumulative effects of war and imposition of new economic and political models.

UNAMIR's mission was to disarm the militias and the RPF combatants infiltrated throughout Rwanda, and especially in Kigali. To carry out that mission successfully, the Rwandan population had to have confidence in the fairness and the neutrality of the mission and its commander. Unfortunately, both the UN mission and its military commander, General Dallaire, were perceived to favour the invading army of Rwanda Patriotic Front. During that period and after when a referee in a football (soccer) game was biased in favour of one team or another, spectators would often boo and call him "Dallaire."

To comprehend the Rwandans' profound distrust of the UN mission in Rwanda it is important to take into account a murder committed just before the mission arrived in the country. On October 21, 1992—Dallaire arrived on October 22—Melchior Ndadaye, the first democratically elected Hutu president of neighbouring Burundi, was savagely assassinated by Tutsi officers who dominate the Burundian army. Ndadaye's assassination was greeted with joy by pro-RPF Tutsis in Rwanda. Shortly thereafter, the RPF reinforced its links with the Burundian junta, especially regarding military issues.

"Burundi had been an example for us," a Rwandan in Montreal declared. "Here was an elected president in Burundi. We all thought that there was a chance that similar things could happen in Rwanda. Maybe we could do as they had done. But Melchior Ndadaye's assassination shot down all our hopes and aggravated ethnic tension in Rwanda. It became obvious to us that the Tutsis did not want democratic rule. From that moment on, opposition parties began to share the fears of President Habyarimana's party. We were not only afraid that the Tutsis would take power; we also began to fear the way they wanted to rule Rwanda. Ndadaye's assassination and the massacres in northern Rwanda since the invasion on October 1, 1990 gave us a pretty good idea of how they wanted to run the country. Looking back now and seeing what the RPF has done, I can say that our fears were well founded."

Following the assassination of the Burundian president, 375,000 Hutu refugees fled to Rwanda and joined the one million internal Rwandan refugees whom the war had displaced since 1990. At the same time RPF and Burundian military leaders met to co-ordinate activities and to convince Rwandan Tutsis living in Burundi to join the RPF army.[6]

UN peacekeepers with their large Belgian contingent thus arrived in Rwanda at a time when mistrust and suspicion of the RPF and its mainly Tutsi supporters had reached an all time high. Their arrival also coincided with the departure of French troops, which the anti-RPF parties had counted on. Thus Belgian troops perceived to be pro-RPF replaced French troops considered to be pro-Habyarimana.

The first important action of the UN military mission, which included more than four hundred Belgian troops, was to escort a battalion of six hundred armed RPF soldiers from Rwandan Patriotic Front headquarters in Mulindi to Kigali. They also had to supervise their settlement, which some described as "triumphant," in the parliament building in Kigali, the *Conseil national du développement* (CND). This operation known as "Clean Corridor" left an image of a Belgian-dominated UNAMIR escorting the invading army to a symbolic and strategic position in the country's capital. Upon arrival RPF soldiers immediately dug trenches around the building, which was not exactly a gesture likely to herald in a peaceful transition.

The image of a pro-RPF United Nations mission coincides with most observations gathered since the tragedy. Both Force Commander Roméo Dallaire and the UNAMIR forces were unacceptably close and in collusion with the Rwandan Patriotic Front.

"Roméo Dallaire was very close to the RPF," says Gilbert Ngijol, political assistant to Jacques-Roger Booh-Booh. "He let the RPF get arms. He allowed UNAMIR troops to train RPF soldiers. United Nations troops provided the logistics for the RPF. They even fed them."

The Secretary General's Special Representative to Rwanda, Jacques-Roger Booh-Booh, confirmed this when he broke ten years of silence regarding Rwanda in an interview published in Africa International. "In the field, he abandoned his work as military commander and got involved in politics; he violated the principle of UNAMIR's neutrality and became the objective ally of one of the parties in the conflict."[7]

A Rwandan refugee living in France recalled that, "Roméo Dallaire was always at the home of Hélène Pinske, a Québec woman married to a Tutsi minister by the name of Landouald Ndasingwa. Unlike Landouald, who knew that the minority could never democratically govern the Hutu majority, Hélène never hid the fact that she hoped the RPF would win. 'By the will of God, we're going to win,'" she declared when the RPF arrived in Kigali.

According to James K. Gasana, Rwandan Defence Minister until July 1993, the UNAMIR behaved just like another military faction.

> It [UNAMIR] was always extremely amenable with the RPF and even agreed to let it get wood from Mulindi (RPF military headquarters in northern Rwanda), even though there was wood near Kigali. These supply trips to the north escorted by UNAMIR peacekeepers and vehicles enabled the RPF to transport infiltrators and new recruits from the northern area to Kigali. Another illustration of this collusion is that in January 1994, upon an RPF request, UNAMIR decided to shut down one runway at the Kanombe airport that enabled landing and take-off over Kigali. [8]

The closing of that runway at the Kigali airport meant that there was only one direction for airplanes to land when arriving in Kigali. This greatly facilitated the assassination of President Habyarimana when he arrived in Kigali in the evening on April 6, 1994.

Even if Roméo Dallaire, Luc Marchal, Jacques-Roger Booh-Booh, and the others had wanted to stop the increasing take-over by the RPF and effectively disarm it, foreign embassies in Kigali were operating as though the RPF had already taken power. Well before April 6, 1994 the embassies had already been giving regular, unmistakable messages to leaders of the president's party, the MRND, saying essentially that President Habyarimana had to go. James Gasana points out that, "from a diplomatic standpoint, most business involving Rwanda's relations with Western countries and particularly the United States was handled with Paul Kagame at RPF headquarters in Mulindi." [9] The International Monetary Fund followed suit. It even called meetings at the invading army headquarters in Mulindi and expected the Habyarimana government to delegate representatives.

Roméo Dallaire and the UN mission may have been following orders from the UN headquarters in New York not to inconvenience the Rwandan Patriotic Front in any way; Force Commander Dallaire may also have been pursuing the policy adopted by Western embassies in Kigali, and particularly by the American Embassy. But whatever the exact line of command, the overall effect upon the Rwandan people was the same.

For UN peacekeepers to be able to disarm both the militias and RPF infiltrators, an agreement on procedures would have had to be negotiated. No such agreement came about. More importantly, the UN mission and its commander had to demonstrate unwavering neutrality and determination in their efforts to disarm both parties fully and equitably. Nobody believed that they would or could do that in 1994, and nobody believes it now.

Since UN peacekeepers were unwilling or unable to disarm militias and infiltrated combatants, they could not prevent the presence of paramilitary groups from aggravating the anarchy that increasingly plagued Rwanda between January and April 1994.

Now what about those lists Jean-Pierre mentioned? Faustin Twagiramungu dismisses stories about lists, saying that the only lists he ever saw had no more than a few hundred names. Lists of a few hundred names do not indicate the intention of one group to eliminate a large part of the Rwandan population. "People should be wary of dubious documents planted in certain books,"[10] he declared in testimony before the Belgian Senate.

Nothing could be more normal or legitimate for a government at war than to collect the names of people suspected of spying for the enemy. For the record, we should recall American campaigns in the First World War. The very official Creel Committee invited citizens of the United States to denounce people suspected of favouring the Germans. "Report the man who spreads pessimistic stories, divulges—or seeks—confidential military information, cries for peace, or belittles our efforts to win the war. Send the names of such persons, even if they are in uniform, to the Department of Justice, Washington."[11] Consider Virginia's Senator John Warner's advice given on CNN's Larry King show on November 7, 2001: "You must think of yourself as an agent, not to spy on your neighbour, but to judiciously report anything that looks suspicious."[12]

What country at war has not drawn up lists of possible spies? Such practices do not prove anything about a will of some people to exterminate part of the population.

"The Mood for Spy Hunts"
A Poster Displayed in Boston by a Military Intelligence Office

In Comparison: "The Mood for Spy Hunts"
In World War I the hunt for spies in the United States far exceeded the real threat. John Lord O'Brian, who headed the U.S. Justice Department Emergency Division, stated that the blind systematic agitation against what was perceived as a tentacular spy network led to terrible oppression of innocent people.

◆

How and why did Gourevitch's so-called genocide fax mutate into one of the elements of the official narrative?[13] The fax Dallaire sent to his superiors in New York remained more or less confidential until November 1995 when it was mentioned in *The Observer* in London. A copy of it then appeared in a Belgian publication and several questions about it were raised during the inquiry conducted by the Belgian Senate. Although nobody had a copy of the reply from UN headquarters in New York, the contents of the reply were known.

For former Secretary General Boutros-Ghali, "that story of the fax is greatly exaggerated. There was not only one fax. Every day the UN would receive faxes saying 'We heard there's a plot afoot...'" He added that if there was a plot afoot, Security Council member countries were much better informed than the UN Secretary General because, unlike the UN, they have intelligence gathering services. "What's more, they refuse to share their information!"[14]

Late in 1997 and early in 1998, the United States was being severely criticized for its role in the Rwandan tragedy and in the Congo. Hearings in the French National Assembly and the Belgian Senate led to irritating headlines and pointed attacks on the Clinton Administration. In spring 1998, in Washington, the House Committee on International Relations wanted to question the Administration about Washington's inaction during the Rwandan tragedy in 1994. Neither the State Department nor the Defense Department deigned to appear at the public hearings held by the House Committee. Their refusal angered members of Congress.

Astoundingly, Philip Gourevitch's fax machine happened to ring at that very moment and out came the much sought-after UN reply to General Roméo Dallaire. Gourevitch published his "scoop" in *The New Yorker* coincidentally during the very week that hearings were being held in Washington about the United States' role in the Great Lakes region of Africa. Here's how

Gourevitch explained it all. He first quoted UN spokesman Fred Eckhard to the effect that the UN was getting "a bum rap on this," then he added, "Somebody with access to UN files disagreed with Eckhard, and one day my fax machine rang and a copy of the missing ..."[15]

People have not asked Mr. Gourevitch how and why he happened to receive the missing reply, and he has not volunteered to tell us. The fax most likely came from Jamie Rubin, Madeleine Albright's senior press attaché and right-hand man, who at that time was Gourevitch's brother-in-law.

Jamie Rubin is the man whom the Clinton Administration charged in March 1995 with devising a plan to prevent Boutros Boutros-Ghali from obtaining a second term as secretary general of the United Nations. Rubin had contacts in all the major media in Washington and New York and never hesitated to use them to leak information to attack Boutros-Ghali within the UN. His overriding strategy however was to protect and promote Madeleine Albright.[16] Moreover, Jamie Rubin confirmed his tight relationship with Philip Gourevitch to *New York Times* reporter and author Howard French. In a 1997 press briefing while he was accompanying Madeleine Albright in Rwanda and the Democratic Republic of the Congo, Jamie Rubin said to French: "Actually a lot of my take comes from an even better source [than US intelligence], and it comes directly. Philip Gourevitch is my sister's boyfriend."[17]

The State Department and Secretary of State Madeleine Albright were in hot water over Rwanda. The best way to divert the attacks was to pass the buck on to the United Nations and to Boutros-Ghali. At the same time, they could also let Kofi Annan know that he too was on a short leash. Annan after all was responsible for UN peacekeeping operations at the time. The spin given to the fax story in *The New Yorker* could be summed up as follows: We in Washington are not guilty of having supported a murderous invading army that has spread death and destruction throughout Central Africa. It's those incompetent UN bureaucrats and especially that secretary general who did not take the obvious necessary measures to stop those horrible *génocidaires* from carrying out their evil plans. They did nothing even though they were sitting on unquestionable documentary evidence of a planned genocide. They did not even inform the international community.

The strategy used by Washington to hide its own evildoing is tried and proven. In 2002, when it was preparing war on Iraq, Washington launched a similar message: "We don't want to destroy Iraq, take over the country, and put in an American puppet. It's the United Nations resolutions that demanded we do so."

Washington's strategy has unfortunately been quite successful even though it does not stand up to analysis. The power of the United Nations is very limited. The CIA alone spends more in ten days than the UN spends in a year: 1.2 billion US dollars.[18] Ramsey Clark points out that, "since the end of the Cold War the U.S. is so dominant in the UN that it is almost a tool, a small tool, and it has a lot bigger ones like its bombs and its aircraft to get its way around the world."

◆

In that January 11 fax Roméo Dallaire reported that according to Jean-Pierre President Habyarimana did "not have full control over all elements of his old party/faction." He could, and perhaps should, have written that the president no longer had *any* control over the country.

Decision-making power for Rwanda was now everywhere but in the hands of Rwandans in Kigali. Between October 1, 1990 and April 6, 1994 foreign powers led by the United States had effectively disempowered Rwandans who had worked for thirty-five years to build a state apparatus and a society that worked relatively well and met the needs and aspirations of the people of Rwanda. Yet the so-called donor institutions had decided that the economic model had to be changed. A strong state with an interventionist bent was to become a tiny administrative unit, even if it meant

Internal refugee camp just north of Kigali, January 1994
The presence of more than one million internal refugees and refugees from Burundi after the assassination of Melchior Ndadaye made Rwanda a time bomb waiting to explode.

social upheaval and loss of power for the Hutu majority. Next came the political model imposed by Western powers even though the country had been invaded under their noses and with their support and was still occupied by a hostile foreign army. The same powers then forced the Rwandan government to sit down and negotiate the transfer of power to an invading army that, at best, represented a small minority of the Rwandan population.

Time passed and the occupying army continued to take new land. The civilian population was chased out of their homes. The country, its president and government, and all Rwandans who refused to accept being ruled by the invading army were vilified throughout the world. While the occupying army killed, deported, and terrorized the population, right-thinking Europeans and North Americans became international mouthpieces for the attacks while regularly adding their own slander. Their words became daggers aimed at the jugular of Rwandan society. Friendly countries turned their backs after thirty years of co-operation and became cozy with the occupying army, soon to be characterized as a beacon of hope for Africa in the new millennium.

By April 1994, on the eve of President Habyarimana's assassination, Rwanda was in total disarray. The country's leaders had no power to decide on their future. The new political parties were in crisis, jockeying for position and influence. The economy was shattered. The war raged on and more than a million people were displaced. Armed groups were everywhere, each establishing its own laws, while the United Nations peacekeeping mission responsible for disarming them could not, or would not, carry out its mandate.

The amplification of the importance of the dubious story of Jean-Pierre and Dallaire's fax must be contrasted with the trivialization of the crime that triggered the massacres in Rwanda in April 1994.[19] Whereas none of the details or causal links in the former story have been established despite years of court hearings, we know that a sophisticated and well-armed organization planned, organized, and executed on April 6, 1994 the assassination of two African heads of State, and that assassination had terrible direct consequences. Yet the powers that be would rather see that crime remain a footnote in history.

CHAPTER 6

It Shall Be Called a Plane Crash

Important facts can be hidden behind the media and nobody ever sees them.

Ignacio Ramonet, *Le Monde Diplomatique*

How could the Rwandan tragedy have been avoided? The question is often asked, but nobody really seems to want to know. The "right and proper tale" would have it that Rwandan Hutu political and military leaders devised a devilish plan to exterminate the Tutsi minority. If that were true, then the only way to prevent the genocide would have been to arrest and imprison all those leaders before April 6, 1994. Such pre-emptive action would obviously have been impossible. It would follow therefore that everything was cast in stone, that the *génocidaires* would carry out their horrible plan and that these tragedies are innate to the societies in which they take place. A thesis like that is particularly hard to accept since it implies that humanity is bereft of means to prevent such tragedies.

It would have been possible for Rwanda to avoid the advanced state of anarchy it found itself in 1993 and 1994 but that would have required that Western powers just keep out and allow Rwandans to decide their own future. Failing that, it still would have been possible to avoid the massacres simply by preventing the assassination of the presidents of Rwanda and Burundi.

In the evening of April 6, 1994 everybody knew that if it were confirmed that the plane had been shot down widespread violence would break out, particularly in Rwanda. Prudence Bushnell of the American Embassy in Kigali wrote exactly that to Secretary of State Warren Christopher in Washington immediately after learning of President Habyarimana's death. "If, as it appears, both presidents have been killed, there is a strong likelihood that widespread violence could break out in either or both countries, particularly if it is confirmed that the plane was shot down."[1]

If the plane had not been shot down, those massacres would not have occurred! It is as simple as that. Even the late Alison Des Forges stated as much under oath when cross-examined as an expert witness in Arusha.[2] Looking back now, one gets the sad and troubling impression that those who could have prevented the assassination of the two presidents did absolutely nothing. Worse yet, everything has been done to make sure the truth does not come out. The slow but inexorable transformation of that assassination into a simple plane crash is surely one of the worst scandals of our time. When a madman shot at President Chirac on July 14, 2002, his Minister of the Interior and future president of France, Nicolas Sarkozy, rightly declared that, "when someone shoots at the president it is by no means a trivial news item." The same could be said about the attempted assassination of President Reagan in 1981. The world took years to recover from the assassination of President Kennedy in 1963. Inquiries have been conducted, books have been written, and films have been produced. But when two African presidents were shot down in their plane on an international flight, the international community refused to conduct an investigation and the event continues to be described as a "plane crash."

In May 1999 UN Secretary General Kofi Annan acting on behalf of the Security Council requested an independent report into the actions of the United Nations during the 1994 genocide in Rwanda.

The report issued in December 1999 describes the assassination in the chronology as follows: "April 6: At approximately 20:30, Habyarimana and President Cyprien Ntaryamira of Burundi, who were returning from a regional summit in Dar es Salaam, Tanzania, were killed in a plane crash just outside the Kigali airport. Within an hour of the plane crash, roadblocks were set up ..."[3] Another subtitle reads: "Crash of the Presidential plane; genocide begins."[4] The eighty-four-page report does mention that the plane was shot down, yet throughout the document it is treated as a banal affair, both in the description of events and in the conclusions and recommendations. In comparison, discussion of the trumped-up, dubious story of Dallaire's January 11 cable, aka as Gourevitch's "genocide fax," occupies many pages of the document. The authors of the report obviously knew where power lies and had understood the message in *The New Yorker* article, which had appeared just a year earlier.

Indictment documents produced by the International Criminal Tribunal for Rwanda also called the assassination a plane crash, as do most popular books on the Rwandan tragedy. The only time this euphemism is not used to describe the terrible criminal act it was is when the shooting down of the plane is attributed to extremists in President Habyarimana's own entourage. This explanation has been consistently and convincingly refuted. Those who so faithfully espoused it at first no longer dare to make such accusations. This of course has never prevented the Canadian Broadcasting Corporation from repeating the accusation with no additional proof, such as in a feature documentary on May 7, 2002 in which the audience was informed that, "Hutu leaders shot down the presidents and blamed it on the Tutsis." Although prosecutors at the ICTR first tried to use this thesis to prove the guilt of arrested Rwandan leaders, they had stopped even mentioning it by the end of the 1990s because they had no evidence to back the accusations.[5]

No official international inquiry has been conducted into the assassination. After the plane was shot down, French military officers in Kigali met Roméo Dallaire, who as UN force commander was responsible for airport security, and offered to investigate the assassination. France was intimately concerned since the plane belonged to France and the crew of French nationals had been killed. Moreover, French investigators were available nearby. General Dallaire refused the French offer saying that he had already discussed the issue with the Americans who were prepared to dispatch an investigating team from its bases in Germany.[6]

On April 8, 1994 the Security Council demanded an impartial international inquiry into the assassination. On April 12 the Belgian Cabinet also demanded that the International Civil Aviation Organization conduct an investigation into the assassination. On June 25 the Security Council mandated the Secretary General to conduct an inquiry into the assassination. In November 1994 the Security Council created the International Criminal Tribunal for Rwanda with the mandate to investigate acts of genocide or other serious violations of international human rights law committed on Rwandan territory during the year 1994. In September 1995 Zaire demanded that an inquiry be held into the assassination. In October 1995 Kenyan President Arap Moi demanded an inquiry.

This litany of demands prompted Belgian Professor Filip Reyntjens to conclude in 1995 that "in fact, nobody seems to really want to know" who assassinated the two presidents. Reyntjens maintained that all the evidence available tended to incriminate the Rwandan Patriotic Front.[7] Reyntjens however complained that he could not investigate the crime any further. Others took up the investigation independently. Charles Onana, an investigative journalist from Cameroon who lives in Paris, published an important book on the question in which he identifies Rwandan President Paul Kagame as suspect number one.[8] His findings were so forceful and convincing that Paul Kagame and Rwanda sued him for defamation and tried to prevent the book from being published. Legal proceedings were eventually dropped when Onana simply refused to be intimidated. This story shows how sensitive the issue of the assassination is and how everything could change if a serious official inquiry were to conclude that the RPF had in fact shot down the president's plane. Paul Kagame probably dropped proceedings against Charles Onana because he feared that the truth about the assassination might come out during the trial.

Many people who could have helped find the truth have remained silent. Louise Arbour, former chief prosecutor of the International Criminal Tribunal for Rwanda and Yugoslavia, has always meticulously avoided the question, refusing interviews unless for puff pieces vaunting her own achievements. In November 2002 when Ms Arbour was speaking at a public meeting in Paris about the International Criminal Court, she simply refused to answer Charles Onana's question about the assassination. "I don't have the right to speak about that issue since the French Judge Bruguière is still conducting his inquiry."[9] When questioned after the speech, she added that in her capacity as Canadian Supreme Court Justice, she could not discuss such things. Her refusal was of course unfounded. Judge Bruguière had received his mandate to investigate the assassination from France. His work is not related to either the International Criminal Tribunal or the Canadian Justice System.

The assassination of the presidents of Rwanda and Burundi has remained a hot potato for Ms Arbour and she has never discussed it since. It should be remembered that Louise Arbour was the chief prosecutor who in 1997 killed the International Tribunal's only official inquiry conducted by Michael Hourigan, a lawyer from Australia. Michael Hourigan, who was working for the Prosecutor's Office headed by Louise Arbour, concluded that the assassination was most likely sponsored by the current president and strongman of Rwanda, Paul Kagame, leader of the Rwandan Patriotic Front. Indications showed that the RPF received aid from a foreign country.[10] Chief Prosecutor Louise Arbour was initially very enthusiastic about the findings until she spoke with United States Secretary of State Madeleine Albright. Two weeks after

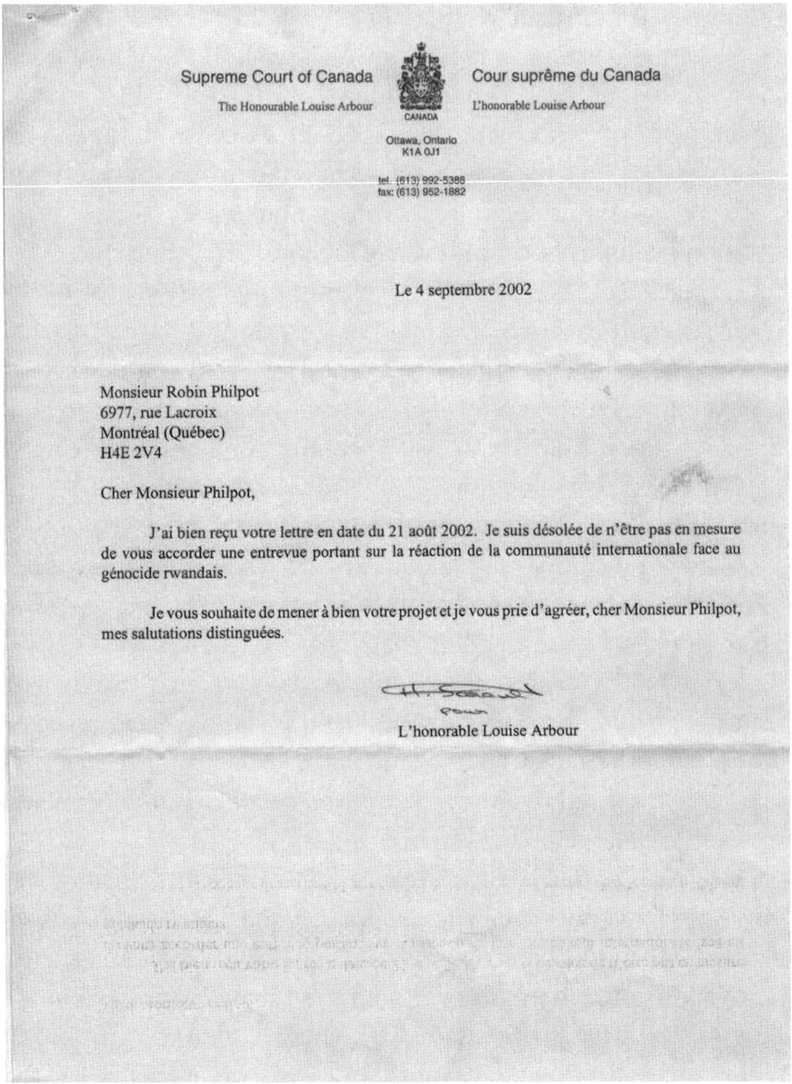

Supreme Court of Canada
The Honourable Louise Arbour

Cour suprême du Canada
L'honorable Louise Arbour

CANADA

Ottawa, Ontario
K1A 0J1

tel. (613) 992-5388
fax: (613) 952-1882

Le 4 septembre 2002

Monsieur Robin Philpot
6977, rue Lacroix
Montréal (Québec)
H4E 2V4

Cher Monsieur Philpot,

J'ai bien reçu votre lettre en date du 21 août 2002. Je suis désolée de n'être pas en mesure de vous accorder une entrevue portant sur la réaction de la communauté internationale face au génocide rwandais.

Je vous souhaite de mener à bien votre projet et je vous prie d'agréer, cher Monsieur Philpot, mes salutations distinguées.

pour
L'honorable Louise Arbour

Letter from Louise Arbour refusing to grant an interview
Former Chief Prosecutor Louise Arbour refuses to answer questions about the assassination of Rwandan and Burundian presidents Juvénal Habyarimana and Cyprien Ntaryamira on April 6, 1994; yet she was the one who killed the only official investigation into that crime by the International Criminal Tribunal for Rwanda.

hearing about Hourigan's report Arbour snuffed it out and imposed a gag order on the report's author. Since then many highly placed members of the RPF who collaborated closely with Paul Kagame have confirmed Hourigan's conclusions. In public declarations, these people explained how they prepared the assassination with the help of Kagame.[11]

In a private interview with Kenyan journalist Ruth Nababkwe after her speech in Paris, Louise Arbour declared that, "it is not clear whether the event in question constitutes a crime within the tribunal's jurisdiction. It is not obvious that the shooting down of the plane carrying the two presidents constitutes in itself a war crime, a crime against humanity or an act of genocide." She then added that the tribunal must "prosecute any person implied in a crime that is serious enough to draw the attention of the international community."

In these unbelievably contemptuous remarks, Louise Arbour gets closer to the truth, namely that assassination of two African heads of state has been made into such a trivial and commonplace event that it is not considered a serious enough crime to warrant the attention of Ms Arbour's "international community." Who is that "international community" and who is responsible for trivializing such a heinous crime? The Belgian peacekeeper who headed the UNAMIR troops at Kigali, Colonel Luc Marchal, answered that question with another question: "Who is powerful enough to have prevented a real international inquiry from casting light upon the events that occurred when President Habyarimana was flying home from a regional summit in Dar Es-Salaam?"[12]

Knowing the truth about the assassination of presidents Habyarimana and Ntaryamira did not appear to be very important for Belgium either. The Belgian Senate held a long series of hearings on the events in Rwanda, and especially on the death of Belgian paratroopers who were accused of shooting down the presidential plane. The Senate did not even bother to discuss the assassination. It would seem that a serious Belgian inquiry would want to investigate that event if only to rule out the accusation that its own troops were guilty.

Michael Hourigan's report for the Tribunal and the French National Assembly's inquiry both implicate "a foreign country." Though it would be very interesting to know whether that foreign country is the United States, fundamentally it matters little. If investigations under way were to conclude that the RPF did in fact plan and carry out the assassination, the United States would necessarily be implicated in the crime since it provided the RPF army with unwavering support from 1990 on, particularly in the period leading up to April 6, 1994 and after. Leaders in the United States are aware of this problem, just as they are aware that the whole tale that they have so carefully helped to stitch together could be unravelled. The crime is now much worse than it was in 1994. First there was the horrible assassination of the presidents of two African countries. Then there has been the cover-up by an army of accomplices who have carefully allowed the criminals to get off scot-free.[13]

Eight years after demanding an inquiry and after creating the International Criminal Tribunal for Rwanda, Boutros Boutros-Ghali was also dumbfounded by silence around the assassination. "Nobody has been able to tell me why no inquiry has been made into that crime," he complained. When I showed him the official UN report that spoke about a "plane crash," he shrugged his shoulders in resignation: "You know, none of these reports are very honest. That's my opinion. They hide a lot of things. The man responsible for peacekeeping operations at the time of the assassination was Kofi Annan."

In a subsequent interview about the assassination and following leaks to *Le Monde* from the Bruguière inquiry, Boutros-Ghali declared: "It is a very mysterious scandal indeed. Four reports have been made on Rwanda: the French Parliament Report, the Belgian Senate Report, Kofi Annan's UN report, and the Organization of African Unity report. All four say absolutely nothing about the shooting down of the Rwandan president's plane. That just goes to show the power of the intelligence services that can force people to be quiet."

The only partial exception was the seven year investigation conducted by French anti-terrorist judge Jean-Louis Bruguière. That investigation implicated current Rwandan President Paul Kagame and the Rwandan Patriotic Front for having planned, ordered, and carried out the April 6 assassination. Yet the Bruguière report has been smothered by the political realignment that France has effected since the election of Nicolas Sarkozy in May 2007 and the appointment of Bernard Kouchner as French Foreign Minister. François Hollande has pursued the policy introduced by his predecessor. Rwanda and the Bruguière report was a serious rubbing point in French-US relations that had to be eliminated. And it was. The conflicting reports produced since then both by France and Rwanda must be seen in that light. Each is devised to pour more mud and sand on the tracks of the criminals.

According to Boutros-Ghali much remains to be found out. "Judge Bruguière, who I invited to a conference in Monaco, told me that according to his investigation, the CIA was involved in that assassination. However, the Anglo-American intelligence apparatus is much stronger than France's. Perhaps the French secret service decided that they have no interest in making the Bruguière report public at that time."

If the CIA was involved in the assassination of Rwandan President Habyarimana in April 1994, as the French judge reportedly claimed, then it is easier to understand why the official story about the Rwandan tragedy continues to call that terrorist attack an "accident" or a "crash." Worse still, considering the terrible consequences that go beyond the wildest predictions of any sorcerer's apprentice, serious questions remain unanswered about the efforts made and means used to erase the tracks leading to the criminals involved in the killing of the two African heads of state and also to misinform and mislead international public opinion about the real causes of the Rwandan tragedy that followed.

CHAPTER 7

How Is the Empire?

We have to go to their schools to learn
how to win even when you are in the wrong.

Cheik Hamidou Kane, *Ambiguous Adventure*

The behaviour of the United States within the UN Security Council between April 6 and mid-July 1994 was what prompted former Secretary General Boutros-Ghali to declare in 1998 that the Americans were one hundred percent responsible for the Rwandan genocide. Mr. Boutros-Ghali expanded on that declaration in interviews in 2002 and 2004. "It was the responsibility of the Americans who were aided by England. But the other member states were too passive. Today it is true to say that the United States acts unilaterally. It is a superpower. But in addition, the abdication and resignation of the other powers must be mentioned."

In his 1999 book entitled *Unvanquished: A US-UN Saga*, Boutros Boutros-Ghali was categorical: "The U.S. effort to prevent the effective deployment of a UN force for Rwanda succeeded with the strong support of Britain."[1] The former Secretary General tends to give credence to the two reasons most often evoked for U.S. opposition to UN action. The first is the Somali fiasco in which eighteen soldiers perished. The second is the Presidential Directive of May 1994 brought down in the middle of the Rwandan crisis, which imposed strict conditions on American participation in UN peacekeeping operations. Boutros-Ghali nevertheless pointed out that Madeleine Albright systematically blocked any kind of military intervention in Rwanda even without United States' participation.

Since the internal discussions of the Clinton Administration were not available for several years, both explanations for American opposition to UN action appeared plausible. The waves of horrifying television images also made it difficult to consider anything other than the propaganda served up by the Rwandan Patriotic Front and its allies, who had managed to win over most Western newsrooms.

Belgian Colonel Luc Marchal's observations about the nature of RPF propaganda were revealing. In a 1998 letter to Alain de Brouwer, another Belgian very familiar with Rwanda, he wrote, "I am fully in agreement with your analysis of the RPF's implication be it before or after the tragedy. I am personally very convinced because I too had been duped by their smart propaganda during the Arusha negotiations. Once I was in Kigali, the gulf that separated what was said and what was really happening became obvious. In fact the RPF movement is totalitarian and it crushes absolutely everything in its way."[2]

Another trusty sign that more was happening in Rwanda than met the eye was the virulent anti-French tone of mainstream U.S. media during the crisis. For example, on May 17, 1994, the *Village Voice* ran a long article entitled "Rwanda's French Connection," in which it accused France of sitting back and letting their Rwandan friends massacre the Tutsis. Yet at that very moment, May 1994, the United States was doing everything in its power to prevent France and all other powers from leading an international force that could have stopped the killing and protected both Tutsi and Hutu civilians. For close observers, the behaviour and declarations of international human rights NGOs at the time was also suspicious, and indicated some high level political strategy. Some British organizations began to vocally oppose any United Nations military intervention arguing that only a victory by the invading RPF could end the genocide. For human rights groups, that position was surprising since it was more about geopolitical positioning than humanitarianism. In hindsight, however, one wonders if these groups should be allowed to qualify themselves as "non-governmental."

An important example is the attempt by Human Rights Watch and other NGOs to prevent Rwanda's Foreign Minister, Jérôme Bicamumpaka, from representing that country before the UN Security Council when it was most important in May 1994. Alison Des Forges and other HRW activists, together with the Louise Mushikiwabo, later to be Rwanda's Foreign Minister under the RPF, participated in a sort of vigilante ambush on the Rwandan delegation at their hotel in New York. Their goal was to prevent the legitimate representatives of Rwanda's Interim Government from making a case to the UN Security Council about the absolute necessity of rapidly redeploying troops in Rwanda so as to save lives and bring about a cease-fire so that the Arusha Peace Accord could be implemented. By paralysing the Rwandan Interim Government they hoped to pave the way for an RPF military victory. (See description of the events by Jérôme Bicamumpaka in Appendix II).

The behaviour of Alison Des Forges of Human Rights Watch at the United Nations heralded an era during which NGOs would literally and figuratively run interference for the great powers at the UN as they advanced their pawns ... and their troops and drones. Anything would go to keep legitimate national representatives from defending themselves before the United Nations and its Security Council. In NATO's rush to bomb and destroy Libya in 2011, as Maximilian Forte points out, "Libya was barred from representing itself at the UN, where shadowy NGOs and 'human rights' groups held full sway in propagating exaggerations, outright falsehoods, and racial fear mongering that served to sanction atrocities and ethnic cleansing in the name of democracy. Nothing could impede a rush to war."[3]

At the same time in May 1994, *The Economist,* whose connections with foreign policy makers in Washington and London are unequalled, called for a clear victory by the Rwandan Patriotic Front. "In the short run, the best hope of peace and of survival for those Tutsis left alive would probably be a quick victory in war for the RPF."[4] Rereading that comment makes it all so simple and obvious to understand and one wonders why there has been so much public fretting and wringing of hands about the "international community's" slow reaction to horror in Rwanda. Unless of course that wringing of hands has been all show aimed to develop some Pavlovian reaction when the word Rwanda is spoken.

Policy makers in Washington and London had a simple straightforward strategy. Why allow a United Nations-sanctioned military force to intervene and hand over initiative to others, and specifically to France? The net result would be that "our boys" in the RPF would be prevented from taking power decisively. We just have to help them win the war and they will be indebted to us forever. They'll guarantee us access to the whole region and keep it stable for years to come. They just have to win quickly. Will many people be killed? Sure they will, but not too many.

This policy had already been introduced in February 1994 when the same Anglo-American tandem had opposed reinforcing the UN military mission known as UNAMIR. At the end of March 1994 UNAMIR was still far short of troops; it reached a maximum of 2500 whereas both the Rwandan Government and the invading RPF had agreed that a minimum of 4500 troops was required. Two weeks after President Habyarimana's plane was shot down, with war at its worst and many civilians being killed, the same two permanent members of the UN Security Council with Belgium's help forced the United Nations to scale back the UNAMIR force to 270 soldiers as of April 21, 1994.

Formerly classified internal Clinton Administration documents were made available in August 2001 following a Freedom of

Information Act request made by the independent National Security Archive.[5] These memoranda, telegrams, working papers, reports, and briefing documents confirm the worst apprehensions about how a superpower develops and applies a foreign policy in which its own strategic interests take precedence over the lives and the peace of a country, its people, and whole regions of Africa. Reading them makes one even more cynical about the hollow apologies made by Secretary of State Madeleine Albright in December 1997 and by President Clinton in March 1998.

The Administration was fully aware of the magnitude of the tragedy unfolding. On April 11, five days after the president's plane was shot down and after Prudence Bushnell specifically warned Warren Christopher about the imminent "widespread violence," a Pentagon memorandum to Under Secretary of Defense Frank Wisner, who was third in charge, warns that "unless both sides can be convinced to return to the peace process, a massive (hundreds of thousands of deaths) bloodbath will ensue... In addition, millions of refugees will flee into neighbouring Uganda, Tanzania and Zaire."

Even though they knew that the massacres would occur and that millions would flee to other countries, the Americans devoted all their efforts to forcing the United Nations to withdraw its UNAMIR troops. That was the priority. A State Department telegram dated April 15 gave specific orders to that effect to the United States mission at the UN and to Ambassador Madeleine Albright.

> USUN [United States UN mission] is instructed to inform UN Security Council colleagues that the United States believes that the first priority of the Security Council is to instruct the Secretary general to implement an orderly withdrawal of all/all UNAMIR forces from Rwanda.[6]

The United States mission was also instructed to ensure the withdrawal took place without discussion and without another Security Council resolution. The priority was not to bring about a cease-fire as was being offered at that very moment by representatives of the Rwandan armed forces.

During this period American diplomats busied themselves as official RPF messengers, delivering its demands to Rwandan government and army officials. The accounts of conversations between diplomats and Rwandan officials reveal the imperial nature of the relationship between the Americans and their Rwandan counterparts. They could best be described as orders, not advice. When Rwandan government and army representatives tried to meet the demands transmitted by the Americans, particularly with regards to a cease-fire, they were casually told to go and talk to Dallaire about it. As we know, however, Dallaire had lost or was losing all his troops and any effective role he might have had in Rwanda.

One of the most public handwringers about the "international community's" inaction has been former Force Commander Roméo Dallaire and his hagiographers. The narrative has it that Dallaire was constantly pleading for more troops but that his pleas fell on the deaf ears of the "international community." That version of the story only took shape with time. Two weeks after returning to Canada from Rwanda, General Dallaire appeared on a major television news magazine on CBC's French-language network. Host Jean-François Lépine asked Dallaire how he reacted to the withdrawal of troops from Rwanda by the United Nations Security Council. He replied simply, "I took part in the decision to withdraw the troops ... I recommended that they leave."[7]

The classified documents also show that the United States supported an RPF victory they wanted to be quick, even though it was known that the RPF represented at best only a small minority of the Rwandan population. Furthermore, a Defense Intelligence Agency document asserts that Rwandan Government forces had no real intention of exterminating the Tutsis, an assertion that starkly contradicts the right and proper tale told ever since.

The Clinton Administration navigated cynically around the word "genocide" throughout this period. Whether they were right or wrong, Pope Jean-Paul II, UN Secretary General Boutros-Ghali, and many others were using the word "genocide" to describe events in Rwanda by the end of April 1994. Washington however meticulously avoided it until June 10. If the Americans had begun talking about genocide they would have been obliged to support a UN-sponsored military intervention in Rwanda. That of course would have prevented the RPF from winning the war, thereby scuttling Washington's long-term strategy. For example, a Defense Department discussion paper on Rwanda dated May 1, 1994 warned Administration representatives against using the term "genocide." "Be careful. Legal at State was worried about this yesterday—Genocide finding could commit US Government to actually 'do something.'"

Other unclassified documents show how the Clinton Administration started adjusting its position when it saw that non-governmental human rights organizations, who had been crying genocide since 1993, could be used to the United States' advantage. The changes started occurring just before a meeting of the United Nations Human Rights Commission. Little by little thereafter the word became the leitmotif of U.S. policy in Rwanda. Since the Administration was counting on a quick RPF victory, the increased use of the term "genocide," which falsely described the situation as the Hutu majority hating and exterminating the innocent Tutsi minority, became the best way to enhance the image of the RPF and bring international opinion to believe that only the Hutu-dominated Rwandan Government forces were guilty of this horrible crime. Moreover, the same unclassified documents prove the Clinton Administration adopted this strategy even though they were in possession of reliable reports and information about massive killing and violence carried out by the Rwandan Patriotic Front.

A spokesperson for Secretary of State Warren Christopher used the expression "acts of genocide" for the first time on June 10, 1994, but only after the U.S. had managed to impose a military embargo on Rwanda. The RPF on the other hand had no difficulty bringing weapons, ammunition, and fighters into Rwanda through Uganda. Though the United States reluctantly agreed upon the creation of a second UN military mission to Rwanda known as UNAMIR II on May 17, which was to reach 5500 troops, they delayed its deployment until the war was over.

The United States finally agreed to a Security Council resolution authorizing the French Opération Turquoise deployed on June 22, 1994. That operation was conceived to create a "secure humanitarian zone" for two months. By this time the term "genocide" had received the blessing of the Clinton Administration. It therefore became easy to depict the French operation as an effort by France to protect its friends, the *génocidaires*. The English-language media immediately and joyfully stigmatized that operation as French colonial support for genocide even though it effectively saved many lives of Rwandan civilians.

The shooting down of the plane on April 6 triggered the tragedy in Rwanda, but the RPF had already prepared to resume the war much earlier. RPF sources now claim that they had four thousand armed fighters in Kigali, yet under the Arusha Peace Accord all weapons in the area were supposed to be deposed and collected by the UNAMIR. Even before President Habyarimana's plane was shot down, RPF troops had started marching on Kigali. In the capital city, the RPF, which had many more arms than the Arusha Peace Accord provided for, positioned its troops for combat during the night of April 6 and were attacking the Rwandan Armed Forces early the next day. The Rwandan Patriotic Front had clearly the broken the Arusha peace agreement and started the war again.

Captain Amadou Deme was a Senegalese army officer and member of the intelligence section of the United Nation Mission in Rwanda under General Roméo Dallaire's command. In a 2007 interview he described the RPF's state of preparedness and deployment on April 6, 1994.

> Early in the morning on April 7, the Katyushas in Kigali were thundering and they went on non-stop. Where did their ammunition come from? What's more, it is an undisputable fact that on the second day, the battalion stationed at the CND in Kigali and the battalion from northern Rwanda met up. In our opinion, they started moving before the attack on April 6. The speed with which the RPF columns reached

> Kigali and its surroundings was dumbfounding. The only explanation is that they were totally prepared to deploy. The other side was not in the same state of preparedness. The Government Forces under attack had been weakened and exhausted, and their leadership and reputation undermined. They had been disarmed and the RPF had benefited from that.[8] (See Appendix for complete interview.)

The unclassified National Security documents also help understand Roméo Dallaire's behaviour during the tragedy in Rwanda and afterwards. His appointment as commander of the UN mission had already helped reduce France's role in that part of Africa. Then in 1994, when Paris was about to launch Opération Turquoise based on a Security Council resolution, General Dallaire publicly opposed the operation, saying that he approved the presence of French-speaking African troops, but not of French troops. Again in August 1994, Dallaire spoke out against extending the mandate of Opération Turquoise in Rwanda. He also threatened to resign if the UNAMIR troops were put under French command.[9]

In an interview with a United Nations official during the same period, Roméo Dallaire declared: "If they land here to deliver their damn weapons to the government, I'll have their planes shot down."[10] When a commander of a peacekeeping mission created by the Security Council dares threaten a permanent member of the Security Council in this manner, he must know that he has powerful friends in high places, including other permanent Security Council members. France unsurprisingly tried to remove Dallaire as commander of the UN mission.

Gilbert Ngijol who was Jacques-Roger Booh-Booh's assistant does not mince his words: "Dallaire was very close to the RPF. He got involved not only in military issues but also in all the political issues which were Booh-Booh's responsibility as the secretary general's political envoy. By insisting that he co-sign all memos with Booh-Booh, Dallaire ensured that he would oversee all messages the political envoy would send."

During the night of April 6, 1994 General Dallaire was invited by a group of Rwandan military officers to discuss the next steps to be taken following the death of the president and the chief of staff of the Rwandan armed forces, Colonel Déogratias Nsabimana, who was also in the plane. There was talk of having Prime Minister Agathe Uwilingiyimana address the population on Rwandan radio. Madame Uwilingiyimana was a member of the opposition MDR party and many were opposed because she was perceived as a relentless opponent of President Habyarimana who had just been killed. Her intervention on national radio would be seen as a provocation and would make things worse. Nevertheless, the next day UNAMIR troops under Dallaire's orders took Prime Minister Agathe Uwilingiyimana to the radio station to address the Rwandan people. She was assassinated during this operation.

Who gave Roméo Dallaire the right to make political and constitutional decisions of this nature concerning the future of Rwanda? Was he now a Rwandan constitutional expert? Was he acting on his own or was he carrying out orders?

When Roméo Dallaire refused the April 7 offer from French officers to investigate the shooting down of President Habyarimana's plane and stated that he had already discussed the issue with the Americans, was he acting on his own or was he carrying out orders? If in these two cases, the answer is that he was receiving orders, where were they coming from?

French investigative journalist Pierre Péan has revealed that at some points Dallaire, instead of reporting to his superiors in Washington, was sending his operating orders with request for instructions to Lieutenant General Daniel Schroeder, head of the so-called humanitarian operation Support Hope, with a copy to Lieutenant Colonel Jim Anderson at the recently reopened US Embassy.[11] Why and when did Dallaire begin reporting and receiving instructions from a U.S. military commander?

Was General Maurice Baril, who headed peacekeeping operations at the UN headquarters, instructing Dallaire? If so, who was telling Maurice Baril what was to be done?

These very important questions remain unanswered. Each time Roméo Dallaire has appeared officially at hearings or in courts,

French investigative journalist Pierre Péan
Pierre Péan has revealed that Force Commander Roméo Dallaire was reporting to U.S. military commanders and diplomats and whereas he was in Rwanda as commander of a UN peacekeeping mission.

the content of his testimony has been so carefully censored that it has been impossible to get to any important details. General Dallaire refused all my requests for an interview. My written requests for written answers to these questions were simply ignored. In the name of history and the truth, he must answer those questions.

"General Dallaire, did you decide on your own that Ms Agathe Uwilingiyimana should address Rwandans on Radio-Rwanda on the morning of April 7, 1994? If not, who made that decision?"

Shake Hands with the Devil came out in fall 2003 and has won many prizes, including Canada's Governor General's award. Yet the questions remain unanswered. Dallaire also maintains the silence about the April 6 assassination.

These questions are important, but the answers have become somewhat academic considering the Americans' determination to see the RPF win a decisive victory and their unwavering support for Rwanda under Paul Kagame ever since. Unless Roméo Dallaire and Maurice Baril can prove the contrary, it can be assumed that both Baril and Dallaire were simply operatives carrying out decisions made at higher levels based on strategic considerations that are becoming clearer everyday.

Roméo Dallaire, appointed Canadian Senator for life, has behaved erratically ever since his stint in Rwanda. Rather than shellshock, his behaviour more likely reveals his inability to look at himself in the mirror after constantly covering up the truth about the tragic events in Rwanda in 1994. It would appear that Roméo Dallaire had a difficult time learning the "art of winning when you are in the wrong," as Cheik Hamidou Kane wrote in his classic novel *Ambiguous Adventure*. On the other hand, it appears that General Maurice Baril had little trouble with the art of winning while in the wrong. He behaved the same way during the refugee crisis in Zaire/Congo in November 1966 (see Chapter 15). For services that Maurice Baril rendered in Africa, and particularly in Rwanda, Canadian Prime Minister Jean Chrétien rewarded Maurice Baril with the plumb job of Chief of Staff of the Canadian Armed Forces in September 1997.

PART 2

CHAPTER 8

The Heart of Dark Imaginations

We were simply saying that culture was more important than politics, and that the slave trade could be explained, first and foremost, by the cultural contempt.

Léopold Sédar Senghor on the origins of Negritude.

For centuries Africa has provided fertile soil for the growth and blossoming of the European imagination. It has also been a powerful source of popular literature of all genres. Ship captains, explorers, slave traders, and pirates have recounted their adventures. Stanley and Livingstone and others wrote of their travels. Early anthropologists wrote learned treatises, though we now know that there was nothing scientific about their work. Nonfiction tended to dominate until the middle of the nineteenth century when novelists began drawing inspiration from Africa. This type of literature continued to grow in the twentieth century, before, during, and after the upheaval that occurred as Africans liberated themselves from colonial rule.

Any body of literature of this magnitude inevitably generates a set of conventions, images, and metaphors. Writers and researchers, including many Africans, have studied and analyzed that literature, first to identify the ideologies and the prejudice therein that allowed Europe—and America—to exploit and rape Africa and Africans with impunity for four hundred years and secondly to determine whether or not the same prejudice pervades modern literature. Among the best known and most eloquent of these are Chinua Achebe, Aimé Césaire, Léopold Sédar Senghor, and Ishmael Reed, to name only a few. In France Pascal Blanchard and Nicolas Bancel have also researched and published the images of empire as reflected in posters and photography. [1] One of the most systematic works published on this question is the well titled, *The Africa that Never Was, Four Centuries of British Writing about Africa.* [2]

The book presents the results of Dorothy Hammond's and Alta Jablow's in-depth study of more than five hundred British publications, fiction and nonfiction, dating from 1560 to 1960. The authors conclude that a literary tradition was developed in Europe and America and that that tradition informs most popular literature on Africa. Though their detailed study focuses on British literature, the authors maintain that, except for a few subtle differences, the same tradition holds for most of Western literature.

Hammond and Jablow showed that fantasies and myths from past centuries developed into a set of awe- and dread-inspired conventions and images from which novelists, travel writers, and essayists draw their inspiration to tell their tales. The conventions are so ingrained that they even withstand powerful changes in political sensitivities such as anti-racism and anti-colonialism. New sensitivities and new political concerns sometimes force writers to perform literary gymnastics, but more often than not they simply morph into a new matrix in which writers further develop the images and metaphors based on fantasies of bygone days. Novelists differ from nonfiction writers only in the measure of their unbridled imaginations.

Hammond and Jablow conclude that the literary image of Africa is a fantasy of a continent and a people that never was and never could have been. Yet when an image is constantly repeated it becomes the substance itself. European ethnocentrism is the constant and unifying theme of this literary convention. "Ethnocentrism created and preserved until today a persistent fantasy: the civilized Briton in confrontation with savage Africans in an Africa that never was." [3]

European perceptions of Africa cannot be addressed without mention of Joseph Conrad whose name is intimately linked with Africa, especially in the English-speaking world. Conrad and his novella *Heart of Darkness*, published in 1902 when Europe's so-called civilizing mission in Africa was at a peak, has become a necessary reference for all people who write about Africa, and specifically about Central Africa and Rwanda. Conrad quotes are *de rigueur* in all popular literature. These writers may be trying to be cute or even erudite, even though anybody who has taken first-year English has read *Heart of Darkness*. It is my belief, however, that modern writers simply do not have the excuse that Conrad had: he was writing at a time when colonialism was at a high-water mark, widely considered to be a good idea. Any prejudice in Conrad's work was common stock. That should not be the case today.

"Conrad did not originate the image of Africa we find in his book," wrote the Nigerian novelist Chinua Achebe in 1975. "It was and is the dominant image of Africa in the Western imagination." [4] Is it too much to ask that modern writers take into account the searing criticisms of Conrad's work and especially those written by African writers before they use him to tell their stories and illustrate their opinions? The fact that they do not consider those who have rejected Conrad is a telling sign of where they are coming from.

Chinua Achebe does not mince his words. In his opinion, *Heart of Darkness* is a thoroughly racist book, "which parades in the most vulgar fashion the prejudices and insults from which a section of mankind has suffered untold agonies and atrocities in the past and continues to do so in many ways and many places today."

The main problem of Conrad's novella according to Achebe is the "dehumanization of Africa and Africans." Achebe states: "the question is whether a novel which celebrates this dehumanization, which depersonalizes a portion of the human race, can be called a great work of art. My answer is: No, it cannot." In the following quote, he highlights the very troubling aspect of *Heart of Darkness,* namely the terrifying thought that Africans were human and even relatives of Europeans, yet somewhat remote.

> The earth seemed unearthly. We are accustomed to look upon the shackled form of a conquered monster, but there—there you could look at a thing monstrous and free. It was unearthly, and the men were—No, they were not inhuman. Well, you know, that was the worst of it—this suspicion of their not being inhuman. It would come slowly to one. They howled and leaped, and spun, and made horrid faces; but what thrilled you was just the thought of their humanity—like yours—the thought of your remote kinship with this wild and passionate uproar. Ugly. Yes, it was ugly enough.[5]

Conrad's defenders would insist that it was Marlow's attitude and not Conrad's in this passage and others. Conrad's prejudice however comes out clearly in other works. The tale he told about his first encounter with a black man should remove any doubts that, as Achebe bluntly put it, "Conrad had a problem with niggers."

> A certain enormous buck nigger encountered in Haiti fixed my [Conrad's] conception of blind, furious, unreasoned rage, as manifested in the human animal to the end of my days. Of the nigger I used to dream for years afterwards.[6]

Conrad is among the most studied writers in the English language. He and his work embody Europe's and America's vision of Africa. Adverse criticism of Conrad like that of Chinua Achebe abounds and is well known. Because of his racism some schools in the United States stopped teaching Conrad in their literature courses. It is surprising therefore that so many writers continue to use him as a crutch when they are writing about Africa. He is regularly quoted, paraphrased, and used as a starting point. Writers compare themselves to him and borrow his images. It would appear that the prejudice towards Africa and Africans contained in his work has permeated so deeply in Western consciousness that it is not even noticed.

Hammond and Jablow identified a literary tradition: in short, a series of metaphors used to describe the African continent and its inhabitants on the one hand, and the relationship between Europeans and Africans on the other. Each metaphor is constructed by the whole body of literature of past centuries.

The most common metaphor identified is what they call the "abysmal gulf" that separates Africa from Europe. Everything African is light years away from Europe: the land, the people, the animals, the vegetation, the institutions, the beliefs, and more. Attempts made to bridge the gulf are all vain and doomed to fail. The qualities and the flaws of the African land mass are even attributed to the people who live there: wild, unchanged, unchanging, unchangeable... The literature abounds in descriptions of the beauty and majesty of African landscape, but these descriptions are used as relief to emphasize how that beauty contrasts with the evil and horror that pervades the continent and its inhabitants.

Africa and Africans are impervious to change and improvements that Europeans have brought. Though some may well have tried to adopt the institutions such as Christianity, European political systems, constitutional rule, and clothing, they have never really succeeded. These efforts have only resulted in pale copies that are beneath the contempt of Europeans and cannot withstand the powerful innate forces of Africa. For example, for a very long time the term "African King" was considered to be an oxymoron, since there were no kings, only despots. The same reasoning applies to African religions, which were no more than superstition, and to polygamy, which was presented as institutionalized lust.

The African languages, cultures, and beliefs made Africans a different order of humanity, an order that is incomprehensible to Europeans. Just as Europeans could not understand Africans, the same holds in the other direction: Africans can never understand Europeans.

The "dark labyrinth" is another common metaphor. Africa is made mysterious, it threatens but also enchants. Death and violence are everywhere. Africa's soil is blood-soaked. Africans are unconscious victims of their own instincts and imbecility. From the earliest contacts between Europeans and Africans, the descriptions of violence and death have been horrific and are presented with the most lurid details. Unlike historical accounts of the bloody wars that tore Europe apart, none of the accounts of similar battles in Africa offers the least social, economic, political or institutional explanation. Africans simply like to kill. They cannot help but do it.

African religion, even after Christianity was adopted, is fundamentally phallic, inspired by fear, fertility, and blood. Descriptions of religion are inevitably embellished with examples of cruelty, bloodthirstiness, and, of course, cannibalism. Images of cannibalism were particularly popular at the end of the nineteenth century, perfectly timed to legitimate Europe's civilizing mission, but they never really disappeared from the literature.

In the "dark labyrinth" Africans are only body and instinct. They are incapable of abstract thinking and cannot make the link between cause and effect. When Europeans venture into the labyrinth, they do so to test character or to find answers about their own identity or about life and death.

Hammond and Jablow identified three other recurring metaphors, one being that of Africa the "strange woman." She draws the European to her only to trap him. This metaphor allows European writers to explore their own fantasies about Africa, but it also reveals their own perception of the relationship between the Western world and Africa. The two other metaphors identified are Africa "the land in amber" and "the antagonist."

In the following pages it will be shown that this literary tradition is still powerful, persistent, and unfortunately altogether too pervasive in the modern popular literature on Rwanda. Readers will note that I have avoided reproducing long quotes from earlier works. Others have quoted them rigorously and at length in accessible books.

Modern writers on Rwanda, though predictably politically correct, sometimes make efforts to break with the tradition by using a cleansed legalistic vocabulary. They liken the Rwandan tragedy to past events upon which a general agreement has been reached, such as Nazi Germany, Nuremberg, and the Holocaust, or by proclaiming loud and strong their opposition to colonialism. Yet old habits die hard. A close look shows that those habits permeate these books to the point that they become their substance. Borrowing from the tradition appears to be a necessary condition for a successful book marketing campaign, and perhaps the best example is Michela Wrong's *In the Footsteps of Mr. Kurtz*, a book on the ... yes the Congo.

Four writers were chosen. Their books on Rwanda have won awards, received enthusiastic praise, and sold well, and they are widely quoted as trustworthy sources. These three works of nonfiction and one novel have helped establish the foundations of the official narrative about Rwanda. Though the four writers come from four different nations—though Québec is not independent, culturally it is a different nation than Canada—the national subtleties that distinguish them are but dust on the bedrock of the popular western literary tradition.

Philip Gourevitch, from the United States, published *We wish to inform you that tomorrow we will be killed with our families, Stories from Rwanda* in 1998. He is a staff writer at *The New Yorker* in which he also publishes articles about Rwanda. Gourevitch was very close to the United States Secretary of State in the Clinton administration, Madeleine Albright. Gourevitch's brother-in-law at the time, Jamie Rubin, was Ms Albright's senior political attaché and head of communications. His book won many awards and was a "New York Times Editors' Choice." As an illustration of the book's significance, a United States immigration judge in St. Paul Minnesota imposed Gourevitch's book as compulsory reading for all attorneys dealing with Rwandan refugees requesting political asylum.[7]

The second book, from Canada, entitled *The Lion, The Fox and The Eagle, A Story of Generals and Justice in Yugoslavia and Rwanda* was published in 2000. The author, Carol Off, is also a television and radio journalist with the Canadian Broadcasting Corporation and has done some television reporting on the Rwandan tragedy and events that followed.

The third book, a novel, first appeared in French in Québec and in Europe. *Sunday at the pool in Kigali* by Gil Courtemanche was published in 2000, has won awards and much praise, and was made into a film in 2006. Gil Courtemanche was a well known Québec journalist who described his book as follows: "This novel is fiction. But it is also a chronicle and eyewitness report." The novel was a best seller in Québec and has been translated into twenty-three languages.

The fourth book, *Rwanda: Histoire d'un génocide*, by the Belgian journalist Colette Braeckman, played a key role in imposing the new paradigm on Central Africa since it was published only months after the Rwandan Patriotic Front took power in 1994. It is not surprising that the author is Belgian. Though Belgium does not wield the power it once did, it still boasts an abundance of "experts" that give the impression of power. Many others defer to the Belgian "experts" in recognition of the former mother country's supposed historical ascendancy. Ms Braeckman is a prolific and high profile reporter with the Brussels daily *Le Soir* and with *Le Monde diplomatique*. Since her 1994 book appeared, Ms Braeckman has published other books and her position on the Rwandan Patriotic Front has changed slightly. However, although she may have changed, the effect of her 1994 book cannot be erased.

CHAPTER 9

Power to Those Who Have It!
- Philip Gourevitch

It is on the Anglo-American race that the hope of the world for liberty and progress rests.

David Livingstone[1]

"Power largely consists in the ability to make others inhabit your story of their reality." That is Philip Gourevitch's definition of power, and that is the power he feels endowed with as he travels through the hills, across the lakes, in and out of the cities and towns of Rwanda, Zaire, Uganda, Tanzania, Europe, and the United States, chronicling his adventures and opinions in a pompously titled book *We wish to inform you that tomorrow we will be killed with our families, Stories from Rwanda.*[2]

More than any other book on Rwanda, Gourevitch's *Stories* reeks of power. By namedropping he makes it clear that he had privileged access to many of the main players in the Rwandan tragedy, including Paul Kagame, Ugandan President Yoweri Museveni, and all the United States ambassadors in the area. Doors were opened so wide for him that in 1997 in the former Zaire he was the one who, with the blessing of Rwandan and Ugandan troops, discovered compromising papers in the late Zairean President Mobutu Sese Seko's palace in Goma. More important to him, it seems, was his discovery of what he calls "the Big Man's diapers" which he takes pains to describe so that he can heap even more scorn on him and, at the same time, on all post-colonial African leaders for whom Mobutu was supposedly the paragon.

Gourevitch is close to power and he has style, but neither enables him to escape the popular literary tradition that hatched during slavery and colonialism. In fact, his proximity to power and his style lead him further into that tradition's worst manifestations.

Ever since the Europeans, and especially the British, set foot in Africa, they have held the kings, chiefs, and leaders in total contempt and systematically displayed that contempt in their literature. So doing, they were able to convince themselves of their own moral and cultural superiority and justify their so-called civilizing mission. Showing contempt for African chiefs and leaders is an insidious but effective way of showing contempt for all Africans. After all, what human beings would ever accept to live under such despots? Even the slave traders and slave owners could stand tall since they too were liberating the Africans from the tyrants. Among this grisly assortment of chiefs, the Europeans were always able to find one or two "good" ones, but who earned their good graces only because they were ready to march to the European drum. The chosen "good" chiefs could expect to be treated with the courtesy due to anybody who remained faithful and in line, respecting his rank, never getting uppity.

Since Gourevitch knew he was close to real power—the administration of "the greatest power on earth" as he likes to gloat—and because he is from the United States where good always prevails, he pushes the old "good-chief, bad-chief" tradition to new limits. He identifies a few good chiefs and lauds their goodness to the point that one wonders why they have not yet won a Nobel Prize. In contrast, the others, who make up the vast majority, are necessarily "bad," but not just bad like hardened criminals, bad like evil, bewitched, incomprehensible, bordering on the inhuman.

The two African leaders to receive Gourevitch's blessings are, predictably, Paul Kagame, now president of Rwanda, and Yoweri Museveni, president of Uganda and number one supporter of the Rwandan Patriotic Front ever since the October 1990 invasion of Rwanda. Blessing is an understatement: Gourevitch waxes hagiographic. Paul Kagame, for instance, is a man who "always sounded so soothingly sane… a man of rare scope—a man of action with an acute human and political intelligence."[3] His grandeur is awe-inspiring. He is one of the best military strategists of our time. "He was an intensely private man; not shy—he spoke his mind without bluster. A neat dresser, married, a father of two, he was said to like dinner parties, dancing, and shooting pool, and he was a regular on the tennis courts at Kigali's Cercle sportif." A description like that could appear in the personal ad section of a paper serving New York's Upper East Side. Carried away by his own eloquence and aware of the people in the United States he wanted to convince, Gourevitch found that he could not help thinking of another "tall skinny civil warrior, Abraham Lincoln." It's hard to beat that comparison.

The other good chief, Yoweri Museveni, is a pragmatic man of enormous energy. He possesses a "frontiersman's inventiveness" and is a champion of free enterprise with an "everyman look that is part of his appeal." When he speaks and when he writes it is "lucid, blunt, and low on bombast." He attacks corruption and bad governance in Africa. He defers to the European by saying that Africa's problems are African. He reads all the latest good American books. He assiduously promotes new products such as a type of toothpaste developed in the Ugandan backcountry. He understands the genesis and superiority of the "great democracies" and places African evolution somewhere between the fifteenth and the eighteenth centuries. For Gourevitch on the other hand, African evolution is somewhere near the end of the Middle Ages in Europe. As a reward for all Museveni has said and done, Gourevitch also gratifies him with a flattering comparison to another mythical American hero: he is like George Washington. Who could ever dislike a man of that stature?

It goes without saying that such high-calibre military and political leaders can only have armies that are "disciplined, polite and benevolent," who have "ideas of right and wrong." They develop "efficient" political and social institutions. In a nutshell, these two countries with two "good" chiefs give promise and hope to a continent that, according to Gourevitch, has little of each. The author's two "good" Africans and their armies are given moral standards and behaviour that must surely be the envy of other modern American commanders like Norman Schwarzkopf, Colin Powell, Wesley Clark or David Petraeus, before his downfall.

The unequalled "goodness" of Gourevitch's two favourites dramatizes the total abjectness of all the other African leaders. President Habyarimana and his entourage are made to be in constant communication with demons and "in concert with the occult." The author gleefully mocks the Habyarimana family's difficulties in giving the late president a proper funeral following his assassination on April 6, 1994. It is a laughing matter for Gourevitch that Habyarimana's remains were transferred first from Kigali to Eastern Zaire and then to Kinshasa before being laid to rest. On the other hand Gourevitch remains suspiciously silent about the assassination that triggered the beginning of the tragedy, except when he infers that President Habyarimana and his inner circle had plotted their own deaths.

When Gourevitch is not busy describing the dying Mobutu's diapers—he could have told us about the diapers of other dying leaders like Ronald Reagan or the Queen Mother, or even his own parents—he holds forth about the "mint black" colour of his Mercedes, the shininess of his Land Rover, his bath oils, and Jacuzzis. Why does he not also describe the bath oils and the cars used by Bill Clinton and Madeleine Albright during their much-praised sweep through Africa with stopovers in Rwanda and Arusha, Tanzania?

Gourevitch's contempt reaches a peak in his treatment of the two Hutu presidents of Burundi who were assassinated respectively on October 21, 1993 and April 6, 1994. Though their assassinations were watershed events, Gourevitch does not deign to name either. They remain the unknown and unnamed assassinated presidents. Dead or alive, Melchior Ndadaye and Cyprien Ntaryamira simply do not fit into "the story of their reality" in which Gourevitch makes Rwandans and other Africans inhabit. If Gourevitch had his way, history will not even retain their names.

There is method in the oversimplification of good versus bad in Gourevitch's book, just as there was in earlier times and earlier books. By focusing on Mobutu's diapers and limousines and on Habyarimana's funeral or lack thereof, the author is simply reinforcing the image of the wonderful renaissance the leaders he has blessed are supposedly bringing about. He makes it into the symbolic burying of the post-colonial leadership, the supposed generation of corrupt despots who rose out of a mafia-like culture. To the very last one, they are "predatory," "monomaniacal" leaders. This generation is being replaced by those Gourevitch has anointed as liberators and thinkers, namely Paul Kagame and Yoweri Museveni. The assassinated presidents of Burundi do not get named so that they will not cast shadows on the two anointed leaders, Kagame and Museveni, who, in fact, were very likely implicated in the assassinations. (For the record, this concealment is contagious: neither Gil Courtemanche nor Carol Off bother to name the Burundian president assassinated on April 6, 1994. They too do not want history to retain the names of those African leaders.)

The "good-chief, bad-chief" formula also enables Gourevitch to put colonial and post-colonial Africa on an equal footing in terms of injustice and hardship foisted upon Africans. For instance he describes the war in Rwanda and the war that followed in Zaire/Congo as a "decolonization process." To bolster his case, Gourevitch surprisingly refers to V.S. Naipaul and his complaints about African "post-colonial mimic men," leaders that supposedly reproduce the abuses they rebelled against. One wonders if by citing Naipaul Gourevitch also endorses that writer's racism, which, despite his Nobel Prize, has been roundly denounced by African and African American writers, including Chinua Achebe and Ishmael Reed.[4] It is outrageous for a writer to use such a thinly disguised reference to monkeys (mimic men) in a book meant to help understand a modern tragedy in Africa? Gourevitch is supposed to be a well-informed writer. Does he not know that Naipaul has declared that blacks were "the most stupid, primitive, lazy, dishonest, and violently aggressive people in the world?"[5]

The theme of the equivalent evils, the two sides of the same coin, the two old mentalities represented by the thirty-five years of African independence and the seventy-five years of colonialism is recurrent in Gourevitch's *Stories*. Once again his madness does not lack method: he can minimize the crimes of colonialism, absolve the perpetrators of those crimes and their successors, and, most importantly, absolve them of any responsibility in current catastrophes.

Another literary convention pervading his *Stories* is that of the "abysmal gulf" separating Africa and the United States. This convention helps the author to enhance the image of the anointed "good chiefs" who operate in such horrible situations and to justify the unjustifiable acts they commit.

Gourevitch sets the stage in the first paragraph of the first page of his first *Story*. He tells of a meeting with three drunken soldiers whose eyes "glowed the color of blood oranges" —all eyes seem to be bloodshot in books on Rwanda—and a pygmy from the jungle who was also drunk. The pygmy hates everything around him and only wants to marry a white woman because, according to the pygmy, "only a white woman can understand my universal principle on Homo sapiens."[6] Under no circumstances could he marry a black woman. Gourevitch concludes this story proclaiming his belief in African humanity. But who is questioning African humanity if it is not Gourevitch himself?

The author punctuates the opening story with a statement of mission that he borrows—oh surprise—from Joseph Conrad's *Heart of Darkness*. Gourevitch's mission, or point of departure, is to soothe people's imaginations just as Conrad's hero Marlow had requested when he returned from penetrating dark Africa. When Marlow's aunt in London insisted on helping him get better, Marlow said, "It was not my strength that needed nursing, it was my imagination that wanted soothing." It should be remembered what tortured Marlow's—and Conrad's—imagination: it was "the thought of their humanity—like yours—the thought of your remote kinship with this wild and passionate uproar. Ugly. Yes, it was ugly enough." It would be difficult to imagine a more effective way of widening the gulf in the American readers' minds between them and Africa than Gourevitch's four-page introductory story with the pygmy.

The tongue ever turns to the aching tooth. Judging by the number of times Gourevitch's tongue turns to the question of African humanity, one can only conclude that he must be terribly troubled by that question. (Only Gil Courtemanche in *Sunday at the pool in Kigali* equals him). In the praise for his book the publisher prepares the reader by saying that Philip Gourevitch "risked life and safety to bring dark truths to a world reluctant to know them... he raises the human banner in hell's mouth, the insignia of common sense, of quiet moral authority."

The two conventions—good chiefs winning out over the bad ones, and the "abysmal gulf"—are the mould into which Gourevitch pours the observations and fantasies of an intrepid American investigator sent to faraway lands as well as the deliberations of the supreme American court of morals. It all leads to the obvious conclusion that good will defeat evil.

The totally unwarranted massacres committed by the army of the Rwandan Patriotic Front against civilians in the Kibeho camp in April 1995[7] are made to be regrettable incidents that resemble those that occurred as General Sherman led the Union army to defeat the Confederates in the American Civil War, or during the liberation of France and Italy from the Nazis: yes errors may have occurred but those errors do not make the cause less noble. The Rwandan and Ugandan invasion of Zaire/Congo in October and

November 1996, the bombing of refugee camps, and the forced return to Rwanda become justice and truth in action. The International Criminal Tribunal for Rwanda becomes a valiant and noble attempt to bring the Nuremberg model to a continent where the rule of law and public morals are established, at best, by criminals, if not by demons themselves.

The *Stories* end like a bad Western. President Clinton lands in Africa in 1998 shortly after his Secretary of State Madeleine Albright paid a visit. Both apologize for the international community's slow reaction to such a horrible genocide and solemnly promise to restore the truth and see to it that people who do not share their views will be put in their place.

On the second last page of the book, Gourevitch first fawns on President Clinton, "as the voice of the greatest power on earth, he had come to Kigali to set the record straight." Then he gives the microphone to a Rwandan Hutu who says: "Here was a politician who had nothing at stake, and who told the truth at his own expense." The concluding words are left to a Tutsi: "Maybe you have to live somewhere far away like the White House to see Rwanda like that."

All that's missing is the sunset and the Marlboro cigarettes.

CHAPTER 10

◆

The Importance of Being Canadian
- Carol Off

Imperialists: All honest, polite, peaceable, charming people.

Gustave Flaubert, *The Dictionary of Accepted Ideas*

Carol Off's essay *The Lion, The Fox and the Eagle*[1] attempts to analyze, appraise, and define the role of Canada and Canadians in international affairs through the two major crises in Rwanda and Yugoslavia. This very Canadian approach to the subject—Canada is always trying to prove it is more than a US appendage—immediately relegates Africa and Africans to supporting roles for two of the author's heroes, Roméo Dallaire, "the lion," and Louise Arbour, "the eagle." Her third hero, "the fox," is Lewis MacKenzie, commander of UN peacekeepers in Yugoslavia. Simply by her take on the subject, Carol Off illustrates the tenacity and the pervasiveness of the literary convention in which Africa is the testing ground for European character.

She starts right off in Chapter 2, entitled *Into Africa,* with a long epigraph from Conrad about "strong, lusty, red-eyed devils" and "violence," "greed," and "hot desire." The reader is left with little doubt about the author's state of mind. She then proclaims that, "*Heart of Darkness* is not so much a place as a frame of mind, a journey into the darkness of the soul as it finally arrives at a place where there are no explanations for anything. Roméo Dallaire entered such a place (Rwanda) in the fall of 1993." Conrad is always there to bolster Carol Off's portrait of Canadians in Africa. She borrows quotes and images from him to widen the gulf that her heroes valiantly, selflessly, but vainly, endeavour to bridge.

In November 1993 Dallaire and his troops "sensed the darkness closing in." As they try to understand what is happening, she opines that the only thing they "could sense was what Conrad described as 'the stillness of an implacable force brooding over an inscrutable intention'." Later the reader learns that Dallaire's mission, which had "tried and failed to stop the dark, random forces of hate and evil," had begun "to morph into something more sinister." The gulf is made so frightful and wide that those who try to bridge it or, to use a less fashionable but more accurate vocabulary, to take civilization across it, are doomed to fail. Indeed, if Conrad did not exist, somebody would have had to invent him.

Like so many others now and in the past Carol Off waxes lyrical every time she mentions the beautiful African countryside. For Off and her Roméo Dallaire, "Rwanda is extraordinarily beautiful." The country is "covered by lush green hills." The vegetation is "deep-blue green" and the "delicious humid climate" has a "perpetual breath of spring." Dallaire and his Canadian assistant Major Brent Beardsley thought, "they were in paradise." As goes the tradition, so goes Carol Off. The majesty and the beauty of the landscape is inversely proportional to the evil it hides, and that evil in all its details inevitably appears a few lines or paragraphs after her descriptions of Rwanda's bucolic surroundings.

To portray the evil Carol Off recycles many of the images and relationships established by her predecessors who wrote during the heydays of slavery and colonialism. The Africans' eyes she imagines are bloodshot and the ground is slick with blood. The Africans' nature is linked to the climate and the land in which they live. For example, she describes the steamy mist that "swirls around the blue-green landscape, creating and otherworldly quality" that results in spiritualism being "deep in the fibre of the country." It is not surprising for a Canadian writer to make these links. English Canadian literature abounds with nativist clichés attributing the courage and energy of Canada's youth to the country's cold and rugged climate and geography. "True north strong and free," goes the English translation of Canada's national anthem.

Carol Off astonishingly uses cannibal imagery in her descriptions. Setting the stage for her hero Dallaire, she writes that Dallaire would have been better prepared for his mission if he had read the report of the 1993 International Commission of Inquiry—that one again (see Chapter 4)—and if he "had known even half of what was being cooked up in Mrs. Habyarimana's kitchen in spring and summer of 1993." Obviously, she would never use such a cooking image when talking about political leaders and their wives such as Laureen Harper, Laura Bush or Cheri Blair. Why then do they come to mind in books on Africa? Former Toronto Mayor Mel Lastman was rightly denounced for saying he saw himself "in a pot of boiling water" before his promotional tour to Mombasa for Toronto's Olympic bid; Carol Off should be denounced too.

A book that so cravenly glorifies two representatives of Canadian institutions in Africa easily falls into the trap of treating African institutions with contempt, be they modern or ancient. This is a very old habit that Off does not even attempt to shed. Religion is superstition, governments are despotic, and European institutions adopted by Africans are mere caricatures.

African Christianity is without a doubt the institution that has been, and is still, the most widely belittled and, according to Hammond and Jablow, "debased" in the popular literary tradition.[2] Though it is admitted that Africans have adopted the rituals of Christianity, they just do not seem to have grasped the meaning. Carol Off expands on this notion when she writes that, "an overlay of rigorous paternalism imposed on the citizenry by the Roman Catholic Church reinforced what was already a system of blind obedience to authority." It would follow that Rwandans are not real Catholics for Ms Off since Christianity is only an "overlay," that cannot resist the onslaught of primal forces. The ancestral traditions of "blind obedience" thus sweep away the poorly stuck "overlay" of our excellent Christian traditions, which seem to be innate for Europeans.

Carol Off gives free rein to her imagination when she describes the Easter Mass on April 3, 1994, just three days before the presidents of Rwanda and Burundi were assassinated.

> It's a country of devout Christians, and they filled the churches. The priests broke bread for Communion and told the congregations Jesus Christ had risen: salvation was theirs. Within the next few days, these Christians would dutifully follow the orders of the government to kill their neighbours—brutally and without mercy—whether they were men, women or babies. Many of the priests would actually help. Not salvation but the apocalypse was upon them.

The author was not in Rwanda on Sunday April 3, 1994. She has no idea what the priests did or what they told parishioners. It is clear though that her goal is to belittle the way Rwandans have adopted Christianity. Furthermore, what better way to trivialize the carefully planned and executed assassination of two African presidents, which she calls a "plane crash," than to tell a terrible tale about what she imagines went on in the churches and in the minds of the faithful three days before the assassination. Interestingly, this exact church scene on Sunday, April 3, is described in almost exactly the same words in Roméo Dallaire's book, *Shake Hands With the Devil* (p. 216). Dallaire published his book three years after Carol Off's appeared, but both had the same ghost writer/researcher, Sian Cansfield. If Random House, who published Dallaire's book, and Vintage Canada, who published Off's book, were not one and the same company, accusations of plagiarism might have been flying. Yet minds seem to meet when it comes to Africa.

As is the wont of many English Canadian journalists, Carol Off uses her references to the Catholic religion in Africa to take a few shots at Québec Catholicism. She uses puns and irony to make fun of the Latin motto Dominican Father Georges-Henri Lévesque had given to Rwanda's National University in Butare when he founded it in 1963. The motto, *Illuminatio et salus populi* or "God is my light and my salvation," given by a Québec priest who supported the Hutus, is contrasted to "darkness" and the "apocalypse" that Carol Off posits as reality. She draws parallels between Québec nationalism and the Quiet Revolution—Father Georges-Henri Lévesque was among the leading thinkers—and Rwanda's social revolution of 1959 that people liken ideologically to the genocide they describe in 1994. Shortly before he died, Father Lévesque denounced this type of post-facto guilt by association that targeted him and others.

As pointed out earlier, since the first contacts between Europeans and Africans, and especially during the nineteenth century and the beginning of colonialism, European literature was terribly simplistic about African chiefs. All were power hungry, dishonest, conniving, contemptible, even laughable, except when they agreed to march to the imperial drum, in which case they were well looked upon. Once again, a gulf separates Europe from Africa. These descriptions of contemptible African chiefs helped to comfort the self-image of efficiency, high moral standards, and universality of the people and institutions hailing from the imperial motherlands. With the stage so carefully set it was easy to take the next step and support the empire's noble colonial mission of civilizing those backward peoples.

Carol Off walks blindly down this road. When President Juvénal Habyarimana took power in 1973, he "was out of the classic African-dictator mould," according to Off. Please expand, Ms Off. She adds that it was the Cold War and "any number of despots could find, and cultivate, foreign patrons who would help them hold onto power." In other words, the imperial powers were being hoodwinked by the African despots. Her version of the late

Rwandan president was incapable of doing anything of any worth. He always "pretends" and is always deceitful. At the request of so-called donor countries, Habyarimana "pretended to pursue economic and political reforms." When he went to Arusha in August 1993 to sign the peace accord, she writes, he took part in "a grand ceremony attended by the major leaders of Africa—none of whom believed the peace agreement would work—and by members of the international community, who breathed a sigh of relief that the worst of the Rwandan crisis was over."

This passage should be read carefully because it reveals the author's deeper thoughts. First, the African leaders do not seem to be part of Carol Off's "international community," even though leaders from Tanzania, Uganda, and South Africa are present. Her "international community" appears to include only the "white" colonial club from Europe and America, just like when Europe began to colonize Africa. Secondly, according to Carol Off, the African leaders signed the agreement but they did not believe a word of it. The accusation is more serious than it appears. She is saying that these leaders were lying and deceiving the members of the "international community," who, as we all know, are selflessly devoted to Africa's wellbeing.

President Habyarimana is nothing but a puppet controlled by his "Lady Macbeth," Mrs. Habyarimana, and her entourage of "red-eyed devils," taken directly from Conrad. As in the nineteenth century, holding an African leader in contempt is the best way to show contempt for the Africans who live under him, but in this particular book it serves other purposes. It helps belittle the assassination of Habyarimana and of his Burundian colleague on April 6, 1994, which for Carol Off was a mere "plane crash." If anyone dared described 9/11 as a "plane crash" into the World Trade Centre, they would likely be committed to an asylum or thrown in jail. It also facilitates the difficult task Carol Off has of exonerating Louise Arbour, one of the two other subjects of her book, for blocking ICTR investigator Michael Hourigan's inquiry into the shooting down of President Habyarimana's plane, the only such investigation undertaken by the Tribunal.[3]

Carol Off has only fine words to describe the Rwandan Patriotic Front leader Paul Kagame, who is like the traditional ally of nineteenth-century colonialists. Paul Kagame is "brilliant," a "great military tactician," thanks mainly to his American training at the US Army and General Staff College at Fort Leavenworth, Kansas. His always "polite and well disciplined" troops are part of a "liberation army" that comes to the rescue and ends the genocide. To help her Canadian and American readers to better grasp the war and who is waging it, she disingenuously alludes to the Second World War and the fight against Hitler. Thus when she depicts the RPF as a "liberation army" ending "genocide," she knows that she has sealed her case. Once again in characteristic English-Canadian style, she is tickled to see France and a French-speaking African country brought to their knees by an English-speaking army trained by the British and the Americans.

Africa and especially Rwanda are pedestals on which she constructs and then exalts the Canadian heroes in her tale. The farther that Rwanda is made to appear from Canada, both geographically and culturally, the more valiant are her heroes. Ms Off lets her imagination fly.

She introduces Roméo Dallaire as a military man "staring down the tunnel of a long, dull finish to his career" when, one fine day, somebody offers to appoint him commander of a mission to a country in Central Africa. We've seen that before: the dull life in the mother country versus adventure in Africa. Carol Off's Dallaire knows absolutely nothing about the geography or the history of this "African country no one needed or cared about." Ignorance about Africa is made into a quality, something to be proud of, whereas for a serious journalist, it would be reason enough to have been refused the job.

We learn that her Dallaire is "smart, hard driving," "trim, handsome," with "boundless energy," a "lion's courage," and "rigorous morality." He "learned his code of social justice from his parents, whose defining experience had been the Second World War." But of course, what better school could he have had considering the parallel Carol Off wants to make between Nazi Germany and Habyarimana's Rwanda? Her exaltation—and imagination—knows no bounds. At one point she portrays Dallaire "marooned in the middle of a country he was hardly able to find on a map a year earlier, with only his NATO training and a personal sense of right and wrong to guide him," at a time when "sinister darkness" is closing in on him. It is curious how the sense of right and wrong seems to be innate for these Canadians. In *Sunday at the Pool in Kigali*, Gil Courtemanche attributes the same high moral qualities to his hero in Rwanda, Bernard Valcourt.

Louise Arbour is the eagle of the tale and the success story in Carol Off's book. She has the same sterling moral character as Dallaire. She is also "pretty," with a "quick wit," "efficient," "competent," and has an excellent legal training, especially since she practiced mainly in Ontario. All these qualities enable her to successfully carry out her mission to eliminate the "culture of impunity" that reigns in the "heart of Africa." Despite the enormous gulf, despite the tribunal's shambles, corruption, incompetence, and inefficiency that Off takes pages to describe, Louise Arbour brilliantly brings order to the court and successfully pursues the noble mission with the help of other fine Canadians, such as Pierre Duclos. A former Sûreté du Québec investigator hired by Louise Arbour, Pierre Duclos had been identified by Québec's Poitras Commission as the policeman who initiated the fabrication of evidence in the Matticks Affair.[4]

Boasting about Louise Arbour, who became a Supreme Court Justice before being appointed UN Human Rights Commissioner, makes Canadians feel good. Louise Arbour surely appreciates getting the credit. She graciously granted Carol Off several long interviews. The purpose of all the flattery is not quite so guileless however. While lauding Ms Arbour she quietly slips in shameless comments about how Africa is different and how, in this different world, Saint Louise Arbour is fully justified to "operate somewhat differently from other courts"—read European courts—and to give herself the "flexibility to hold suspects without charge."

Africa is so different that we are expected to understand and accept that "due process, as understood in North America and Europe, would have made it almost impossible [for Ms Arbour] to arrest the prime suspects," or the "big fish" as Carol Off likes to call them.

CHAPTER 11

Sunday at the Cesspool
- Gil Courtemanche

They think we're simple children:
Watermelon in the sun,
Shooting dice and shouting,
Always having fun.

Langston Hughes, *This Puzzles Me*

To make his case on Rwanda and extrapolate on his own experience in that country Gil Courtemanche chose to write a novel. His novel is also, in his own words, "an eye-witness report,"[1] even though he was not in Rwanda when the events take place. His ploy is clever since he can accuse real people of heinous crimes even while they are being tried in Arusha, sitting in prison or in exile, or living as political refugees in Europe and America. He then hides behind his licence as novelist as soon as someone presents a fact contradicting his allegations. It is also clever because he can abandon all inhibitions to his imagination and fantasies—it could also be described as bragging—about Africa, the Africans, and especially the African women he claims to know.

A work of nonfiction would have required much more research, investigation, and checking of facts, allegations, and quotes, to ensure their veracity. Courtemanche would have had to be rigorous throughout. Knowing that his lack of rigour made him vulnerable to criticism for his unbridled imagination, since he was not in Rwanda in 1994, he tries to pre-empt critics in the preface by referring to the African Rights publication entitled *Rwanda: Death, Despair and Defiance* (African Rights, London, 1995). Readers should of course know what Belgian Professor Filip Reyntjens, known internationally for his work on Rwanda, wrote as early as 1996 about the group African Rights. "As for African Rights, the political and historical analyses made by that group have a flagrant pro-RPF bias that is incompatible with the mission and code of conduct of any serious association devoted to promoting human rights."[2]

Sunday at the Pool has won numerous literary awards and has been translated from French into twenty-three languages. Critics have extolled it as "extraordinary," "elegiac," "astonishing," a "masterpiece," a "fresco with humanist accents," "novel of the year." A close read however leaves no doubt that Courtemanche's novel is a pure reproduction—also a poor reproduction—of the popular literary tradition that Africans have always categorically rejected. Even the supposedly modern narration of his imagined amorous encounters is as old as the hills of Rwanda. Similar titillating accounts appeared in popular British and French literature in the late nineteenth century, such as *L'art d'aimer aux colonies,* which was published steadily until the late 1930s. That book was very popular at the turn of the ... nineteenth century.

Courtemanche unabashedly describes his main character Bernard Valcourt as "sophisticated" and "a man of the left and an enlightened humanist" (unabashedly because Bernard Valcourt is obviously Courtemanche himself).

What shocks and astonishes most is how such "an enlightened humanist" makes his own Western world seem so far apart from and superior to Africa. The former world is "civilized." It is a world of justice and reason and of laws and regulations that are respected, a world of abstract thought and poetry. This world is also sexless, that is, until it comes into contact with Africa.

Africa, on the other hand, is a world of total disorder, a world in which instinct rules, and, in the absence of abstract thought, only concrete words are used. It is a world in which fertile and over-sexed bodies dance, "humans turn into demons," and where there is only "fire and screams rising from the hell [the Rwandans] had created." It is a "hysterical country where madness was settling as the normal condition of life" and a country that "only deserved to die, it had gorged so greedily on lies and false prophesies." That is how Courtemanche describes Rwanda.

The author also uses his characters to widen the gulf between the two worlds, particularly making his hero, Bernard Valcourt, into a stalwart defender of everything that is good. Valcourt is contrasted to the words, actions, experiences, and beliefs of his Rwandan friends, his lover Gentille, and his enemies. Courtemanche's method is well worn as the following examples show.

To defend a dead prostitute, Valcourt risks his life by reporting the incident to the assistant chief prosecutor who he describes as a "vicious hyena" in this "ridiculous republic." Valcourt does not do it because he is brave, as his lover Gentille suggests, but only because he "can't behave any other way," because he "acts by reflex, because that's the way one ought to in a civilized society." Courtemanche does not shy away from using the old colonial word "civilization" when describing his world compared to the uncivilized world he is now living in.

> I'm like a child who follows a book of rules. You excuse yourself when you bump someone by mistake ... you help the blind across the street ... you get up on the bus and give your seat to an old lady ... and when you witness a crime you go to the police so the crime will be solved and in due course justice will be done. No, my darling. I'm not brave. I'm just trying to do things right, and here, that's not easy.

Further on, he says that he would go and testify before the courts and stand ready to serve justice "if ever justice exists here as it does in the vicinity of Lafontaine Park, Monsieur Deputy." The Parc La Fontaine is a large city park in Montreal.

For the Westerner Valcourt/Courtemanche justice and citizenship along with the incumbent rights and duties come naturally. They are totally ingrained in his culture, which it seems only Westerners can assimilate. They are like a book of rules—in the original French version they are a catechism—learned from infancy by all. On the other hand, the book of rules in Rwanda, its catechism, according to Courtemanche, is hate, violence, bewitchment, all contained in a culture of impunity, a culture of lies and concealment transmitted from one generation to the next.

The author's cultural arrogance and superiority has sadly been seen before. Rudyard Kipling was the most notable representative with his "White man's burden." In the French tradition, Roger Caillois was a flag bearer of this cultural superiority. What is the difference between Valcourt's statements and those of Caillois that Aimé Césaire so roundly denounced in his landmark *Discourse on Colonialism* published in 1955. Caillois, a member of the Académie française, blindly and bluntly defended the cultural, scientific, and religious superiority of the West.

> That discipline of life which tries to ensure that the human person is sufficiently respected so that it is not considered normal to eliminate the old and the infirm ... whether for biological or historical reasons, there exist at present differences in level, power and value among the various cultures. These differences entail an inequality in fact. They in no way justify an inequality of rights in favour of the so-called superior peoples, as racism would have it. Rather they confer upon them additional tasks and an increased responsibility.[3]

For Caillois it was the "discipline of life," for Courtemanche, "a book of rules," but in both cases they smugly consider it superior. Césaire points out that the "increased responsibility" that Caillois would grant to his superior culture is nothing more than the task of ruling the world!

The "civilized" culture also includes morals and ethics. Valcourt is a man tortured by the great moral and existential questions of our time, and the concomitant quest for good, whereas he is surrounded by reckless, happy-go-lucky, simple-minded Africans.

For example, Courtemanche's noble but tormented hero, Valcourt, is contrasted to the AIDS-infected tobacco vendor, Cyprien, who is always happy and carefree, whose ambition is "to have fucked (all the women) before dying," and who likes Valcourt because he "could listen for hours and hours and talk without ever preaching." Cyprien tells Valcourt: "I'm going to tell you what always gives you such a long, serious face ... What I want to say is, you get us thinking. We feel from your eyes what you see in your head. You see dead bodies, skeletons, and on top of that you want us to talk like we're dying. I'll start doing that a few seconds before I die, but until then I'm going to live and fuck and have a good time."

Without Valcourt, Cyprien cannot think. Even though he is dying, he lives on happy-go-lucky, fucking, laughing, and drinking, with no worries about tomorrow, no thoughts about the people around him.

This type of infantilization of Africans is also not new. The French tradition has its *"petit noiraud"* advertisements (*"Y a bon BANANIA," "chocolat battu et content"*). The Anglo-American tradition has its minstrel shows, Amos and Andy, blackface. Loathsome though it may be, it is a not-too-subtle way for Courtemanche to demonstrate his own contempt for the African republic he so obviously scorns. The representatives of the republic are all "rotund," "fat," "dripping with sweat," and they choke in their too-tight suits, and hard collars that make their necks bulge. Government ministers, bureaucrats, and soldiers are unfailingly drunk, weaving about unsteadily, laughing with their "eyes rolling up in their sockets" while dancing and "dispensing HIV like parish priests their indulgences." Contemptible, the whole lot for our "sophisticated man of the left."

Gil Courtemanche infanitilizes all Africans, including his former colleague at CBC/Radio-Canada, Léo Kalinda, who was originally from Rwanda. Even though Kalinda, like Courtemanche, strongly supported the Rwandan Patriotic Front's take-over of Kigali, he is not spared. The author of the *Sunday at the Pool* transposes a real event that took place in 1987 to the 1994 period.

"Léo, who was making a film on the great Rwandan democracy, was moving about from table to table distributing smiles and lies like a Negro Maurice Chevalier in a bad musical comedy." Not far from the minstrel show! Is it possible for an African to be an intellectual? Courtemanche thinks not since he puts the word "intellectual" in quotes whenever it is beside the word "African."[4]

Describing Africa through the story of a woman—Africa 'the strange woman' as described by Hammond and Jablow—may be old and worn out, but it always makes for titillating copy, whatever the historical period. The European or North American man discovers himself and really becomes a man through his experience with an African woman. (In the same vein, Kipling wrote: "Ship me somewhere east of Suez, where the best is like the worst, Where there aren't no Ten Commandments, an' a man can raise a thirst.") The author then uses his experience to explain Africa to his readers. The reader inevitably learns more about the writer than about Africa, whereas the writer falls head first into the worst clichés.

The avowed mission of the author of *Sunday at the Pool* is to "write this country's [Rwanda's] story through the story of Gentille and her family," which is a cliché in itself. Then wittingly or not Courtemanche trots out every imaginable cliché and stereotype. Justin, the almost bestial African lifeguard who hits on a white woman from Québec has "an enormous penis," and he is contrasted to Jean Lamarre, her "over-modest husband who always came to bed clothed in pyjamas and never took them off, even when laboriously making love to her." The white characters' bodies are never described, but the Africans' bodies are all described to the last detail. The authors' friends' bodies are beautiful, his enemies' bodies, ugly; but all African bodies are caricatured.

Courtemanche's obsession with African bodies is a backdrop that provides relief for the work of the European mind. Valcourt is a man of letters and of intellect who is able to teach his lover Gentille "to come with words," which it seems no African could do. Gentille, who is "like the fruit of the red earth of this hill, a mysterious mix of all the seeds and all the toil of this country" in which the women "had only concrete words," only learns abstract thought and the beauty of poetry thanks to the good efforts of the poet and humanist Bernard Valcourt, and to his favourite writer, Paul Éluard.

Courtemanche's arrogance knows no bounds. What could he know about poetry in African languages like Kinyarwanda, Swahili or in any other, which he neither spoke, read or understood? What does he know about the relations and emotions among Africans? And what does he know about African art and creativity? Either he knows very little or he holds them in such contempt that they warrant not a word. One might also presume that Paul Éluard, who along with others signed the denunciation of the human spectacles prior to the 1931 French colonial exhibition, would have been disgusted to be conscripted into Courtemanche's tale.

As in all popular books on Africa, the images of the bucolic African countryside and luxuriance help magnify the endless descriptions of violence, death, and sex. In this book such descriptions border on necrophilia. Either the novelist did not know that war means gory death—despite modern American propaganda—or, like Conrad and Gourevitch, Courtemanche was also troubled with African humanity. The answer is in the question itself, and there is little doubt that Courtemanche had a problem with African humanity. Over and above the countless bestial adjectives and metaphors used, the author alludes to the inhumanity of Rwandans at least fourteen times, such as in the following excerpt from the original French version which the translator chose to exclude fearing perhaps that it could get the author into trouble, or that he might be accused of plagiarizing from Conrad: "*Valcourt fut horrifié par la pensée que rien dans cet homme ne lui avait paru humain...*" ("Valcourt was appalled at the thought that nothing in this man appeared to him to be human...")[5] The other thirteen references appear in English.

Borrowing from Chinua Achebe's important essay on Conrad, I would ask the same question: how can a novel that celebrates the dehumanization of a portion of the human race be so widely and uncritically praised and translated into so many languages? Why has serious literary criticism glossed over such prejudice in *Sunday at the Pool.*

The slave trade, slavery, and colonialism existed because in the eyes of the slave traders, slave owners, and colonizers Africans were inferior and less human. Slavery and colonization were therefore a blessing for these beings.

If *Sunday at the pool in Kigali* had been written in 1902, it would have been swept away by the epic cultural and political fight that ended colonialism and resulted in African independence. Today we would view the novelist and his book as underpinnings of colonialism that are much better forgotten. But the novel appeared in 2000, forty years after colonialism supposedly ended. That the book and its author were so widely eulogized speaks loudly to our refusal to recognize the seriousness of the crimes committed not so long ago; it has also heralded the period now becoming known as the New Scramble for Africa.

CHAPTER 12

◆

An Avatar of Colonial Europe - Colette Braeckman

After a short period of dormancy and a little self-doubt about its erstwhile imperial mission, the West may be ready to resume its old domineering monologue in the world.

Chinua Achebe, *Home and Exile*

When Colette Braeckman published her book *Rwanda, Histoire d'un génocide,* immediately after the Rwandan war in October 1994, she donned the cap of both reporter and editorialist. As with all war correspondents, she lines up facts, offers hypotheses, and provides quotes from leaders who, it seems, had no other choice than to grant her interviews, considering her position as reporter for the Brussels daily *Le Soir* and the influential French monthly *Le Monde diplomatique.* Her writings abound with information, but are short on truth, the first casualty of all wars. When Ms Braeckman editorializes, she has the self-righteousness of Rwanda's former imperial masters, a blatant bias in favour of the Rwandan Patriotic Front, and a marked indulgence towards her fellow Belgians, and particularly the Belgian troops.

Her very favourable treatment of Paul Kagame and the Rwandan Patriotic Front faithfully follows the popular literary tradition:

President Kagame can do no wrong (Ms Braeckman apparently changed her position several years later but never admitted any mistakes). All the other leaders, starting with President Habyarimana, are insulted and slandered. It would hold that such contemptible leaders could only lead even more contemptible people.

The Belgian troops on the other hand are lily white for Ms Braeckman. She indignantly reports that, as early as 1990, Rwandans had dared to accuse Belgian soldiers of going after Rwandan teenage girls, and even raping some. Everybody knows of course that European and American soldiers in Africa would not think of behaving that way. Yet she shows no indignation, nor does she even mention that before leaving Rwanda the Belgian troops ransacked their Kigali hotel and the international airport, spreading their excrement throughout. She also omits to mention and get indignant about the Belgian soldiers who shredded a Rwanda flag before the very eyes of Rwandan troops.[1] Should we be surprised that the Belgian troops had earned such a bad reputation by the time they left Rwanda?

Ms Braeckman lines up her facts and blindly develops theories to reinforce her belief that the Rwandan Patriotic Front "liberated" Rwanda between 1990 and 1994. Writers should know that they have to tread carefully when publishing books so soon after a major international crisis as their premises and assumptions can prove to be false or unfounded thus discrediting the entire book.

That is what happened to Colette Braeckman who claimed unequivocally that the assassination of President Habyarimana on April 6, 1994 was planned and carried out by "Hutu extremists" in the president's own entourage. Taking that as the Gospel truth, she elaborated on the mindset, motives, and acts of all the Hutus who governed both Rwanda and Burundi from 1990 to 1994. Within months of the publication of her book, several reliable analyses and investigations showed that the assassination had not been carried out as she assumed. Large sections of her book thus became false and utterly irrelevant. Such glaring errors should have eliminated Colette Braeckman as a serious source of information and analysis on Central Africa. Yet the contrary has occurred and she has remained a major source for French-language media worldwide.

The author similarly went overboard trying to prove that the Rwandan Patriotic Front was not an ethnically driven formation. Her method was to quote and promote the Rwandan Hutu leaders who agreed to participate in the government set up by the victorious RPF army. These included Prime Minister Faustin Twagiramungu, Interior Minister, Seth Sendashonga, Justice Minister Alphonse-Marie Nkubito, and President Pasteur Bizimungu. Unfortunately for her—and for her book—every one of these people fled the country, was assassinated or imprisoned in the months and years after her book appeared. All have been accused of embracing the "ideology of genocide," while some have been accused of committing genocide. As a result, more sections of her book become irrelevant.

Another striking case of the war correspondent's bias is her claim that the million internal refugees who fled northern Rwanda to camps around Kigali during the war between 1990 and 1994 were unwitting victims of the Habyarimana government's Machiavellian tactics and were not real victims of the invading RPF's violence and terror tactics. War correspondents are always affiliated with one side or the other, and few doubt the importance of their role in influencing the outcome of the war. Think of Winston Churchill in the Boer War, Rudyard Kipling, Peter Arnett in the first Gulf War, and many more. In most cases, their affiliation and even their bias are admitted and known. That is not the case with Colette Braeckman who claims to be a neutral observer.

Ms Braeckman most glaringly embraces the popular literary tradition on Africa when she ventures away from journalism to explain the origin and causes of the Rwandan tragedy. At the end of her introduction entitled "Once upon a time" she reveals her real thoughts about Africa and Africans. As she tells her tale, these thoughts reappear constantly, either as rhetorical questions or in carefully selected quotes in the book.

> It was not a question of war or political repression. It was about wiping out a whole people in the name of ethnicity, and erasing every trace of their existence from man's world. Are we faced with the last avatar of pre-colonial Africa, of "savagery?" ... Demons are dancing in people's heads. Madness is stalking everybody. The thrust of blood, fever and angst had burst through all bounds.[2]

"The last avatar of pre-colonial Africa," suggests Colette Braeckman. Though she throws in a question mark, her opinion is clear. It means that the "savagery" she describes is a reincarnation of Africa from before the Europeans civilized it. Africa was just morphing back to what it was before Europe began its mission to civilize the heathen peoples. Despite the Europeans' valiant efforts their mission just did not succeed in containing the Africans' barbarian nature. Left to themselves when they became independent, they could simply not control their instincts which, to use Ms Braeckman's words, "projected them beyond good and evil."

The reporter Braeckman also hazards a few guesses about the philosophical origins of the tragedy, but takes care to distance herself, though very slightly, by quoting European missionaries in Rwanda.

> The missionaries recognized the beast that ran wild in the country. The mad look of the militia men, the peasants' relentless glare, the radio lie machine, the intellectuals' sophisms aimed at manipulating the masses left no doubt what was happening. They saw before them their old opponent, the prince of Darkness, the Wicked One. "The Devil is back on earth," they exclaimed.[3]

Man, according to Ms Braeckman, was thus projected beyond the idea of good and evil despite the fact that Rwandans had been Christianized and had received many years of training in human rights laws, the law of war, and the necessary protection of women and children. "Is it possible," adds Braeckman "that the sudden contract of these ancient closed societies with the European world, the colonial conquest, and the social distortions it provoked had suddenly broken ancient cultural taboos? And that the graft of Christianity had not only failed to take root but had also provoked a total and self-destructive rejection one century later?"

In short, for Colette Braeckman, Christianity was grafted onto the African body but the graft didn't take, because it was impossible. The African body rejected the graft and destroyed itself at the same time. In case the reader missed the message Braeckman adds a quote from a Rwandan bishop: "The Christian message did not sink in. After a century of evangelizing, we have to start all over again."

For Carol Off, Christianity was an "overlay" that could not withstand the primary African forces. For Gil Courtemanche, the Rwandan "catechism" was hate, violence, witchcraft and lies, and churches were crematoriums. For Philip Gourevitch, Rwandans ran like herds to be baptized, blindly following a converted chief. This band of four agrees on one point: Rwandans were simply incapable of embracing Christianity correctly. Though they may have adopted the rituals, they were "never quite able to free [themselves] from the compelling forces of [their] environment and the dark inheritance of [their] forefathers," as an earlier eulogist of Empire wrote in 1958.[4]

Over and above their presumption that they can judge the religious practices of Africans, these four writers make statements that contain an even more sinister message. If a link were to exist between the supposed rejection of the meaning and values of Christianity and the "savagery" these authors enjoy describing, then a corollary would be that Africans could have avoided it all if only they had been able to assimilate the Europeans' religion correctly. Either salvation can only be found in Jesus or Europe abandoned its civilizing mission too soon.

The idea repeated *ad nauseam* that Africans have not properly understood the Christian message is profoundly and disgustingly ethnocentric. Historically, for every Christian who in the name of his or her religion has fought for peace, human equality, justice, and freedom, at least ten Christians have, in the name of the same religion, declared wars, invaded and conquered countries, massacred innocent people, enslaved millions of people, colonized entire peoples and countries, opened concentration camps, and bombed civilians. To claim or even to hint that massacres in Rwanda are proof that the Christian message did not sink in is to ignore and hide 2000 years of history.

The best answer to this argument came from Muhammad Ali. When he was visiting the World Trade Centre in New York after the 9/11 attack in 2001, a reporter asked him how he felt about the suspects sharing his Islamic faith. Ali answered pleasantly: "How do you feel about Hitler sharing yours?"

In addition to parading as a theologian who judges religions, Ms Braeckman forays into the field of African art and culture and imagines a causal link with the violence. Independent Rwanda, she maintains, has scarcely any symbolic representation. Its figurative art is "shabby and infantile." She then asks, rhetorically as usual, whether the absence of means of artistic expression might also be "a source of violence," the theory being that, since symbolic expression including language is not possible, Rwandans turn quickly to murderous acts.

Peoples who have been dominated or colonized and who have fought or are fighting to maintain their dignity have all heard this talk before. So many have been told for such a long time that they have no literature, no culture, no history and thus they really don't even deserve to exist.

Colette Braeckman's book was published in 1994, some thirty-four years after Belgian colonialists left Africa. In her book the author creates a historical paradigm in which the past thirty years in Rwanda are presented as an uninterrupted slide into hell, and she never stops repeating it. "For thirty years, Rwanda was permeated by a genocidal culture. ... In thirty years, propaganda had rooted out the meaning of good and evil." Her message could not be clearer. Before 1960, when the Belgians held sway in that part of Africa, Rwanda was protected against the evils it encountered. Since then, Rwandans have been left to themselves and look what happened.

Ms Braeckman speaks about "a last avatar of pre-colonial Africa." It would be difficult to find a better "avatar of colonial Europe and its civilizing mission" than Ms Breackman herself.

PART 3

CHAPTER 13

◆

International Criminal Justice as "Battering Ram"

The commander in chief had spoken and declared the previous verdict unattackable, holy and superior to mere mortals – and how could his subordinates dare to contradict him.

Émile Zola, *J'accuse*

The one point that the Nuremberg Tribunal and the ad hoc criminal tribunals for the former Yugoslavia and Rwanda have in common is that both involve what is known as "victors' justice," notes Ramsey Clark who was present at Nuremberg in 1945 and was lead counsel for the late Seventh-day Adventist Pastor Élisaphan Ntakirutimana. It is a question of power over principle, in which the goal is to demonize the enemy.

"It's worth remembering," adds Ramsey Clark, "that at several occasions during the Nuremberg trials, Hermann Goering shouted out 'what about Hamburg,' which was a notorious early 1943 heavy bombing of a civilian city; and he shouted out 'what about Hiroshima.' He could have added Berlin and Dresden."[1] The former United States Attorney General recalled those incidents to show that, because victors' justice is the exercise of power rather than the pursuit of justice, only the actions of one side are addressed, which more than corrupts justice. "Victors' justice is not founded in truth which involves the fundamental principle of equality, which is not only the mother of justice, it is essential to truth. Selectivity is inherently false because it does not present the whole truth you might say, the whole picture."

The Nuremberg tribunal created after World War II still has credibility and rightly so. It criminalized wars of aggression and reinforced the notion of national sovereignty, both fundamental to the preservation of peace and cornerstones of the Charter of the United Nations. Unlike Nuremberg, however, the International Criminal Tribunal for Rwanda omits reference to wars of aggression and foreign intervention and, because of that omission, legitimates them. The ICTR was unquestionably designed to punish one side and protect the other.

A criminal court is a great way to destroy one's enemies, insisted Ramsey Clark. "You can now tell the world that these vicious Serbs are the guilty ones, who did all this murderous killing, and not us who broke up Yugoslavia piece by piece." By the same token in Rwanda, the horrible "*génocidaires*" are the guilty ones, not we who destroyed Rwanda by blindly supporting an invading army.

Both the former chief prosecutor of the International Criminal Tribunal for Rwanda, Louise Arbour, and UN Secretary General Boutros Boutros-Ghali tended to agree with Ramsey Clark about the injustice inherent in the selectivity of ad hoc criminal tribunals.[2] Louise Arbour admitted that the fact Rwandans, Serbs, and Croatians, were the only ones called to account for their actions made their singling out less just, but she maintained that it did not make them less guilty. Whereas Justice Arbour continued to laud the ad hoc tribunals as trailblazers for the International Criminal Court—fangless with regards those who hold real power —, Boutros Boutros-Ghali and Ramsey Clark were much less optimistic about the tribunals, and much less naive.

Louise Arbour's apparent naïveté probably hid other motives. In a public address in Paris on November 21, 2002 Ms Arbour invoked Canada's Charter of Rights and Liberties adopted with Canada's 1982 Constitution to reinforce her defence of the International Criminal Court. That should have been a red flag for anybody who still believed in Ms Arbour's integrity. Canada's Charter of Rights was in fact at the heart of a "constitutional coup d'État" by the government of Pierre Elliott Trudeau aimed at taking away the recognized sovereign constitutional powers of the Québec National Assembly specifically in areas of language and culture.[3] Ms Arbour studiously avoided mentioning that. She also avoided mentioning that Québec's National Assembly voted almost unanimously to reject the 1982 Constitution and the accompanying charter. In addition, on the twentieth and thirtieth anniversaries of its adoption by Ottawa, the Québec National Assembly reiterated its rejection. Opposition to Canada's Charter of Rights and its Constitution, mainly from Québec, focuses on the transfer of power from people and their elected representatives to judges appointed by the Canadian Government. Similarly, opposition to the International Criminal Court is based on the fear that power has been transferred away from sovereign nations and their leaders to a new international body run by appointees who owe their appointments to the good graces of the great powers.

Secretary General Boutros-Ghali believed that the United States favoured the creation of ad hoc tribunals for the very reason that only Rwandans and Yugoslavians would be prosecuted. At the same time they vigorously fought the establishment of the permanent International Criminal Court, which would be able to prosecute American citizens. "They consider themselves to be above the law," said Boutros-Ghali.[4]

Ramsey Clark insists that the problem dates much further back. "There would be no UN had it been implied in any way in the Charter that there would be a criminal tribunal. If it had been put in directly, the meeting would have been over. People would have packed their bags in Washington before the San Francisco meeting and left. The United States would have been the first to leave.

The U.S. won't sign the treaty today. It's not peculiar to the U.S.," he added. "Power does not like to judged; it is determined not to be judged and if it has the power, it won't be."

The only court referred to in the Charter and Statutes of the United Nations was the International Court in The Hague, which had no criminal jurisdiction and only dealt with civil business of limited scope. "Its judges have been disciples of the government that is responsible for their appointment," points out Ramsey Clark, and they only arbitrate cases the UN member countries agree to submit to it. Former Attorney General Clark maintains that the International Criminal Tribunals for Rwanda and Ex-Yugoslavia are simply not authorized by the United Nations Charter, and are therefore not legal.

The contradiction is glaring. The most stubborn opponent of the International Criminal Court is the country that proposed the two Security Council resolutions creating ad hoc tribunals for Rwanda and Yugoslavia. Moreover, the chief proponent was the United States ambassador to the UN, Madeleine Albright, who soon after became secretary of state, and for whom the tribunals became a legacy.

The United States' domination in the creation and funding of the ICTR has affected all the work the tribunal has conducted in both Arusha and The Hague. This was illustrated by a highly symbolic event in 1998 when President Clinton swept through Africa that year he stopped over in Arusha, Tanzania, just as his wife did a year earlier. During his stopover, tribunal staff, realizing that the real boss was in town, raised the Stars and Stripes where the UN flag should have been flying.

The English legal system was adopted rather than the continental legal system. The power to establish the facts and lay charges was therefore given to the Chief Prosecutor whose position became the most important and powerful at the tribunal. As a result, no prosecutor has been appointed to the tribunal without being vetted by the United States State Department. The fawning behaviour of most prosecutors towards the United States and its foreign policy indicates that they knew to whom they were indebted. Carla Del Ponte, who succeeded Louise Arbour as prosecutor, was one exception and she paid the price.

The tribunal's first prosecutor, Richard Goldstone from South Africa, published a self-aggrandizing book entitled *For Humanity* in 2000.[5] The book abounds with obsequious and disingenuous compliments about the United States' role in the International Criminal Tribunal and particularly about Madeleine Albright's own personal appointee, David Scheffer, who was seconded to the prosecutor's office as special advisor immediately after Goldstone got the job. The South African prosecutor spent much of his time in Washington and New York attending cocktails and other who's who events. His cocktail circuit was so busy that Secretary General Boutros-Ghali informed Goldstone that other Security Council members were complaining about his too intimate relationship with the Americans. Boutros-Ghali shared that opinion.

The most troubling aspect of Richard Goldstone's book is his description of how the prosecutor's office obtained information from the CIA to prepare the indictments. Goldstone speaks of the CIA as if it were a database available for anybody to interrogate and obtain reliable information. You just punch in a question and out comes the answer. How can a man who was granted such power over people's lives pretend to be so naive. Is it just another way to dissimulate pro-CIA propaganda? It may have escaped Mr. Goldstone, but an intelligence outfit like the CIA is not known to be an objective supplier of reliable information. It provides information, true or false, when that information can be used to achieve its strategic goals and protect US interests and investments. Unlike the ostensible mission given to the international tribunal, justice is not the CIA's top priority.

Richard Goldstone's blind faith in the United States' desire for universal good reaches new heights in his conclusion. He expresses contentment at seeing the United States and Europe bomb the hell out of the former Yugoslavia. "Never before had a nation used military force against a sovereign foreign state for the sole reason that the human rights of its citizens were being violated."[6] Yes, Virginia, there is a Santa Claus.

The man who opened the prosecutor's office in Kigali clearly wanted to please his former superiors when he wrote his book *For Humanity*. Buried in fawning anecdotes about the powers that be in New York and Washington can be found one short paragraph to tell the tale of the Rwandan tragedy. The main omission in that short paragraph tells more than the whole book about what really happened and about the issue his superiors did not want to be discussed.

"On the night of 6 April 1994 the gruesome genocide began in Rwanda," writes Richard Goldstone. He proceeds to tell the tale that the reader surely knows by heart. In other words, one fine April evening Rwandan Hutus decided to eliminate the Tutsis. Not a word about the assassination of two African heads of state. Not a word about the war waged since October 1990. Such a cavalier attitude towards crucial facts is criminal, especially when it comes from a man supposedly devoted to justice. It is chilling to think that he was given the power to choose the people to be charged and prosecuted by the ICTR.

Louise Arbour replaced Richard Goldstone in October 1996. All accounts of Ms Arbour's appointment concur on one point: United States Secretary of State Madeleine Albright tested her, interviewed her, and handpicked her for the job. It could be added that Louise Arbour is indebted to Madeleine Albright for her nomination to the Canadian Supreme Court and later to her position as United Nations High Commissioner for Human Rights. When Canadian Prime Minister Jean Chrétien appointed her to the Supreme Court he left no doubt that Louise Arbour's international notoriety gained with the tribunal was the main reason she was fast-tracked to the prestigious position.

Louise Arbour's name was not even submitted for the tribunal position by Canada's Department of Foreign Affairs. When Richard Goldstone announced his departure, he recommended appointing a prosecutor who mastered French. The United States would never have tolerated having a French national appointed since France was a serious rival in Africa and in the Balkans. The candidate therefore had to be a French speaker who was loyal to the United States and had a healthy distrust of France. That kind of French speaker can be found in Ottawa. Some say they can be found in Belgium too.

In keeping with the wishes of those who appointed her, Louise Arbour regularly made loud and damning declarations against France, while carefully protecting the United States. In December 1997, for example, she went to Paris and accused France of boycotting the international tribunal and protecting war criminals. She denounced France's "remarkable defaulting at all levels," compared to the outstanding co-operation offered by the United Kingdom, Canada, and the United States.[7]

The ICTR's subordination to United States' foreign policy stands out especially in the prosecutors' refusal to indict criminals from the Rwandan Patriotic Front and to prosecute the perpetrators of the April 6 assassination of President Juvénal Habyarimana. Considerable evidence of massive RPF crimes against the Rwandan civilian population has been collected. All fingers point to the RPF and Paul Kagame as the sponsors of the April 6 assassination. If however the prosecutor were now to charge a member of the RPF in relation to that crime many years after the fact, it would represent a terrible admission of the ICTR's failure. Worst of all would be the fact that the whole tale developed to explain the Rwandan tragedy and the horrible war in the Congo would disintegrate like a sand castle on an abandoned beach.

In June 2013 Judge Frederick Harhoff of the International Criminal Tribunal for Yugoslavia created a stir when, in a letter to his colleagues, he criticized the President of the tribunal, U.S. Judge Theodor Meron. His criticism focused essentially on the political intervention in the judicial process in favour of the United States and Israel resulting in the acquittal of high-ranking Croatian and Serbian military and political personnel. Harhoff concluded his letter saying, "The worst of it is the suspicion that some of my colleagues have been behind a short-sighted political pressure that completely changes the premises of my work in my service to wisdom and the law." [8]

That Harhoff's letter, particularly the phrase "short-sighted political pressure," created a stir eighteen years after the ad hoc tribunals were created is the most surprising. It is more a sign of the willful blindness of the hundreds or even thousands of people who have built well-paid careers and earned well-padded pension funds out of the international law boondoggle than of any revelations contained in the letter. The political nature of the ad hoc tribunals and the International Criminal Court has never been a secret; some people close to the tribunals even boast about how they have used them to advance the interests of the United States and its allies, including NATO.

David Scheffer was the first United States Ambassador-at-Large for War Crimes Issues in the Clinton Administration's second mandate. Before that, between 1993 and 1996, he was senior advisor to the U.S. ambassador to the United Nations, Madeleine Albright, and then on the Deputies Committee of the National Security Council. In his capacity as ambassador-at-large, Scheffer was involved in the creation of the International Criminal Tribunals for the former Yugoslavia and Rwanda, the Special Court for Sierra Leone, and the Cambodian court, and in negotiations leading up to creation of the International Criminal Court. In 2012 Scheffer published *All the Missing Souls, A Personal History of the War Crimes Tribunals.* [9]

If any doubts linger about how foreign policy trumps international justice, this book should dispel them. For example, in the months prior to the NATO bombing campaign against Yugoslavia in 1999 in support of the Kosovo Liberation Army (KLA), the Chief Prosecutor for the International Criminal Tribunal for the former Yugoslavia, Louise Arbour, was busy preparing indictments against Serbian leaders. Ms Arbour claimed that Kosovo was under the tribunal's jurisdiction and that the KLA was not a terrorist organization, but rather an armed force resisting Serbian aggression. Louise Arbour would end up indicting President Slobodan Milosevic on May 22, 1999 while the bombs were still falling on Belgrade. Here is how David Scheffer described the role of the international tribunal:

> By then, the tribunal was a potent judicial tool, and I had enough support from President Clinton, Secretary of State Madeleine Albright, Secretary of Defense William Cohen, and other top officials in Washington **to wield it like a battering ram in the execution of U.S. and NATO policy**. (our emphasis)

International criminal justice with its lofty principles becomes "a battering ram" to be wielded "in the execution of U.S. and NATO policy." Who could have said it better than Scheffer himself?

How does this "wielding" of the "battering ram" work in practice? One example is how the United States paved the way for Louise Arbour to indict the Serbian President Milosevic. Until February 28, 1998 both Washington and the president of Serbia considered the Kosovo Liberation Army to be a terrorist group. As long as that label applied, the International Criminal Tribunal and its prosecutor, Louise Arbour, had no jurisdiction over fighting in Kosovo. Seeing the advantage of adding another weapon to the combined U.S.-NATO bombing capacity, Washington simply lifted the terrorist label from the KLA and redefined it as armed resistance, thereby making it possible to indict the president of Serbia. David Scheffer: "If there had been no Balkans conflict of the 1990s, there might never have been the metamorphosis of the KLA from terrorist organization to armed force in the eyes of Washington policy-makers."

Washington's ejection of Carla Del Ponte as Chief Prosecutor for the Rwandan tribunal is surely the best example of how the United States ensured the tribunal would continue to be the "battering ram" it needed in the execution of its foreign policy in Central Africa. David Scheffer's successor as ambassador-at-large for war crimes issues, Pierre-Richard Prosper, appointed by George W. Bush in 2001, did the wielding this time round. Prosper had previously been prosecutor at the International Criminal Tribunal for Rwanda in the case of Jean-Paul Akayesu before becoming special counsel and policy advisor to Scheffer and then replacing him. He later was a chief foreign policy advisor to 2012 Republican presidential candidate Mitt Romney. Ambassador Prosper was the man who conducted the operation to remove Carla Del Ponte.

A Swiss national, Carla Del Ponte was appointed to replace Louise Arbour in 1999 and in December that year she began special criminal investigations of officers of the Rwandan Patriotic Army led by Paul Kagame. Reacting in an April 2000 interview to revelations about how Louise Arbour had suppressed investigation into the shooting down of the presidential plane, Carla Del Ponte declared, "If it is the RPF that shot down the plane, the history of the genocide must be rewritten."[10] This was not going to sit well with the United States. Carla Del Ponte's spokesperson, Florence Hartmann, a former reporter for *Le Monde,* wrote a book in which she described the meetings at the State Department in Washington in May 2003 that resulted in Del Ponte's removal.

The backdrop is the war on Iraq launched in March 2003. Prosper convoked Carla Del Ponte and a Rwandan delegation from Kigali to meetings in May 2003. For over a year, Rwanda had been obstructing the tribunal and deploying its de facto control by disallowing prosecution witnesses to go to Arusha. The RPF hoped to force Del Ponte to abandon special investigations of RPF military officers. The Rwandan officials, together with U.S. Ambassador Prosper, insisted that Rwandan authorities alone should be responsible for investigations into RPF crimes. In meetings over a three-day period, which Hartmann described as an "ambush" (*guet-apens),* an "agreement" was supposedly reached that eliminated Prosecutor Del Ponte's authority to investigate RPF crimes and forced her to transmit to the Rwandan authorities any information gathered to date. Carla Del Ponte left for The

Hague and received the "agreement" by fax; she promptly disavowed it. Washington then moved quickly with its British allies to evict Del Ponte from the Rwandan tribunal leaving her with responsibility for the ICTY only.[11]

It was 2003. The United States and the United Kingdom had invaded Iraq and Washington was busy signing bilateral agreements to obtain immunity for United States nationals from criminal charges that might be laid by the International Criminal Court. Rwanda broke ranks with all other African countries and heartily backed U.S. and U.K. aggression in Iraq and signed the bilateral agreement with Washington; in return Kigali obtained immunity for RPA officers, an end to the Congress-imposed weapons embargo, and substantial military aid in the war it was waging in the Congo. Therewith vanished any hopes that the International Criminal Tribunal for Rwanda would investigate RPF crimes, including the April 6, 1994 assassination of two African heads of state. The ICTR would continue to be wielded like a "battering ram," just as it was devised to be when it was created in November 1994.

◆

From the beginning Ramsey Clark doubted the ICTR would be able to answer people's questions about the tragedy; the reasons he advanced also explain why the accused were not likely to get fair trials. "I wouldn't underestimate the central wrong of selecting people for prosecution. It's enemies they're choosing," he said. "It really is war by other means and it's very cruel. In a sense the power of charging is placed in the hands of the Rwandan Patriotic Front, because it controls the facts. The prosecution could not proceed without it; cases couldn't be presented without it."

The vast majority of facts required to make a case or to defend someone remain in Rwanda. In the trial of Pastor Élisaphan Nkatirutimana, for whom Ramsey Clark was counsel, all prosecution witnesses came from Rwanda, but not one defence witness could appear in court in Arusha. Defence counsel knew who the witnesses were and knew that they would be ready to testify, yet to oblige them to do so would endanger their lives. If defence counsel even tried to talk to the witnesses, even indirectly, their lives would be in danger. The Rwanda tribunal simply never had the power to make people testify, nor to guarantee witness protection. It did not even have the power to find witnesses, be it for the prosecution or for the defence.

Louise Arbour became very well known because she indicted and oversaw the arrest of some important people in Europe to the unanimous applause of the international media. Ever since, each time Ms Arbour appears in public it is said that the "little lady" was so bold that she made dictators tremble. She made just as many spectacular arrests in Africa, though they received less publicity. The goal was always the same: obtain international attention for herself and the tribunal, whose reputation was not good. The best example in Africa was Operation NAKI (NAirobi-KIgali) on July 18, 1997. Ms Arbour had seven people arrested in Nairobi. She then had these "big fish" as she called them forcefully transferred to Arusha in flagrant violation of the ICTR's own internal regulations.

The main problem was that only two of the seven were indicted before being arrested. The five others were arrested, transferred by van to Arusha, and held for months without even being told why they had been arrested. One man, Esdras Twagirimana, was held for two months without ever being charged. When the tribunal finally admitted its error, it sent Mr. Twagirimana back to Nairobi where he was arrested again and had the ICTR monetary compensation confiscated.[12]

Louise Arbour claimed that the ICTR was obliged to use methods that other courts could not think of using. Her opinion was that the ICTR required greater flexibility to arrest and hold suspects without laying charges. The ICTR simply could not observe due process as it is applied in Europe and North America.[13] African prisoners charged by the Rwanda tribunal have also often been denied the right to a lawyer of their choice, whereas the

European branch of the same tribunal, in a typical double standard, granted this right to prisoners from the former Yugoslavia. The Arusha branch blithely chose lawyers for prisoners against their will. The effect was often disastrous. For example, on January 24, 2003 the forty-five-year old Anglican bishop Samuel Musabymana died in prison. The ICTR had appointed a lawyer whereas the bishop wanted to retain the services of the Canadian lawyer Peter Zaduk. Without a lawyer Bishop Musabymana was unable to obtain the medical care required, nor receive visitors. His family in particular was systematically kept away.

Africa is supposedly different and so unfortunately "our justice system" has to be applied differently. If the representatives of such an august international institution think in fact that Africa is so different, then it would be only logical to ask them to recuse themselves, knowing that they have neither the means nor the understanding and experience to carry out their mandate adequately. That of course has never happened. It appears that they want it both ways. On the one hand, they claim to apply a legal system and means that they consider to be universal, infallible, and the height of civilization. Anybody coming from a Northern country can do it. They study a few months, read a few books and are sent out in the field to indict, arrest, and prosecute Africans. None of them speak or understand any African language. That seems to matter little since "civilization" comes naturally to them. On the other hand, the ICTR apologists behave and talk as though Africa were totally different. Africans are not like us, they will say; they have no democratic culture, no culture of the rule of law. It is the culture of impunity that rules. In short, they are not civilized like we are, and we are thus obliged to waive due process and the rule of law, but of course this is all done in the name of justice and freedom, which we all agree upon.

"If you look at the trials, they have all the trappings of colonial power, of European power, of the European system," observes Ramsey Clark. "If you looked at pictures of colonial courts at higher levels, and at this court, and analyzed them, you would not see much difference in them. And every significant aspect, with the exception that some of the judges are African, but all trained in Western Law, you would see the procedures, the structure and the results are a continuum of colonial law applied under new circumstances. I don't think they are fooling themselves, they know what they are doing."

The colonial mentality pervading these operations is barefaced and brazen. Rwanda also set up courts, though with little success, to judge the one hundred fifty thousand prisoners packed in small jails for many years. After Paul Kagame and the Rwandan Patriotic Front took power, the Justice Ministry was a shambles. Most of the staff, lawyers, and judges were in exile or in prison themselves. A large number of people had to be trained to take on responsibility for the legal system. Canadians, Belgians, and Americans jumped at the opportunity to develop a program for recruiting and training Rwandan jurists. It was important to prove that these countries had been right in supporting the Rwandan Patriotic Front.

William Schabas, a signatory of the January 1993 International Commission of Inquiry report examined in Chapter 4, headed the training program. Candidates, to be accepted, had to answer a short questionnaire prepared by Canadians, which included the following questions:

- What is the capital of Canada?
- Jean-Paul Sartre is the author of (a) *The Second Sex* (b) *The Outsider* (c) *Being and Nothingness.*
- The author of *The Republic* is (a) Plato (b) Aristotle (c) Euripides.[14]

Could a more Eurocentric set of questions be imagined?

Here is a modest proposal. All lawyers, judges, civil servants, army officers or anybody else applying for international work in Africa—or in their own countries—must answer the following questions before their applications will be considered:

- What is the capital of Zambia?
- Ferdinand Oyono wrote: (a) *God's Bits of Wood* (b) *Ambiguous Adventure* (c) *Houseboy*?
- In what era of African history was Sundiata a leader: (a) 16th century (b) 13th century (c) 19th century?
- What modern country bears the name of the kingdom Sundiata led: (a) Ghana (b) Rwanda (c) Mali?

◆

Those who devised the tribunal claimed in the founding resolution (Resolution 955 (1994)) that it would "contribute to the process of national reconciliation and to the restoration of maintenance of peace." Added to justice and truth, that makes for a tall order. Moreover, that order emanates, not as it should, from the General Assembly of the United Nations representing all states on an equal footing, but from another organ, the Security Council, with five permanent and ten temporary members. The Security Council created the tribunal under Chapter VII of the Charter of the United Nations entitled "Action With Respect to Threats to the Peace, Breaches of the Peace, and Acts of Aggression." In short, the tribunal was created as an instrument to carry out the Security Council's policing or coercion functions, whereas by their very nature these functions should be totally separated from justice. As early as 1995 John Philpot wrote:

> It takes mental gymnastics for a jurist to justify the creation of a court as an appendage to an international organ of policing and coercion. In this active international policing role, an international criminal court cannot meet the requirement of neutrality and independence which must be the hallmark of any tribunal, and all the more of an international tribunal requiring the respect and support of all nations.[15]

The tribunal was also devised with a territorial and temporal jurisdiction that eliminated the fundamental question of who initiated the war, i.e., the crime against peace, "the supreme international crime." The wording effectively hammered a wedge between international law and international humanitarian law. Under the former, a serious tribunal would have necessarily investigated the initial crime, the invasion of October 1, 1990, whereas under the latter, it could pretend that nobody had started the war or fall back on the mantra, "international humanitarian law is not concerned about that question."

People following the crisis in the African Great Lakes region since 1990 know that the invading army, those who wanted regime change in Rwanda, were also determined to rewrite the history of the region, as is the case in all wars of aggression and conquest. That army and its supporters, including several of the main non-governmental human rights organizations, were already rewriting history in the years leading up to 1994 (see Chapter 4). They were therefore quick to declare that an official historical record already existed based on the idea of genocide; the corollary was that anybody questioning the new official history was a "negationist," a term that was already being bandied about in September 1994. Underlying the Security Council's desire to "contribute to the process of national reconciliation and to the restoration and maintenance of peace" is the idea, as noted by jurist David Paciocco, that developing an official history and a common memory is instrumental in achieving that goal.

David Paciocco holds that a major problem with the International Criminal Tribunal for Rwanda and with all international criminal law is their penchant "to conduct inquiries into historical events, rather than simply trying those accused."[16] Based on his experience at the Rwandan tribunal, David Paciocco, now a judge of the Ontario Court of Justice in Canada, wrote:

> To begin with, there is an inherent risk of prejudgment. International criminal trials invariably turn on the interpretation of historical events that are already believed to be understood. If the decisions of a tribunal do not conform to those expectations, the credibility of the tribunal can be compromised. Yet if a tribunal allows such expectations to influence outcomes, the law itself is compromised. Indeed, it is defeated and undermined. The trial process becomes an

> instrument for confirming a preordained result, rather than a process for adjudicating an allegation according to rules. If expectations are permitted to predetermine results, there is, in effect, no international law—only the pretence of it.

Justice Paciocco notes also how attempts to write history in trials at the ICTR were stymied by facts that told another story. Early on prosecutors introduced evidence that would lead to believe that President Habyarimana's plane was shot down by extremists in his own camp who intended it to be the signal to start eliminating Tutsis. The hope was to bolster the historical theory that the killings were planned well in advance. A few years later, however, prosecutors dropped that angle of attack as more substantial evidence pointed to the RPF as being at the origins of the presidential assassination. Prosecutors have surprisingly been able to keep a straight face.

Another distortion that results from trying to establish a historical record is the excessive use and abuse of expert witnesses. David Paciocco: "These witnesses are, in effect, permitted to give advice, under oath, to the Tribunal about what it should find... [they] are treated, in effect, as privileged, forensic investigators. They do not simply furnish their evidence to the Prosecutor for presentation, as ordinary investigators do. They furnish conclusions directly to the tribunal, using tools of deduction, hearsay and access to undisclosed documentation." Whereas the tribunal welcomes these experts with open arms based on the notion that they will have answers about the historical events, none of them are neutral reporters since they all have careers and reputations to maintain. Paciocco concludes: "The problem with this kind of thinking is that the trial of a man whose liberty is at stake should never be seen as an inquiry into history. It is about whether he will be punished and forever stigmatized with the most outrageous slur that civilization knows how to cast upon him."

United Nations representatives, echoing the tribunal's founding resolution, have constantly reiterated that although suspects were being tried, the most important goal was to foster national reconciliation. David Paciocco remarks that while the aim was national reconciliation the means to achieve that aim involved prosecuting genocide suspects. This probably explains why the tribunal launched a PR campaign in which it boasted about the number and rate of convictions,[17] which had been predicted by Ramsey Clark when he stressed that both the tribunal and the prosecutor's office had a mission to convict people and that an ad hoc tribunal that failed to convict would be a total failure.

Courts are established to administer justice according to principles of equality and the presumption of innocence. That they measure success, not by the quality of the justice administered, but rather by the number of convictions chalked up is a travesty. More importantly, what if suspects are acquitted? What if the worst charges are judged to be unfounded? What happens to the official historical record? What happens to peace and reconciliation?

That is probably the worst nightmare haunting the ardent supporters of the Rwandan tribunal and the RPF government: the absence of adjudicated facts to underpin an official narrative rapidly erected upon the tragic Rwandan wasteland and then trumpeted throughout the world. Yet that is what has happened. On the fundamental allegation, "Conspiracy to Commit Genocide," the man who has been constantly accused of being the "brains" behind the massacres, the "biggest fish," Théoneste Bagosora, along with his three co-accused were all acquitted of that charge.[18] Equally important, the tribunal gave lie to the oft-repeated story of a plot to commit genocide conceived and executed by the *Akazu* or little house, the term used to describe a group of people belonging to the families and entourage of President Habyarimana and his wife, Agathe Kanziga. Although the indictment of the alleged ringleader of the imagined *Akazu,* Protais Zigiranyirazo, President Habyarimana's brother-in-law, even specified the names of many people who supposedly belonged to that group, the tribunal acquitted him on that count.[19]

A great irony of the Rwandan tribunal is that although a preconceived official historical record pervaded the minds of those who devised and presided over the tribunal's destiny, the historical record that has been established totally contradicts the earlier "official" one. French historian Bernard Lugan, also an expert witness but who, to his credit, changed his opinion as new facts became available, summed it up brilliantly in his 2007 book *Rwanda: Contre-enquête sur le genocide*:

> The real history of the Rwandan genocide is being written before the ICTR during the long trials underway. Day after day, a totally different vision of the dramatic events appears, a vision that profoundly challenges the basic premises advanced a decade earlier. Yet the indictments remain cast in past certainties [...]. Those accused thus must submit to procedures that violate their rights, since they are tried based on obsolete indictments.[20]

Which version will history retain? Will it be the official narrative that can be found in the mainstream media, most popular books, and movies, and which has held sway since 1994 and even before? Or will it be the account that can only be established by carefully studying the reams of sworn testimony by the accused and by both defence and prosecution witnesses during those long trials and appeals that began in 1996? Chances are that on the short term, the former will prevail. However as Mark Twain put it, "a lie can travel way around the world while the truth is still putting on its shoes."

CHAPTER 14

◆

From his Rwandan home, Banished a Wand'rer Came

While a tall white woman
in an ermine cape
Looked at the blacks and
Thought of rape.

Langston Hughes[1]

Jean-Paul Akayesu was the first man in history to be convicted of genocide, rape, and other crimes against humanity by an international criminal tribunal, yet he vehemently—and convincingly—proclaims his innocence. The former burgomaster of Taba Commune located some twenty-five kilometres west of Kigali is purging a life sentence in Mali. I visited Jean-Paul Akayesu for five days at the Masion centrale d'arrêt in Bamako in November 2002. At the time he was imprisoned with three other Rwandans who have been in Mali since they were transferred from the United Nations prison in Arusha, Tanzania, in December 2001. They were later transferred to another United Nations prison in Koulikoro, Mali.

Though it might appear to be an oxymoron, the Maison centrale d'arrêt in Bamako could be described as a humane prison.

Unlike prisons in countries with a punitive culture like the United States and Canada, the idea of sensorial deprivation is non-existent. Prisoners feel the elements, the wind, the heat, and the rain. It is also more humane because Mali has no capital punishment. People never serve more than fifteen years in prison. It would seem that Malians believe in rehabilitation. Prisoners generally appear healthy and well. Fights are rare and prison guards are not known to push prisoners around. Visitors are received courteously. Though Bamako is dustier, more expensive and much larger than when I had last visited the city in 1974, I still felt safer than I do in some large American cities, even in the prison.

What's more, the Malians do not seem to have succumbed to the demonization of Rwandan Hutus, which has made them into monsters in Western public opinion.

The decision to send sentenced prisoners to Mali was made by the Clerk's Office at the ICTR in Arusha. Three other countries, Sweden, Belgium, and Norway, had offered to hold the prisoners but the clerk refused, saying that since they were African they should be imprisoned in Africa.

The decision might initially appear to reflect a real sensitivity towards Africans. After all, Mali and Rwanda are African countries located near the Equator. Yet in terms of being uprooted, sending Rwandans to prison in Mali is comparable to locking up an Inuit from Nunavut in Arizona. Jean-Paul Akayesu found the transfer very difficult: "In May and June, just before the rainy season, I thought the heat was going to kill me." Rwanda is located on a high plateau and the temperature is generally between 10 and 25°C, whereas in Mali, even in the "cool" season, the temperature often goes up to 35 or 40°C. Rwanda is always green, Mali is almost always dry and dusty. Rwanda is Christian, Mali is Muslim.

For prisoners convinced of their innocence, the worst problem is the distance from their families and the isolation that makes communication with the outside world almost impossible. When I visited Jean-Paul Akayesu in November 2002, I was only his

Jean-Paul Akayesu, Maison centrale d'arrêt, Bamako, Mali
Like many wrongly convicted people, Jean-Paul Akayesu gathers documents in the hope that his case will be reopened so that he can prove his innocence and be able to join his family dispersed throughout the world.

second visitor since he had arrived a year earlier. "When the tribunal sent us to Mali," he said, "they just wanted to make us disappear from the news. If we were in Europe or in North America, we wouldn't be isolated. In those places we would have telephones, visitors, and all the means of communication. Here travelling is difficult and expensive. How can we make our cases known from here? How can we ever hope to reopen our cases?"

"It's banishment to the penal colony all over again," wrote his fellow prisoner Alfred Musema in a moving open letter written the day after he was "deported to the unknown." His open letter of course was never published. "Unjustly sentenced to life in prison is the same as being sentenced to a long slow death. While I was writing 'Courage!' they were writing 'Silence! You're going to die, slowly.'" Surprisingly few people have in fact remarked on the colonial nature of these new forms of UN-sanctioned penal colonies, where prisoners are moved about from one country to another at the behest of the big powers.

Banishing prisoners to Mali is the logical follow-up to the decision to put the tribunal in Arusha, Tanzania. UN Secretary General Boutros Boutros-Ghali regrets that decision. "The original idea was to put the tribunal in The Hague," he said in an interview. "I said, No. It was an African problem. Setting up the tribunal in Arusha was a simple question of dignity. That is why I chose Arusha. In fact it was a mistake, my mistake. To create a tribunal, you need all the surroundings and background: a cultural background, a legal background, media facilities, and more. They all contribute to a tribunal's work. Arusha had none of this. It was empty. And it is considered to be marginal. The tribunal should have been created in a big city that would take an interest in it. The psychological support of a big city, its cultural infrastructure, is necessary for the institution, for the judges, the lawyers, the media."

"And what about the accused and the convicted?" I asked the former Secretary General.

"For everybody," he replied. "None of us, jurists included, had given any thought to the parallel and paralegal aspects, such as political and material questions. So we convict somebody. Where is he to serve his sentence? Who is responsible for overseeing his imprisonment? Why? None of this has been studied seriously."

Boutros-Ghali's candour is admirable and appreciated. Yet it came a little late for Jean-Paul Akayesu who is sentenced to life virtually incommunicado in a remote jail, while his name and his case are regularly cited in all the major North American and European media and used in all international law faculties and international studies departments. His candour also came late for the many prisoners who have been acquitted in Arusha but who have nowhere to go because no countries will accept them.[2] The United Nations and particularly the member countries that so enthusiastically supported the creation of the international criminal tribunals must have presumed that being charged was the equivalent of being guilty and nobody would be acquitted. Whatever happened to the presumption of innocence?

◆

Jean-Paul Akayesu was shocked when I showed him the front page of *The New York Times Magazine* of September 15, 2002, with a photoshopped photo of the only woman held by the International Criminal Tribunal for Rwanda, Pauline Nyiramasuhuko, with its screaming title "The Minister of Rape." When he saw the reference to his own conviction, which the *Times* article described as a breakthrough in international law, he shook his head in protest and said, "That's all they wanted! The tribunal desperately needed a precedent and jurisprudence on which they could build and develop international law. I wasn't even accused of rape, only of being burgomaster during a time when rapes were supposed to have been committed near the Taba commune office."

On the question of rape Akayesu is categorical. "There were no rapes in my commune. I would have heard about them. And I declared that under oath before the Tribunal in the name of God almighty. Witness JJ could not even identify me, even though she had told the Prosecutor that she would be able to recognize me." (The witnesses' real names are not divulged.)

The story of how Jean-Paul Akayesu came to be charged with rape is itself mind-boggling. "I was in the middle of my trial in March 1997 when Hillary Clinton showed up in Arusha during her tour of Africa. My trial was interrupted for her visit. Hillary Clinton concluded her speech by offering the tribunal six hundred thousand U.S. dollars if it introduced rape charges in the trials in Arusha. In June 1997 the Prosecutor Pierre-Richard Prosper, who was working under Chief Prosecutor Louise Arbour, had my indictment amended to include rape, even though he had already completed his case against me. This was all done despite the fact that nobody had talked about rape before my trial began."

In addition to Hillary Clinton an important American feminist organization requested the right to intervene as an *Amicus Curiae* or friend of the court. That request further pressured the tribunal to convict people of rape.

The order of these events is crucial to understand why and how the rape charges were introduced in the Arusha trials. Two prosecution witnesses against Jean-Paul Akayesu had made sworn statements to the prosecutor during investigations prior to his indictment and arrest. The prosecutor disclosed the statements to defence counsel as required. Neither statement mentioned anything about rape or anything about crimes of a sexual nature. The witnesses had met investigators from the prosecutor's office in the Rwandan commune of Taba in November 1995. One witness made charges against Burgomaster Akayesu but made no mention of women being raped. When she arrived in Arusha in 1997, the issue of rape had become more important and so she ended up adding accusations of rape, but only after having been sequestered with the prosecutor for two weeks. "Witness H was a former student of mine," recalled Jean-Paul Akayesu. "The prosecutor said she was unable to appear for those two weeks because she was sick, but I know that it took that much time for them to convince her to testify that she herself had been raped."

With time proof of false testimony and fabrication of evidence came to the fore. For example, a Rwandan Tutsi from Taba, who had attended meetings during which false testimony was prepared to convict Akayesu, provided a sworn statement corroborating the point that the issue of rape had not even been raised before 1997. "Sometime early in 1997, if I remember correctly, they began to talk about rape witnesses. Before that time, there was no talk about evi-

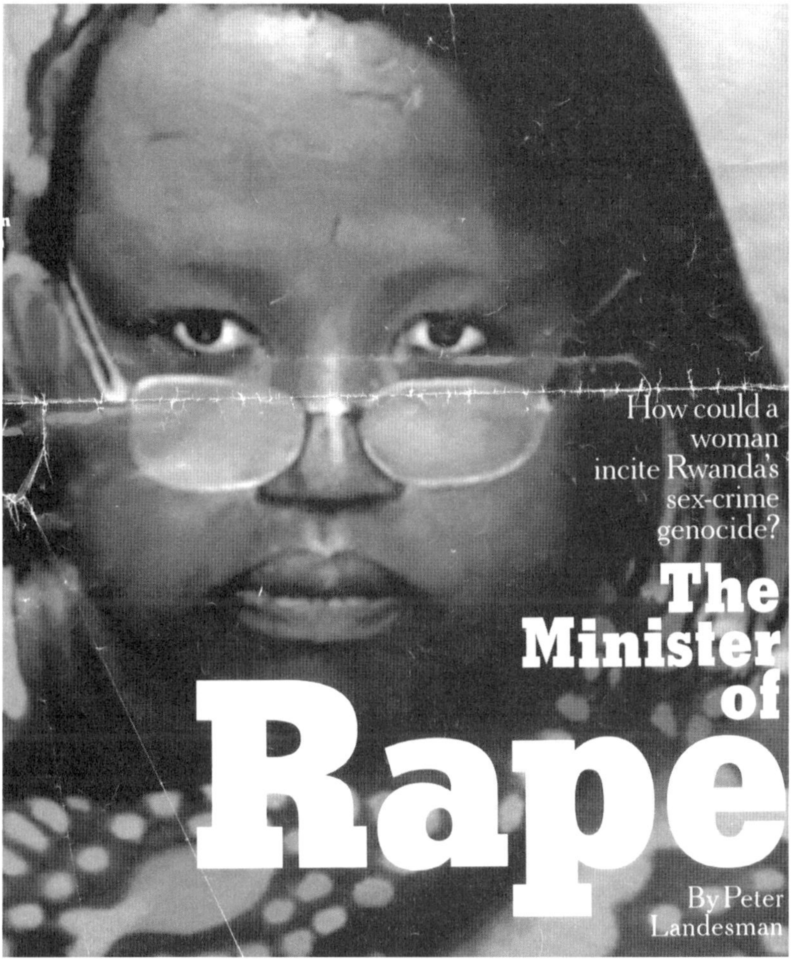

Front Page of *New York Times Magazine*, September 15, 2002
Jean-Paul Akayesu was shocked at the front page and feature article that considered his case to be a breakthrough in international law.

dence of rape. Mr. Karanwa told me that there are widows and others who are easy to manipulate so that they will testify about rape."[3] The Appeal Court in The Hague simply refused to receive witness BBB's statement that would have exonerated Jean-Paul Akayesu.

Ramsey Clark thinks that the people working for the tribunal wanted to introduce rape charges in Akayesu's case, and in all the others, to ingratiate themselves to those who funded the tribunal in the United States, and especially Secretary of State Madeleine Albright for whom the tribunal was to be a legacy. This interpretation concurs with that of Boutros Boutros-Ghali who complained about the tribunal's chronic lack of funds and its irrelevance in international public opinion. Nobody wanted to go there and nobody was interested in the tribunal. The solution was therefore to hype it more—to sex it up, as the British would say—by adding charges that would catch the eye of North American public opinion.

Jean-Paul Akayesu's conviction was little more than a formality. "It just takes one woman to come to court and declare 'I was raped' or 'I saw somebody being raped,'" noted Akayesu. "There's just no way to defend yourself against such accusations." Akayesu's complaints take on real meaning in light of declarations made by former ICTR judge Madam Navanethem Pillay during a promotional tour of Canada in November 1997 before the defence began its case. On CBC radio Judge Pillay declared that there were two hundred thousand victims of sexual violence in Rwanda as well as a political strategy of sexual violence against women. No evidence to this effect had been presented in court. She was only repeating the prosecutor's declarations. What ever happened to the cornerstone of the legal system Judge Pillay belongs too, namely the presumption of innocence? Ms Pillay was judge in the Akayesu case. She was later appointed United Nations High Commissioner on Human Rights, replacing ... Louise Arbour.

Where do the stories of rape come from? Is there any truth to them? Jean-Paul Akayesu answers straightforwardly. "Intermarriage between Hutus and Tutsis was very common. You also have to realize that marriage in Rwanda is not the same as in the West. Two young people may decide one day that they are going to form a couple. They then go and see their parents who organize a wedding for them. A Tutsi girl could have been engaged to, or going out with, a Hutu boy. As the RPF army advanced the couple would have fled with the rest of the population, first to southern Rwanda and then to neighbouring countries like the Congo. When the RPF won the war, they convinced the Tutsi girls to leave their husbands. A full-fledged campaign was developed to get those girls to accuse their fiancés of rape. Often the girls were already pregnant. When they gave birth the RPF said that the newborn were the children of rape. Judging by *The New York Times Magazine* article (The Minister of Rape), it appears that they succeeded in demonizing us," observed Akayesu.

For anybody who knows anything about the inextricable relationship between rape and race in the minds of white Americans, there is something dubious in all the horror stories told about the rape Rwandans were supposed to have committed. For the first time in world history, after centuries of slavery, racism, masters' "rights" or *droit de cuissage*, and colonialism where sexual domination was an integral part of colonial domination, an international criminal tribunal largely funded by the United States and urged on by the wife of a U.S. president from the South, sentenced a man to life for rape as a war crime, and that man is an African who claims to be innocent. Sadly, it brings to mind Billy Holiday's *Strange fruit*, and the lynching of African Americans unjustly accused of rape.

In a 1987 essay on white America's vendetta against African American men Ishmael Reed wrote: "An audience of white and Asian feminists attending a rape awareness workshop held in Berkeley last October said that they imagined the 'stereotypical' rapist as black, until they were informed by Sallie Werson, a women's center counselor, that seventy-five to eighty percent of rapists are white."[4]

In a book entitled *Color of Rape, Gender and Race in Television's Public Spheres*, feminist author and professor Sujata Moorti expands on the question and reaches similar troubling conclusions.[5] Moorti analyzes the manner in which the major American television networks deal with the subject of rape. Focusing on three highly publicized rape cases that occurred between 1989 and 1991 and the narrative that developed out of them, Sujata

Moorti concludes that, "the only consistent feature is the demonization of black masculinity."

The author agrees with many other scholars who have shown that issues of rape and race are always entwined in American public discourse. Moorti contends that, "anxieties about black sexuality continue to shape contemporary television representations. Consequently, the myths of the black male rapist, black male bestiality, and black female promiscuity inform the images of black women and men in rape narratives as well as the black male and female experience in the legal and criminal justice arenas."[6] She also maintains that the racism that resulted in the famous 1931 unjust conviction for rape of the nine "Scotsboro boys" still prevails today in media representation of rape.[7]

Since her book appeared her conclusions have become more significant. The group of young black men arrested, convicted and locked up for gang rape of the New York Central Park jogger—one of the cases studied by Moorti—were all absolved of that crime when another man confessed the crime and DNA analysis corroborated his confession. The story had provoked hysteria throughout the United States. Pundits, politicians, and the general public let their imaginations run wild as they used that rape case to expound on black male violence in inner city America. Jungle imagery and vocabulary were of course used to make the case.

We now know that that's not what happened and that the New York Police had obtained forced confessions. All the young men are innocent and have sued for damages, yet in 2013 the case was still not settled. Who can erase the horrible demonization of African-American men that went on for more than ten years? Who can return years of their lives to the five young men falsely accused, convicted, and imprisoned?

The way the media dealt with that case, which eventually took an unpredictable turn, reinforces one of Sujata Moorti's principal conclusions. The media narrative of rape cases makes no attempt to understand the rape phenomenon or to grasp the raped woman's situation. The raped woman "becomes a symbolic cause to discuss other social issues" or to express obsessions. The Central Park jogger case provided excellent material for people to complain about black-male ghetto violence.

This is the very American context in which the introduction of rape charges in Jean-Paul Akayesu's case, qualified by *The New York Times* and many other media as "the legal breakthrough," should be understood. As was the case with the Central Park jogger, as was the case with the "Scotsboro boys," the rape stories from the Rwandan tragedy become a symbolic cause to discuss a supposed African culture of violence and oppression—the underlying theme being Western/white moral superiority—at a time when the same Western powers, and particularly the United States, want to legitimate their direct control over African resources and African countries.

The September 2002 *The New York Times Magazine* front-page feature on "The Minister Of Rape" is the most glaring example of the rape story distortions.[8] Ten pages of text complete with photos tell the story that is amplified by commentary from American anthropologists, jurists, and psychiatrists all of whom are grimly astonished by the incomprehensible dark and evil nature of the crimes alleged to have been committed. Though the article is long on the details of what these specialists imagine to be the Rwandan mind, it is short on facts. Therein, it faithfully follows the popular literary tradition on Africa developed during the slavery and colonialism that would have Africans killing each other—in this case raping each other—because they can't stop themselves from doing it.

The *Times* reporter fails even to mention the shooting down of President Habyarimana's plane that triggered the tragic events. As for the October 1990 invasion of Rwanda—had there been no invasion, there would have been no massacres—the event is alluded to as follows: "As tensions increased around 1990, ..."

Who could imagine a major media or anybody describing relations with Japanese Americans, or Canadians, up to and including their internment with the phrase, "As tensions increased around

December 7, 1941," without mentioning Pearl Harbour? What would be said if the September 1939 Blitzkrieg on Poland were to be described in the popular press as "increased tensions between Poles and Germans." Though the invasion of Rwanda on October 1, 1990, was of exactly the same nature for Rwandans as Pearl Harbour for Americans and the Blitzkrieg for Poles, *The New York Times* called it "increased tensions".

Gore Vidal called the *Times* the Typhoid Mary of American journalism in reference to the New York cook who between 1900 and 1907 went about her work gaily and spread the disease to everybody she came in contact with. With globalization, it would seem that the disease now goes beyond United States' borders. The same article or excerpts from it appeared in many papers including *The Toronto Star* and *The Montreal Gazette* in Canada, and *Le Courrier international* and *Le Figaro* in France.

◆

Jean-Paul Akayesu was elected burgomaster of Taba in 1993, the chosen candidate of the main party opposed to President Habyarimana, the Mouvement Démocratique Républicain (MDR). The party leader, Faustin Twagiramungu, who became prime minister of Rwanda in July 1994 following the RPF military victory, insists that Akayesu is innocent of all charges: "We chose that man to be our candidate because he was liked and trusted by the Tutsis."

Jean-Paul Akayesu described how he behaved during the crisis. "I spared no efforts to prevent the massacres. I issued orders not to let any killer come into Taba. We fought against the militia thugs in Taba. Some were even killed. But with only six policemen, how could I fight against armed gangs? There was widespread fighting and killing in Kigali. People were fleeing from Kigali to Taba, older people, men, women, children, pregnant women too. Taba was considered a safe haven."

The term "genocide" was generally unknown to Rwandans before 1994. "We had learned about the genocide against the Jews in school," Akayesu said, "but I was well into my trial before I knew anything about the legal meaning of the term, that it is a systematic attack on Tutsis and that I was supposed to have incited people to massacre my fellow Tutsi citizens. I did exactly the opposite! For example, the very day that massacres began in Taba, I had met a hundred or so people gathered around a Hutu who had been killed. The killers had taken off because they knew I was going to arrest them."

Akayesu points out that the cumulative effect of years of war, President Habyarimana's assassination, rumours of massacres and violence at the hands of the RPF army, and the fighting and shooting in Kigali that could be heard as far as Taba had prompted thousands of people to flee towards his town. In May 1994 some 140,000 people, internal displaced persons or refugees from the RPF-imposed war, all in need food and shelter, were in and around Taba commune. "With only six policemen what could I do to stop the killings?"

Now Akayesu knows the legal meaning of the term "genocide" and is serving a life sentence for that crime, yet he categorically rejects the use of the term to describe the Rwandan war. "There were Hutus and Tutsis in the whole Rwandan state apparatus, in all the political parties, including the president's party, and in the famous Interahamwe. Even the leader of the Interahamwe was a Tutsi. Do you think it is possible to plan to eliminate the Tutsis without them knowing? Would it even be possible? I do not think so. Look at President Habyarimana's own political entourage and you'll see that there were many Tutsis who were his good friends. Who could have planned to eliminate the Tutsis without them knowing about it?"

When the Court of Appeal in The Hague brought down its verdict, Jean-Paul Akayesu thought about Dreyfus who had been wrongfully convicted one hundred years earlier. "Like Dreyfus, I have been the victim of injustice from the very beginning, and I have never ceased denouncing it and proclaiming my innocence. When I was arrested in Lusaka on October 10, 1995 they also arrested a government minister, a prefect, some senior civil servants. All the others were released. I was held. They continued to hold me because they had to fabricate evidence and that was easy to do to a burgomaster who lived with, and was elected by, the people. But it makes no sense at all. They release the prefect, the senior civil servant, and the minister, all of whom could have decided on or planned a genocide, but they hold the burgomaster of a small town who has a mere six policemen working for him." After that, the tribunal appointed defence counsel against Akayesu's will and violated all their own rules and procedures. Then there was the appeal.

The burgomaster of Taba was the first to be convicted by an international tribunal that, for its own credibility and to justify 350 million dollars already spent, needed to obtain a conviction that would not be overturned. It is not surprising therefore that the Appeals Chamber had prepared its ruling on Jean-Paul Akayesu's appeal early in March 2001 before his appeal brief had even been translated from French into English for the judges. One judge knew absolutely no French.

The final ruling came down on June 1, 2002. Three months earlier, a Tutsi (witness BBB) had contacted Jean-Paul Akayesu's family. When Akayesu filed BBB's sworn testimony before the Appeals Chamber with details showing that almost all evidence presented during his trial had been fabricated, the Court refused to consider it and did not bother to hold a hearing to examine the seriousness of the testimony.

After he was arrested in 1995 Jean-Paul Akayesu believed he would be released within a couple of weeks. He told his wife exactly that. After eight years behind bars he had become extremely bitter about the International Criminal Tribunal for Rwanda. "It is a tribunal with a mission! An ad hoc tribunal created to punish Rwandan Hutus. There have been serious and credible revelations about President Habyarimana's assassination and the abominable crimes committed by the RPF. The tribunal has ignored them all. It is cultivating impunity for the current Rwandan government."

Despite his bitter experience, Jean-Paul Akayesu has not lost hope. He is like many other political prisoners or wrongfully convicted people who gained notoriety over time. He carefully gathers his documents together. He is always writing and preparing for his case to be reopened, confident that he will end up proving his innocence and that he will be able to join is family that is now dispersed throughout the world.

In the meantime, however, the name Akayesu is being heard and read in law faculties throughout the world. The Rwandan tribunal's first decision bears the name *Akayesu*, the first case in which genocide was dealt with in an international tribunal, and the first case in which rape was included as a charge under the Genocide Convention.

In a major work entitled *International Criminal Law*, law professor Alexander Zahar critically examined the *Akayesu* judgment and made comments that should give pause to all those who enjoy citing it cavalierly.

"From a jurisprudential point of view," writes Zahar, "the most striking aspect of the *Akayesu* judgment is the slightness of its legal sources. The bibliographical citations in the judgment suggest that research facilities in Arusha were scarce at the time. But *Akayesu* also makes several pronouncements on the law that are not reasoned and were not necessary."[9]

Alexander Zahar also casts a long shadow over the *Akayesu* case's "most remarked-upon contribution to genocide law," namely its interpretation of articles in the Genocide Convention to include sexual assault. He maintains that the *Akayesu* Trial Chamber did not consider whether the physical and mental harm caused by rape constituted a threat to the existence of the group targeted. "It resorted instead to assertions and metaphors and to conclusions of fact that went well beyond the evidence heard by the court." Zahar adds, "a streak of legal activism persists in the work of the tribunals. The *Akayesu* judges perhaps felt that they were in tune with the times, but the uncharted reaches of international criminal law demand a far more conservative attitude."[10]

CHAPTER 15

"Watch out for Africa!" Closing in on the Congo

American domination—the only domination
from which one never recovers.
I mean from which one never recovers unscarred.

Aimé Césaire, *Discourse on colonialism*

France our most inveterate enemy.

Benjamin Franklin, 1747

One Friday November evening in 1996, the 8th to be exact, Canada's Prime Minister Jean Chrétien and his wife Aline were quietly watching the CNN news at their Lake Harrington cottage just north of Ottawa. The non-stop images of people suffering near Goma in Eastern Zaire were so stirring that the Prime Minister decided Canada should mobilize and lead a multinational force to protect Rwandan refugees whose camps were being mercilessly bombed.

Instead of taking a well deserved prime ministerial rest, Prime Minister Jean Chrétien first bounced the idea off his closest advisors, his wife Aline and his nephew Raymond Chrétien, who was then Canada's Ambassador to Washington and who had just been appointed as the special United Nations envoy to the African Great Lakes region. The Prime Minister then picked up the phone to build up a "good head of steam" among other middle powers like Canada before approaching Washington. He lined up the presidents of Brazil and Argentina who agreed to participate in the planned Canadian-led force. With them on side, Jean Chrétien was ready to call Bill Clinton and persuade him to support the Canadian initiative. The week's work ended happily with a Security Council resolution on Thursday November 14 establishing a multinational force with ten thousand troops that would be led by the Canadian General Maurice Baril. This force to be immediately deployed was to enable the 1,300,000 Rwandan refugees to return home.

Surprise! The very next day, with the cameras of the world well focused, thousands of Rwandan refugees started crossing the border from the Congo into Rwanda. Then two weeks later, another huge group returned from Tanzania. On December 12 special UN envoy Raymond Chrétien informed the Security Council that it was no longer necessary to deploy the multinational force since the refugee problem was being settled by itself. "As soon as the Security Council resolution was adopted, Kigali activated the rebels in Eastern Zaire who then attacked the refugee camps. The militias fled thereby liberating the refugees to go home," Raymond Chrétien told the United Nations press corps. At the very same time, General Maurice Baril, who headed the multinational force, declared: "I must now recommend that my government terminate the mission."

Mission accomplished! Applause please!

That is the narrative that we are expected to believe. But what really happened?[1]

Here is how a humanitarian worker with a major non-governmental organization replied to that narrative. "General Baril was a damned liar when he said there was no longer a refugee problem in the Congo and that the troops in the multinational force could go home. He's a murderer!" The Montreal-based humanitarian

Rwandan refugees at Zaïre-Rwanda border, November 1996
When the RPF bombed refugee camps in eastern Zaïre (now the Congo) some of the 1.3 million refugees were forced to return to Rwanda or to flee west farther into the forests.

worker, who asked not to be named, was working in Kigali and Goma during this period and was posted at the Rwanda-Congo border when the refugees were forced to return to Rwanda. "When the city of Goma fell the troops divided the refugee camp in two," he added. "Some 300,000 or 400,000 refugees fled toward the forests to the west, whereas between 250,000 and 300,000 refugees headed towards Rwanda. Everybody knew that it happened that way. Satellite photos showed it clearly. Those photos were sent to all humanitarian groups and to General Baril. He had the same photos we had."[2]

Another eyewitness described the events in exactly the same way. The French daily *Libération* published his description on March 10, 1997. "Can we believe General Baril when he declared in mid-December that there were no refugees left in Zaire. After all he had spent only half a day on the road to Masisi in the vehicle of a rebel Tutsi army officer and had not seen any refugees. That declaration which officially terminated the multinational force caused the death of thousands of refugees. There's no way he could be unaware of their presence."[3]

Six years later Ambassador Raymond Chrétien, interviewed at the Canadian Embassy in Paris, admitted that the refugee problem in the Congo only appeared to be settled when his mandate ended in December 1996.

> A bit of the problem was settled. It was the tip of the humanitarian iceberg, but a huge part of the problem was not solved. Many refugees headed for the forest and have probably been killed since then. A million people dead! Not much has been said about that. But there was an international consensus that 500,000 refugees returned to Rwanda. After that, there was no political will to deploy the multinational force.[4]

Though one might be tempted to congratulate Raymond Chrétien for his honesty about his and the mission's failure, it is much too little and much too late. What's more, his excuse about a so-called "international consensus" is a fable. That so-called consensus was totally fabricated.

Léon Kengo Wa Dondo was prime minister of Zaire between 1994 and 1997. According to him, "Zaire's 1995 census established that there were 1,300,000 Rwandan refugees in Zaire. Only a very small number of refugees returned to Rwanda in November 1996. The idea of taking advantage of the presence in Zaire of Rwandan refugees accused of genocide to justify military intervention by Uganda, Burundi, and Rwanda and then to transform the invasion into what appeared to be a civil war in Zaire was well planned in advance."[5]

According to eyewitnesses, all the pieces were in place to film the refugees' return and broadcast it around the world—the accurate term to describe the refugees' return is "forced repatriation" or "*refoulement*." Yet here's the spin that was prepared: the refugees were being freed from the yoke of the genocidal Hutu militias and returning happily to their homes in Rwanda.

The 1951 Geneva Convention on refugees specifically prohibits forced repatriation.[6] All countries involved in the November 1996

Raymond Chrétien, special envoy of the UN secretary general in the 1996 refugee crisis
Six years after the RPF bombed refugee camps in Zaïre, Raymond Chrétien admitted that following the failed operation for which he was responsible, "A million people were dead!"

operation signed that Convention. But who really cares about the rule of law anyway?

Reporters were lined up at the Rwanda-Zaire border well before the refugees were forced to return. Until then they had had very little freedom of movement—reporters had been prevented from going near Goma when that city was taken a few weeks earlier—but now they were given full access to observe and film the whole operation. Their total freedom to cover the operation contrasted with the way they were corralled like cattle before the operation, and after it was over. "Obviously, we used the media," recalled Raymond Chrétien in reference to his 1996 United Nations mission to Central Africa.

"CNN's Christiane Amanpour was particularly well informed about the operation before it began," observed the humanitarian worker who was at the border. "She obviously had access to privileged information. She was not interested in any of the less glamorous aspects of the operation. Her work was frankly dishonest." He pointed out cases of refugees being tortured by the Rwandan Patriotic Front army and the fact that the RPF formally prohibited anybody from providing water to refugees for the first twenty-five kilometres on the Rwandan side of the border. Many refugees were suffering from cholera so the RPF goal was to let them die from dehydration.

The bias of CNN's Christiane Amanpour observed by people on the spot is not surprising. Shortly after the events took place, Ms Amanpour married Jamie Rubin, Madeleine Albright's mover and shaker and press attaché. Jamie Rubin is likely the man who leaked the so-called genocide fax to his then brother-in-law Philip Gourevitch of *The New Yorker* and he was evidently quite intimate with CNN's star reporter. Promoters of the "right and proper tale" about Rwanda constantly refer to the very sinister *akazu* or "little house" to describe the Habyarimana family and their entourage who are supposedly responsible for everything that happened in Rwanda. It would seem however that the United States can still teach the *akazus* of the world a few things, namely how to use family ties to stage events and not be seen.

At the very moment in mid-November 1996 the tragic refugee operation was underway, French journalist Jean Daniel was meeting the assistant Secretary of State, John C. Kornblum, in his Washington office. His account of that meeting is chilling.

> "France? We want to get along with France. Chirac? A man of good will. We like him. But: (1) no question of keeping Boutros-Ghali; (2) no question of keeping Mobutu in power... Let's get together again in six months time. We'll see if I am mistaken. Watch out for Africa: France has it all wrong. The strong man is in Uganda, not in Kinshasa."[7]

Jean Daniel, in his own words, left that meeting "floored by the cynical detailing of events to come and the arrogance of the vocabulary used."

The United States' offensive against France in French-speaking Africa is the backdrop to the destruction of refugee camps in eastern Congo/Zaire and it also explains why the ephemeral Canadian-led multinational force that was supposed to protect the refugees was sent home so soon.

"Who bombed the Sake and Mugunga refugee camps near Goma?" asked Zaïre's former Prime Minister Kengo Wa Dondo, even though he left little doubt that he believed the United States was directly implicated. Eyewitness accounts of the taking of the city of Goma on November 1, 1996 emphasize the speed of the operation, which relied on heavy military materiel, the simultaneous attacks from different points, and rockets launched from gunboats on Lake Kivu. The Zairean armed forces panicked. Another witness tells of the arrival of heavy American cargo planes in Kigali every night during the last two weeks of October 1996. The arms were apparently being delivered to the war in eastern Zaire.

Many sources point to elite U.S. troops, including African Americans, and U.S. weapons in eastern Zaire. According to the French daily *Le Monde*, French intelligence sources claim that American soldiers were secretly buried in that area of Zaire.[8]

Marie Béatrice Umutesi wrote a moving account of her life as a refugee, first in Rwanda and then in Zaire, in a book eloquently titled *Surviving the Slaughter: The Ordeal of a Rwandan Refugee in Zaire.* She shows that the operation was coordinated and that the return was illegally forced upon the refugees. At the end of October 1996 conditions in the huge Mugunga refugee camp had become unliveable. The population had tripled and the RPF army allied with Zairean rebels were closing in on the camp.

> A few days before the destruction of the camp at Mugunga, a mission of American soldiers came by. With the help of megaphones, they asked the refugees to take advantage of their presence in order

> to go back to Rwanda, because afterwards it would be too late. It was after this that there was a massive return. The only exit that wasn't blocked by the rebels was the one that led back to Rwanda. Even though they controlled the movements of the people and could take whomever they wanted aside and kill them, they let the great majority of the refugees pass. At all the other camp exits, they shot anyone who moved in sight ... Several weeks after the destruction of Mugungu, the NGOs said they buried 6,700 bodies.[9]

These observations are revealing. What is equally revealing is the unbending U.S. opposition to efforts by France and the European Union to establish a multinational force for Zaire at the end of October and in early November 1996. From November 4 through November 8 the headlines basically resembled this headline from Le Monde: "*La France a du mal à convaincre l'ONU de l'urgence d'une intervention au Zaïre.*"[10] (France is unable to convince the UN that intervention in Zaire is urgent).

Now the convenient narrative would have us believe that where France ran into a wall, Canada's Jean Chrétien easily convinced the UN to intervene. He even did it while resting and relaxing at his Harrington Lake cottage. Sometimes one wonders how gullible these leaders think we are.

Jean Chrétien looked as though he succeeded in mobilizing the UN simply because Washington told him to play that role so as to short-circuit France's efforts. The Canadian prime minister went along of course, just as all sidekicks do. CBC's flagship program *The Fifth Estate* on November 18, 1997 reached exactly the same conclusion: the operation was orchestrated by Washington to make it look as though Canada was leading. To say Prime Minister Chretien "succeeded in mobilizing the UN" was a lie. The only thing he succeeded in doing was to kill the hopes of seeing a real multinational intervention at a time when the refugee crisis made it absolutely crucial.

The same reasoning applies to Raymond Chrétien's nomination as special envoy of the UN secretary general, and to Maurice Baril's appointment to command the stillborn multinational force.

That reasoning also helps us understand their behaviour. Jean Chrétien, Raymond Chrétien, and Maurice Baril were little more than operatives in a major American initiative aimed at knocking Mobutu out of power in Zaire and replacing France as the main foreign power operating in that country. Moreover, for services rendered—more accurately, for services that were not rendered—Maurice Baril was appointed Chief of Staff of the Canadian Armed Forces a few months later and was appointed UN envoy to the Congo in 2003.

In late October 1996 Emma Bonino, the European Commissioner for Humanitarian Action, and Aldo Ajello, special European Envoy in the African Great Lakes region, were both calling desperately for the establishment of a multinational force to be led by France, Belgium, and South Africa. Each call was bluntly rejected by the United States. "I see no usefulness in external military intervention in Zaire," repeated the United States' Ambassador to Rwanda, Robert Gribbin.[11]

Raymond Chrétien acknowledges that he was called on to be the UN special envoy to make the Americans happy. "When Boutros Boutros-Ghali appointed me, he wanted someone who could work with the Americans." Raymond Chrétien added that he "insisted that all other international envoys be pulled out. I didn't want Ms Emma Bonino or anybody else circulating there while I was carrying out my mandate."[12] In other words Raymond Chrétien did not want any other official representatives such as the ones sent by the European Union to appear to have any power to settle the problem. France was therefore effectively sidelined since its voice was being heard through the European Union.

It should be pointed out that Rwandan refugees fleeing the murderous attacks by the Rwandan Patriotic Army had a completely different perception of Emma Bonino. Pierre-Claver Ndacyaysenga described her arrival at the infamous Tingi Tingi refugee camp a few months later:

> As [Emma Bonino] descended from the airplane on Sunday, February 2, she was greeted by a crowd of thousands of emaciated refugees who, hands forming visors over their sunken eyes, looked at her like children waiting for their mother to feed them. Faced with so much misery, which she qualified as inhuman and unacceptable, she could not hold back her tears. She also acknowledged the mistakes of the international community, which had claimed that all Hutu refugees had returned to Rwanda. The visit of this compassionate woman in whom we invested our hope of survival had some positive impact, although it was not as great as we had wished for. After her visit, we noticed an improvement in the quantitative distribution of food and medical care, as well as in the general media coverage of our ordeal.[13]

As commander of the stillborn multinational force Maurice Baril played exactly the same role as Raymond Chrétien. Here is how the Québec City daily, *Le Soleil,* reported the dealings that preceded Baril's appointment as commander. "United States and Canadian government and military officials met at the White House to discuss the multinational force, but Washington still had reservations about the chain of command of the force and had no intention of seeing the United Nations lead it. The principle of a Canadian command corresponded to the American wishes that France would only have a secondary role in the international force to be set up."[14]

Former Prime Minister Kengo of Zaire pointed out in an interview that the Security Council resolution adopted on November 14, 1996 called for the deployment of a multinational force to enable the refugees to "return to their country peacefully, safely, and with dignity." The force was mainly made up of American, Canadian, and British troops with a small French contingent. "But Paul Kagame never wanted the refugees to return to Rwanda peacefully, safely, and with dignity," Kengo insisted. "He wanted them to return to Rwanda as stragglers, one by one, at his mercy. The international community just let him do as he liked."

The safe and peaceful corridor was never set up, and it is easy to understand why not. If the refugees had returned "safely, peacefully, and with dignity," they would have been able to demand that their property and belongings be returned to them, but most of all they could have demanded free, democratic elections. They would also have been in a position to demand a place at an international negotiating table aimed to promote Rwandan national reconciliation after six years of war. That would have complied with the second point in Raymond Chrétien's UN mandate, which was to organize an international conference.

Democratic elections—one man, one vote—would have been the death knell of the RPF regime and of Paul Kagame. From the moment the Rwandan Patriotic Front invaded Rwanda on October 1, 1990 everybody knew that the RPF, which was more than ninety percent Tutsi, could never win elections in Rwanda where only fifteen percent of the population were Tutsis. Furthermore, national reconciliation would also have meant the end of the hunt for *génocidaires* in Congo/Zaire, and thereby eliminate the main pretext used to justify the military intervention in the Congo of the Ugandan, Burundian, and Rwandan armies with U.S. backing.

How could the policy that was so clearly and cynically described to Jean Daniel in November 1996—"France has it all wrong, no question of keeping Mobutu, the strongman is in Uganda, not Kinshasa"—be implemented if Paul Kagame were to be voted out of power and if there were no more "*génocidaires*" to send the armies after?

Former Prime Minister Kengo made an understatement when he said, "Paul Kagame never wanted the refugees to return to Rwanda peacefully, safely, and with dignity, and the international community let him do as he liked." Would it not be more accurate to say: as self-proclaimed leader of the international community, the United States, with the support of Canada and the United Kingdom, told Paul Kagame to invade Zaire, to attack and bomb the refugee camps and force some of them to return to Rwanda? Paul Kagame willingly followed orders. The United States, Canada, and the United Kingdom, it should be remembered, were to provide ninety percent of the 10,000 troops in the ill-famed, stillborn multinational force that would have had the power to save the lives of hundreds of thousands of Rwandan refugees and of Congolese people. Moreover, it could have prevented the unparalleled massacres wrought upon the refugees and all of the Congo in the following years.

As is too often the case in major humanitarian crises, some humanitarian professionals, for reasons that are hard to grasp, always seem to do everything in their power to see that the maximum number of people die. The ubiquitous Belgian ex-Senator, Alain Destexhe, a former secretary general of Doctors Without Borders, is a perfect example. Destexhe fought hard against deployment of a multinational force in Eastern Zaire. The terms used in his opinion article published on November 14, 1996 are staggering. The humanitarian Destexhe wrote in *Le Monde* that the refugees would never return to Rwanda "unless they are forced or are starved into doing so." He also proposed forcible return saying that, "sometimes a painful political solution is preferable to a policy of compassion."

Philip Gourevitch, who also favoured the "painful political solution," managed to present the bombing of the refugee camps and the forced return as a humanitarian military mission because all the refugees are basically, in his opinion, *"génocidaires."* He describes refugee camp life as a sort of Eden in Africa and belittles the tragedy of the refugees most of whom are probably dead now: "living in a refugee camp was not a bad economic proposition for a Rwandan (...) Food was not only free, but ample; malnutrition rates in the camps were far lower than anywhere else in the region, on a par, in fact with those of Western Europe. General medical care was also as good as it got in central Africa (...) The birth rate in the camps was close to the limit of human possibility."[15] In short, they were multiplying like rabbits!

The demonization of Hutu refugees was central to the United States' plan to remove Mobutu from power in Kinshasa. On May 5, 1998 in Washington the House of Representatives' International Relations Committee held hearings to find out why the Clinton

Administration had done so little to prevent the massacres in Rwanda in 1994 and later in the Congo. Neither the State Department nor the Defense Department appeared at the hearings even though they had received formal requests. Only the chief of staff of USAID, Richard McCall, testified. When he was asked why the United States was not pushing for negotiations between Hutu rebels in the Congo and Paul Kagame's government in Kigali, McCall replied angrily: "They're not 'rebels' ... They're *génocidaires*. It would be totally offensive to negotiate with them. I would blow the roof of any building I was sitting in if that were suggested to me."[16]

Starting in 1995, recalled former Prime Minister Kengo wa Dondo, the government of Zaire was getting messages from Washington demanding that Mobutu announce his decision to leave. "Essentially the message went like this. If President Mobutu were to announce on his own that he was stepping down, the United States promised to grant him all the honours due to a veteran head of state. If not, his body would be dragged through the streets of Kinshasa." In April 1997, when it became obvious that Mobutu was not about to obey Washington's ultimatum, President Clinton personally wrote to Mobutu and threatened to let the "rebels" led by Laurent-Désiré Kabila and the Rwandans take power in Kinshasa. Mobutu still refused to obey and so he was removed, according to plan, on May 17, 1997.[17]

A word is in order about the use of the term "rebels" in Central Africa ever since 1990. Any careful observer will have understood that when the term is used by U.S. State Department officials and the major media it in fact describes armed troops that were either full-fledged, uniform-bearing troops belonging to the Rwandan Patriotic Army or Rwandan and Congolese paramilitary troops funded, armed, and led by members of the RPA. Under no circumstances could the term "rebels" be used to describe the Rwandan refugees on Congolese soil fighting against the forces of Paul Kagame. "Rebels" are the good guys and they must be on 'our' side. For nearly twenty-five years well-funded and organized armed forces have torn apart Central Africa, yet they are still being described as rebels. As Noam Chomsky and Ed Herman wrote in *Manufacturing Consent*, "We can even read who are U.S. friends and enemies form the media's use of the word." The manner in which the word "rebels" has confused people about Central Africa suggests that its later use in Libya and Syria to describe armed terrorists or proxy armies might come from a manual of best practices in Information Dominance.

The other feature of the cynical plan unveiled to Jean Daniel in November 1996 by Assistant Secretary of State Kornblum was the removal of Boutros Boutros-Ghali as UN secretary general. On November 19, 1996 in New York, while the refugee crisis raged, U.S. Ambassador to the United Nations Madeleine Albright vetoed the renewal of Boutros-Ghali's mandate, the man she liked to call "Frenchie."[18] Here is how the former secretary general described the behaviour of the United States. "They didn't want someone who would question their decisions. They wanted everything, and everything at once! You know, when people have power ... I have worked with absolute rulers all my life. They cannot accept discussion; they cannot accept even a minimum of contradiction. I want that! And that's all. What? You want to discuss the issue? I am the God of Gods, and I will have what I want. And you're saying that you would like to think about it for a while?"[19]

Washington offered Boutros Boutros-Ghali the same honours it offered Mobutu. President Clinton would receive him at the White House, American universities would grant him honorary doctorates, and more, but in return he had to step down as secretary general of his own volition. Boutros-Ghali replied that he did not accept tips.

◆

Under President Juvénal Habyarimana, Britain had no diplomatic representation in Kigali. By 2002 London's Ambassador to Rwanda was the most important diplomat in the country according to former Rwandan Prime Minister Twagiramungu.

Raymond Chrétien returned to Rwanda as UN special envoy twenty years after having been Canadian Ambassador to the region. He noted that one of the main differences in Kigali was that English had taken over from French, and his negotiations with the Rwandan Government were conducted in English. Rwanda had adopted English as the official language along with Kinyarwanda and French as early as January 1996. That decision also shows whom the new government wanted to please.

Before, during, and after the Rwandan tragedy of 1994 and its continuation in the Congo, the media in English-speaking countries loudly denounced France's guilt and established a sinister "French Connection" by dishonestly using grisly pictures and sensational headlines combined with innuendo and direct accusations. With its imperialist motives, undercover actions, and basically fascist goals, France was made to be the overseer of a genocidal state. Worst of all, it seemed, was the fact that France had continued to honour the bilateral agreements it had signed with Rwanda. In the name of noble and just causes such as human rights and anti-colonialism, everything had to be done to get France out of Rwanda and, for that matter, out of Central Africa. Certain NGOs with their fake neutrality jumped into the fray and launched their own attacks against iniquitous France. If ever a French official or journalist dared to speak publicly about the existence of an English-speaking plot and offensive conducted through a Tutsi "rebel" front, they were ridiculed. It was as if France was the only country to have a vested interest in this part of the world that supposedly was of no interest to anyone, the only one with ulterior colonial motives.

While France was being made to look so bad, the United States was carefully conducting a major offensive in French-speaking Africa following the demise of the Soviet Union. American officials made no bones about it. In March 1993 Under Secretary of State George Moose declared to the Senate that, "we have to ensure that we have access to the tremendous natural resources in Africa, a continent that accounts for seventy-eight percent of the world's chrome reserves, eighty-nine percent of platinum reserves and fifty-nine percent of cobalt reserves."[20] After the Afro-American summit in Dakar in May 1995 the late Ron Brown, Secretary of Commerce, made the following challenge: "America is going to be demanding of Africa's traditional partners, starting with France. We are no longer going to leave Africa to the Europeans."[21] And when Secretary of State Warren Christopher visited Africa in October 1996, he clarified the United States' political goals in Africa: "The time is up when Africa could be divided into spheres of influence, when foreign powers could consider whole groups of countries to be reserved for them. Today Africa needs the support of all its friends rather than the exclusive patronage of a few."

For a big power, even if it is the biggest and most influential in the world, it is no minor undertaking to lead another country to break its long-standing ties with other countries, to replace the official language in use for nearly a century, to reject administrative, educational, and military structures adopted since independence or earlier, and to start doing business in a different way. It is, in fact, a major and difficult shake-up that affects all aspects of the country, of neighbouring countries, and of groups of countries. That is the shake-up that the United States planned and announced for Africa. It was also a warning to all the French-speaking countries that were part of an organization created thanks to the vision of an eminent African poet and political leader, Léopold Sédar Senghor.

The American offensive against France in Africa explains why an unusual number of Canadians were appointed to important positions in the Central African crisis. Roméo Dallaire, Maurice Baril, Louise Arbour, and Raymond Chrétien are the best known. Rarely have we seen so many in a major international crisis. Canadian nationalists sometimes like to credit Canada's supposed lack of a colonial history, the country's peace-keeping experience or its enhanced international role. All three reasons are far-fetched or false, particularly the claimed lack of a colonial history—what about Britain's/Canada's colonization of Aboriginal lands and the conquest and colonization of Québec?

The image of an innocent Canada unsullied by its colonial past should have been relegated to the storybooks after what the Canadian army did in Somalia in 1992 and 1993. (Lest we forget, Canadian soldiers beat a 16-year old boy to death; investigation also revealed many more cases of brutality.) As for peacekeeping, aside from Roméo Dallaire and Brent Beardsley, none of the Canadian Forces were in Rwanda before August 1994 because Canada did not want to send troops there. Those who, on the other hand, try to defend the idea of Canada's enhanced international prestige have been left out in the cold as the United States proceeds to do what it wants when it wants and only calls on Canada when it needs a good sidekick.

The United States whose citizens are strangely proud to speak only one language desperately needed a loyal French-speaking country in the 1990s. In the 1960s James Minnifie wrote a searing attack on Canada and its role as a front for the American empire in his book entitled *Peacekeeper or Powdermonkey*. Add a French-speaking veneer and a deep-set distrust of France and Washington had exactly the wolf in sheep's clothing it needed.

Dislike and suspicion of France in English-speaking Canada are nearly 250 years old, yet they reached new summits during the political reign of Pierre Trudeau, especially as the Québec independence movement gained ground. That visceral distrust of France became an integral part of Canada's foreign policy. On the other hand, Quebecers committed to a strong French-speaking Québec know that their future is intimately linked to the international prestige of France and the French-speaking world. Solid and trusting relations with France are therefore crucial.[22]

Need we recall that the Francophonie Summit, which the late president of Senegal, Léopold Sédar Senghor, had envisioned in the early 1960s, became a reality only in 1986 because of Ottawa's profound suspicions about France's motives. Ottawa politicians perceived France as a hostile and irredentist empire at work in

Québec. The Canadian Government, for its part, likes to treat Québec as little more than a large municipality. A whole generation of Canadians, especially in the armed forces, foreign affairs, and the judiciary, have been raised and trained to distrust everything that is French. To reach the top in any of these fields, French-speaking officers, diplomats, and jurists are expected to toe the line, not once, not twice, but constantly, failing which suspicion is immediately cast upon them, especially by the media.

Louise Arbour, Raymond Chrétien, Maurice Baril, and Roméo Dallaire are all products of these Canadian institutions. While carrying out their respective mandates, each one succeeded in provoking France, blocking it or keeping that country on the sidelines. Each time France proposed a solution to the Rwandan crisis and its sequel in the Congo, the United States and the United Kingdom opposed it. And each time a Canadian was standing there fronting the storm for the Anglo-American alliance or the Anglosphere.

Senghor saw the group of French-speaking countries as a way to counter the cultural and economic domination by English-speaking countries—mainly the United States—which he saw developing in the 1960s. He would surely have seen that whenever the French-speaking world suffers a setback, French speakers throughout the world, and not only in France, lose ground.

Despite appearances and Canada's superficial bilingualism adopted in order to block the Québec independence movement, Canada has always fought tooth and nail against the French language both within the country and in foreign affairs. Hence when the tally is taken of Canada's "successes" in beating back the French language, it will be important to include the country's efforts in Central Africa that started with the war in Rwanda in 1990.

CONCLUSION

As if it were deliberate, just before and just after African countries became massively independent, African prehistory, which was also making a revolution, imposed itself or, more exactly, imposed Africa as the birthplace of humanity.

Léopold Sédar Senghor[1]

The world must take another look at the Rwandan war. First to avoid visiting the same tragedy on other countries, be it in Africa or other continents; and secondly to silence those who would invoke Rwanda as justification for brazen military intervention cloaked in humanitarian cant. The hypocritical apologies of U.S. leaders regarding Rwanda also need to be revisited and reassessed so that we will understand how a terrible tragedy has become a useful imperial fiction. Madeleine Albright told the Organization of African Unity in December 1997: "We, the international community, should have been more active in the early stages of the atrocities in Rwanda in 1994 [...] Yes, mistakes were made, but we are not responsible." President Bill Clinton, the most unwavering supporter of Paul Kagame, told Rwandans in Kigali on March 25, 1998: "It is important that the world know that these killings grew from a policy aimed at the systematic destruction of a people [...] Never again must we be shy in the face of the evidence."[2]

Between 1990 and 1994 the Anglosphere and Europe effectively wrung all decision-making powers out of the Rwandans' hands.

This contrasted with the period following the social revolution in 1959 and independence in 1962 during which Rwandans had built a society and a state capable of meeting the needs and aspirations of the Rwandan people.

The so-called donor countries decided in the late 1980s that the economic model had to change. A strong state apparatus that intervened in the economy had to make way for a skeleton state through privatization and outright withdrawal from certain sectors. Although those who wield money and power simply "invited" Rwanda to join the movement, their barely veiled big stick left little doubt about the consequences of a refusal: disobey and you will be shunned by the "international community"—a modern euphemism for the retired expression "the civilized world." You will become the world's dinosaurs. Rwanda rushed to comply.

It was supposed to be just an economic model. Yet it engendered profound political and sociological transformations in Rwanda, not the least of which was a transfer to private interests of the hard-won power Rwandan Hutus had managed to obtain as a result of the 1959 social revolution. Rwanda was, as René Lemarchand reminds us, the only country in Africa, along with Zanzibar, where revolutionary change occurred. The new model represented a major step backwards and a reinforcement of the Tutsi minority's economic power as Tutsis already dominated the private sector. For the people with money at the International Monetary Fund and the World Bank, a model is a model, is a model! It must be applied across the wall. When they decided to impose the model on Rwanda, did they consider the impact it would have on the country? Most likely not. If they did, then their decision was even more sinister.

At the same time France joined a growing crowd and "invited" African countries to adopt a new political model that, since it came from Europe and North America, was nothing less than God's gift to humanity and democracy. "The winds of freedom blowing East must inevitably blow South too," they said. From now on, everybody had to hold free elections and establish a multiparty system whether they were at war or not. The same model was to apply across the board, whatever the country's history, demographics, economy or traditions. Well, not exactly everybody. Uganda's President Yoweri Museveni had established a total dictatorship, but eyes were averted and he was lauded for his initiative. Africans were not exactly "invited" either; as with the economic model, a big stick was held over their heads in case they failed to comply and establish a multiparty system. Rwandans, under President Habyarimana, went along with the "invitation" as best they could.

As if these transformations were not enough, U.S.-trained officers led a foreign army to invade the country while everybody watched and some applauded. The foreign army occupied Rwandan territory and very soon the United States and others told Rwanda to sit down and negotiate with the invading army that had just launched a murderous war. "Peace process" and "power sharing" became the new buzzwords.

The invaders then unleashed new "punitive" attacks, occupied more land, drove the civilian population out, and activated armed clandestine cells among the Tutsi minority. They continued to enjoy unbending support from the Anglosphere while zealous international brigades of human rights organizations, officially non-governmental, provided grist for their mill.

As the ill-named "peace process" followed its course and formally sanctioned the occupation of Rwandan territory and the de facto removal of President Habyarimana from power, Melchior Ndadaye, the first Hutu president elected in neighbouring Burundi, was brutally assassinated by the Burundian army dominated by the Tutsi minority. Ndadaye's assassination confirmed the worst fears haunting Rwandans: it revealed to all that the Rwandan Patriotic Front, whose members openly celebrated the assassination of Melchior Ndadaye, was not interested in a democratic Rwanda but rather a return to a pre-1959 feudal order in which the Rwandan Tutsi minority, who represented less than fifteen percent of the population, would once again dominate the

Hutu majority. For decades Western countries, and particularly the United States, had lectured the world on democracy—the political system in which the majority expresses its will in free elections. Now the United States led the Western countries in the defence and support of an army that, at best, represented a small minority of the population and whose leaders could never hope to win a democratic election.

This was the situation in Rwanda on April 6, 1994 when the president of Rwanda, Juvénal Habyarimana, and his Burundian counterpart, Cyprien Ntaryamira, were assassinated. Political power was no longer held by Kigali, but rather by Washington through a proxy army. The economy was in a shambles, crippled and drained by the war and the displacement of more than one million internal Rwandan refugees camped around Kigali, one million peasants who no longer worked their land. The newly created political parties were in crisis, all jockeying for anointment by international decision-makers.

Following the assassination of the two African heads of state, the United States and Britain, knowing fully well that violence, death, and destruction would ensue, prevented the United Nations from intervening in Rwanda so as to advance their own strategic interests in Central Africa. Their goal was obvious: help the Rwandan Patriotic Front win a decisive and, they hoped, quick victory in Rwanda. Yet the decisive victory the British-American tandem was counting on did not come quickly. Four long months would go by, which is not surprising: a people who freed themselves after centuries of domination never willingly abandon their freedom.

On the evening of April 6, 1994 the RPF broke the truce and resumed war. Killings occurred in Kigali, as predicted by U.S. diplomats. Yet, the United States and Britain pursued their policy of favouring a decisive and imminent RPF victory. Remember what former UN Secretary General Boutros Boutros-Ghali wrote: "The U.S. effort to prevent the effective deployment of a UN force for Rwanda succeeded, with the strong support of Britain." For the British-American tandem, strategic imperial interests prevailed over human life, especially when those human lives were African.

That is the most serious crime committed in Rwanda in 1994: in the name of strategic imperial interests, hundreds of thousands of Rwandan Hutus and Tutsis were sacrificed.

We now know what happened in Rwanda in the years leading up to the April 6, 1994. Although the official narrative would have it that the assassination of two African heads of state that evening is still a mystery, all serious investigations point to the Rwandan Patriotic Front and Rwandan strongman Paul Kagame as the culprits. They are the ones who broke the Arusha Peace Accord, prepared and executed the missile attack on the Rwandan president's plane, and resumed war in Rwanda until they took power. They are also the ones who invaded the Democratic Republic of the Congo and who have pursued a murderous and destructive war ever since.

Why then are Rwandan Hutus throughout the world treated as the only culprits? Why are they constantly demonized and hunted throughout the world? Why do we sit straight-faced as the Rwandan government and its supporters continue to justify their war on the Congo and the concomitant pillage by referring to the fleeing *génocidaires*?

Here is where the second crime committed in Rwanda lies. It is the cover-up and the protection of the criminals responsible for the tragedy. The means deployed have been impressive. Altogether, it would make for an excellent case study in Information Dominance: how to impose an official narrative about good Rwandan Tutsis defeating horrible Rwandan Hutu *génocidaires*, who are worse than the worst in modern history, the Nazis.

Though this big lie has been repeated ad nauseam, absolutely nothing in the Rwandan tragedy can be likened to the Nazis' planning and launching of a war and mass extermination of Jews. If in fact there was a comprehensive policy developed and implemented in Rwanda and Central Africa, it was the one hatched by cynical minds in Washington and London and their proxies in the RPF as they reengineered the political and economic order of that part of Africa. Since then powerful people such as Bill Clinton and Tony Blair have endeavoured to cover their tracks by promoting what they describe as the "Rwandan miracle," yet it would be more accurate to speak of a Rwandan counter-revolution and nightmare.[3]

"Watch out for Africa! France has it all wrong. The strongman is in Uganda, not in Kinshasa," forebodingly trumpeted the Under Secretary of State in November 1996. For imperial decision-makers in Washington and London, the massive deaths in Rwanda and then in the Congo will have been at best "collateral damage," at worst, a necessary sacrifice in the development of a new imperial discourse.

It has become common to smile smugly at the mention of imperialism, even among the liberal left. The imperial narrative that prevailed from 1850 through 1960 is considered quaint and antiquated; its ugly head would never rear again because the imperial hypocrisy of those times has been exposed and those old empires, dismantled. We can laugh now at David Livingstone who declared in 1866: "It is on the Anglo-American race that the hope of the world for liberty and progress rests ... the inborn energy of English colonists would develop resources ... By linking the Africans to ourselves ... it is hoped that their elevation will eventually be the result."[4] We can also snicker at his fellow traveller and contemporary, Samuel Baker, who maintained that "England (...) possesses a power that enforces a grave responsibility. She has the force to civilize. She is the natural colonizer of the world ... to wrest from utter savagedom those mighty tracts of the earth's surface."[5] Rudyard Kipling summed it up best when he took up the "white man's burden," as did so many Englishmen as they took over Africa and Asia. How terribly backward those imperialists were! We are modern; we have put all that behind us.

Sadly that is not the case. The story of the imperial burden or imperative and the responsibility for Europeans and North

Americans to bring freedom and progress to the peoples of the world may have been refashioned and couched in a new vocabulary, but the reality and consequences are no less devastating. The imperial imperative pervades popular literature as shown in Part 2 of this book. It also informs supposedly serious position papers destined to provide justifications and legitimacy to decision-makers who have the power to bomb or not to bomb, to invade or not to invade, to protect killer regimes or not to protect them. Rwanda, which has been made to be synonymous with "genocide" and the necessity to intervene, has become the touchstone for the "thinkers" of this new imperialism.

Michael Ignatieff is a failed Canadian politician yet some powerful people still consider him an important thinker. The UN Security Council invited Ignatieff to make a presentation on military action against Syria in September 2013. After lamenting the problems Western Powers had in obtaining popular consent for military intervention in Syria, he claimed that popular will should not dictate how governments should act. Then came the necessary reference to Rwanda in 1994 during which, according to him, neither the U.S. Congress nor the Canadian Parliament would have agreed to act. This reference to Rwanda allowed him to add that nations' executives should be free to act without obtaining democratic approvals especially in cases of humanitarian emergencies as in Syria. In short, because of Rwanda we should bomb Syria.[6]

Michael Ignatieff worked hard to develop the new imperial discourse and the so-called "Responsibility to Protect – R2P" while he directed the Carr Center at Harvard's Kennedy School of Governance. One of the first fellows he recruited was Roméo Dallaire. While there he also worked closely with the Center's founding Executive Director, Samantha Power, who Barack Obama appointed as U.S. Ambassador to the United Nations in 2013. For Ignatieff and Samantha Power, Rwanda is always the starting point to justify military action. Samantha Power, who was Senior Director to the National Security Council before her nomination as ambassador to the UN, constantly invoked Rwanda to justify military intervention in Libya. To drive the point home, they and other "humanitarian interventionists" have attached Roméo Dallaire's name and photo to all Responsibility to Protect or R2P initiatives. The message does not fall on deaf ears. Just days before NATO began bombing Libya, the president of the Libyan League for Human Rights called for intervention saying, "there will be a real bloodbath, a massacre like we saw in Rwanda." In fact the only massacre in Libya was that of Libyans bombed and murdered by NATO and their "rebel" allies. As Max Forte wrote, "Everywhere is Rwanda for the humanitarian imperialist." [7]

Shortly before the invasion of Iraq, Michael Ignatieff, in a *New York Times* piece ominously titled *The Burden,* spelled out the humanitarian interventionist creed, which was then still a work in progress. Note how he used the term "burden" unabashedly, even calling it "noble" later on in the article.

> The semi-official ideology of the Western world—human rights—sustains the principle of self-determination, the right of each people to rule themselves free of outside interference. This was the ethical principle that inspired the decolonization of Asia and Africa after World War II. Now we are living through the collapse of many of these former colonial states. Into the resulting vacuum of chaos and massacre a new imperialism has reluctantly stepped—reluctantly because these places are dangerous and because they seemed, at least until Sept. 11, to be marginal to the interests of the powers concerned. But, gradually, this reluctance has been replaced by an understanding of why order needs to be brought to these places [...] Bringing order is the paradigmatic imperial task. [8]

Let us apply Ignatieff's thesis to Rwanda, which he so often cites. Rwanda was one of "these former colonial states" that supposedly "collapsed." That collapse resulted in a "vacuum of chaos and massacre" and the "new imperialism stepped in," although not directly as it would elsewhere, such as Iraq and Libya. It stepped in "reluctantly"—oh yes, of course—because, according to all official statements, Rwanda is "dangerous" and "marginal to the interests" of the United States. (Remember how "reluctant" the British empire was in the 1880s, "an empire acquired in a fit of absence of mind.")

We all know that the Rwandan state did not collapse on its own and that the vacuum of chaos and massacre did not occur all by itself. Above all, we know that the reluctant new imperialism did not bring order, which is supposedly the "paradigmatic imperial task." The new imperialism in fact reinstalled a regime controlled by the Tutsi minority through which it would be able to impose a new domination of the region. It also engendered a convenient disorder that facilitated a more brazen exploitation of Africa's natural resources than has ever before been foisted on the continent.

The old imperial narrative has made a comeback. Recycled and rebranded, it has been regurgitated in the vast majority of popular books, reports, and articles on Rwanda. It is the thread that holds the "right and proper" tale about Rwanda together. Worst of all, and probably owing to our lack of vigilance, it has been potent enough to open the doors to a new and brutal scramble for Africa and the development of a new form of colonial domination. For most Rwandans, that is exactly what occurred starting on October 1, 1990, though this time with fewer Belgians and more Americans.

NOTES

Introduction

1. Edward S. Herman and David Peterson, *The Politics of Genocide*, New York, Monthly Review Press, 2010, p. 12.
2. On the pretention of the Rwandan Patriotic Front that all Rwandan Hutus, Tutsis, and Twas lived happily together before European colonialists arrive, Serge De Souter sets the record straight in *Rwanda: Le procès du FPR, mise au point historique* (L'Harmattan, 2007). He situates the current catastrophe in a long series of conflicts that began well before colonialism. "Historically, the notion that the three groups lived together in peace and harmony is indefensible. It would be a great exception in the history of humanity." On the same point, see also monumental work, *Proverbes du Rwanda* by Pierre Crépeau and Simon Bizimana (Musée Royal de l'Afrique Centrale, Annales, 800 pages.
3. René Lemarchand, "Revolutionary phenomena in stratified societies: Rwanda and Zanzibar," in *Civilisations*, Vol. 18, No. 1, Institut de Sociologie de l'Université de Bruxelles, 1968, pp. 16-51.
4. Supporters of the official narrative have widely—and dishonestly—misinterpreted this term. In his authoritative 1970 book *Rwanda and Burundi*, René Lemarchand defined *inyenzi* as follows: "the term inyenzi is currently used within and outside Rwanda to refer to small-scale Tutsi-led guerrilla units trained and organized outside Rwanda and varying in size from about six to ten men... It literally means cockroaches." (p. 198).
5. "Ed Broadbent et la crise rwandaise : un rapport préparé avec insouciance" *La Presse*, September 6, 1994, B3, (Ed Broadbent and the Reckless Report on Rwanda).
6. John, Philpot, "Le Tribunal international pour le Rwanda, La justice trahie," in *Études internationales*, vol. XXVII, No. 4 December 1996, Institut québécois des hautes études internationales.
7. Pablo Neruda, *Canto General*, translated by Jack Schmitt, University of California Press, 1991, p. 169.

Chapter 1

1. "The Minister of Rape," *New York Times Magazine*, Sunday, September 15, 2002, p. 1.
2. Yoweri Museveni, *What is Africa's problem*? University of Minnesota Press 2000, p. 106.
3. *Ibid.*, p. 178.
4. *Ibid.*, p. 132.
5. *Ibid.* How to fight a Counterrevolutionary Insurgency, pp. 132-140.
6. J. R. Seeley, *The Expansion of England, Chicago and London*, 1971, p. 12.
7. See Maximilian C. Forte, *Slouching Towards Sirte, NATO's War on Libya and Africa*, Baraka Books, 2012, p. 24.
8. For a full discussion of the role of NGOs and humanitarian organizations, see Maximilian Forte, *Slouching Towards Sirte, NATO's War on Libya and Africa* (Baraka Books, 2012), Chapter 5, Humanitarianism and the Invention of Emergency, pp. 237-267.
9. Fashoda was a fort located on the Upper Nile (Now in Sudan). French and British military missions met there on September 18, 1898. France wanted to set up a series of forts from west to east across Africa—Dakar to Djibouti. The British wanted to build a railway from Uganda to Egypt and link its "possessions" in Africa from south to north—the Cape to Cairo. In November 1898, France withdrew from Fashoda and conceded it to the British. It was subsequently decided that the headwaters of the Nile and the Congo rivers would delineate the British and French spheres of influence.
10. Pierre Péan, *Carnages, Les guerres secretes des grandes puissances en Afrique,* Fayard, 2010, pp. 425-457. Péan provides a clear explanation of the United States' strategy in Eastern and Central Africa at the turn of the 1990s and examines specifically the role played by Roger Winter and the United States Committee for Refugees from before the founding for the RPF. For a discussion of the United States' strategic goals in Africa and its objectives with AFRICOM, see Maximilian Forte, *Slouching Towards Sirte, NATO's War on Libya and Africa* (Baraka Books, 2012), particularly Chapter 4, A War against Africa: AFRICOM, NATO, and Racism.
11. McNair Paper Number 44, Chapter 6, October 1995. Institute for National Strategic Studies.
12. Aimé Césaire, *Discourse on Colonialism*, Monthly Review Press, 1972, p. 15.
13. Valens Kajeguhakwa, *Rwanda : de la terre de paix à la terre de sang et après?*, Éditions Rémi Perrin, 2001, p. 223.
14. William Cyrus Reed, Exile, Reform and the Rise of the RPF, *Journal of Modern African Studies*, Vol. 34, No. 3, 1996, pp. 479-501.
15. Panikos Panayi, ed. *Minorities in wartime : national and racial groupings in Europe, North America, and Austrialia during the two world wars*, Oxford (England) Berg, 1993, p. 3.

16. J.S. Woodsworth, *Strangers Within Our Gates*, cited in John Herd Thompson, *Ethnic Minorities during Two World Wars*, Ottawa, 1991, Canadian Historical Association.
17. Roger Daniels, *Concentration Camps: North America, Japanese in the United States and Canada During World War II*, Krieger Publishing, FL USA, 1981.
18. *Enjeux nationaux et dynamiques régionales dans l'Afrique des Grands lacs*, Journée d'Étude, Lille, June 20, 1992, under the direction of André Guichaoua, URA Tiers-Monde/Afrique.
19. James K. Gasana, *Rwanda : du parti-état à l'état-garnison*, L'Harmattan, 2002, p. 89.
20. Gasana, *op. cit.*, p. 76

Chapter 2

1. RFI – Radio-France international, Rwanda/Entretien, "Patrick Karegeya: 'Nous savons d'où les missiles sont partis,'" 9 July 2013, http://www.rfi.fr/afrique/20130708-patrick-karegeya-nous-savons-missiles-sont-partis (our translation)
2. Joyce Leader, The Rwanda Crisis: The Genesis of a Genocide, A speech delivered at Penn State University, April 5, 2001.
3. James K. Gasana, *op. cit.*, p. 74.
4. See Guy Bouthillier and Édouard Cloutier, *Trudeau's Darkest Hour, War Measures in Time of Peace 1970*, Baraka Books, 2010. When Noam Chomsky received a complimentary copy of this book he replied, "All new to me."
5. See Chapter 14: Jean-Paul Akayesu was then held at the Maison centrale d'arrêt, de Bamako, Mali. He claims to be innocent. I interviewed him in prison in November 2002.
6. James K. Gasana, *op. cit.*, p. 205.
7. Interview with Faustin Twagiramungu, November 2002 in Brussels.
8. https://peaceaccords.nd.edu/site_media/media/accords/Rwanda_Peace_Accord.pdf
9. Carol Off, *The Lion the Fox and the Eagle*, Vintage Canada, 2000, p. 25.
10. Jacques Castonguay, *Les casques bleus au Rwanda*, Paris, L'Harmattan, 1998, p. 89.

Chapter 3

1. *The National Post*, October 12, 2002, p. A1.
2. Interview with Ambassador Raymond Chrétien at the Canadian Embassy in Paris, November 21, 2002.
3. Discours de son excellence Monsieur le premier ministre Pierre-Célestin Twigema à l'occasion de la cérémonie d'ouverture du Tribunal pénal international pour le Rwanda, Arusha, le 8 janvier 1996.

4. Interview with Pierre-Célestin Rwigéma, January 23, 2003.
5. Rémi Korman, "La construction de la mémoire du genocide des Tutsi du Rwanda. Étude des processus de memorialisation," http://www.fondationshoah.org/FMS/IMG/pdf/15-_Korman_ok.pdf.
6. *Le Point*, Radio-Canada, September 14, 1994. The interview can be heard in its entirety in French at www.barakabooks.com.
7. Requests for interviews with Roméo Dallaire must go through his lawyer Harvey Yarosky. According Mr. Yarosky, Dallaire refused to meet me because he was finishing his book on Rwanda. A set of written questions were forwarded to Dallaire, but he still refused to answer.
8. Interview with Gilbert Ngigol, Paris, November 23, 2002.
9. Justice Arbour also refused to grant an interview for this book. When I met her at a public meeting in Paris, she claimed that because of her current position she cannot answer specific questions about the Tribunal. However, the Paris-based Kenyan journalist Ruth Nabakwe interviewed her and provided me with the cassette.
10. *The Politics of Genocide* by Edward S. Herman and David Peterson is a must-read to understand the use and abuse of the word "genocide" and its derivatives. They remark in their concluding notes: "During the past several decades, the word 'genocide' has increased in frequency of use and recklessness of applications, so much so that the crime of the twentieth century for which the word originally was coined often appears debased. Unchanged, however, is the huge political bias in its usage, and it remains as true today as it was in 1973 or 1988 that 'We can even read who are U.S. friends and enemies form the media's use of the word.'" (The quote is from Chomsky's and Herman's classic *Manufacturing Consent.*)
11. *Le Devoir,* January 29, 1993, p. 6. (See chapter 4.)
12. Linda Melvern, *A People Betrayed, The Role of the West in Rwanda's Genocide*, Londres, Zed Books, 2000, p. 56.
13. *The Gazette*, February 8, 1997, B3.
14. RPF Press Release, February 8, 1993, "Resumption of hostilities in Rwanda," in James K. Gasana, *Rwanda. Du parti-état à l'état-garnison*, Paris, L'Harmattan, 2000, p. 183.
15. Aminata Traoré, *Le Viol de l'imaginaire*, Arles/Paris, Actes Sud/Fayard, 2002, p. 69.
16. Marie Béatrice Umutesi, *Surviving the Slaughter, The Ordeal of a Rwandan Refugee in Zaïre*, preface by Catharine Newbury, University of Wisconsin Press, 2004, p. 26. Originally published in French under the title *Fuir ou mourir au Zaïre, Le vécu d'une réfugiée rwandaise*, L'Harmattan, 2000.

Chapter 4

1. *Le Devoir,* Montréal, February 1, 1995. Father Georges-Henri Lévesque founded the National University of Rwanda.
2. Interview with the author, Brussels, November 23, 2002.
3. Reed, William Cyrus, Exile, Reform and the Rise of the RPF, in *Journal of Modern African Studies,* Vol. 34, No. 3, 1996, p. 496.
4. The authors of the report are Jean Carbonare, Agir ensemble pour les droits de l'Homme, Paris; Philippe Dahinden, jurist and journalist, Lausanne; René Degni-Segui, Dean of the Law Faculty, Abidjan; Alison Des Forges, Africa Watch; Pol Dodinval, M.D., Liège; Éric Gillet, FIDH, Brussels; Rein Odink, Jurist, Amsterdam; Halidou Ouedraogo, Judge, Burkina Faso; André Paradis, General Manager, Ligue des droits et libertés, Montreal, William Schabas, Law Professor, Université du Québec à Montréal.
5. Robin Philpot, "Ed Broadbent et la crise rwandaise : un rapport préparé avec insouciance," *La Presse,* September 6, 1994, p. B3.
6. *La Presse,* September 14, 1994, p. B3.
7. "Atrocities and the Law, A Canadian lawyer puts his legal skills to work literally uncovering and confirming evidence of human rights abuses in the African country of Rwanda," by William A. Schabas, in *Canadian Lawyer,* August/September 1993, p. 36.
8. *La Presse,* September 14, 1994, B3.
9. Vienna Declaration and Programme of Action, World Conference on Human Rights, Vienna, 14-25 June 1993
10. Gasana, *op. cit.* p. 183.
11. Pierre Péan, *Noires fureurs, blancs menteurs, Rwanda 1990-1994,* Mille et une nuits, 2005, pp. 133-159.
12 http://www.asser.nl/upload/documents/DomCLIC/Docs/NLP/UK/Vincent_Brown_and_others_HighCourt_Judgment_8-4-2009.pdf
13. Alison L. Des Forges' curriculum vitae submitted to Citizenship and Immigration Canada in the case against Leon Mugesera, 1995.
14. Canada's Federal Court of Appeal in the case of Leon Mugesera examined the 1993 International Commission of Inquiry report closely. The accusations against Leon Mugesera, who was extradited from Canada to Rwanda in 2012, were based on a conclusion of the International Commission of Inquiry about a speech he had made in November 1992. The Federal Court of Appeal, which freed Mugesera, reached devastating conclusions regarding the International Commission of Inquiry. The Supreme Court of Canada overturned that decision, but based its ruling not on a full review of the evidence but on the grounds that, according to the Supreme Court, the Federal Court of Appeal should have deferred to the decision of the Immigration arbitrator, an employee of the government, not a judge.

Justice J.A. Létourneau concurred with his colleagues saying, "I cannot but express my bewilderment not only at the ease with which Mr. Mugesera's speech was altered for partisan purposes by the International Commission of Inquiry, but especially at the ease and confidence with which the alterations of the text were subsequently accepted, with the consequences that we know." [255] "As my colleague pointed out, conclusions sometimes erroneous, sometimes hasty and speculative, sometimes doubtful, with a weak foundation, often reasserted and reiterated by others without discrimination and any other attempt at authentication, have generated a belief in a non-existent reality..." [256]
Interestingly, the Federal Court of Appeal also established that the commission had received a transcript of the speech translated from Kinyarwanda from an unidentified diplomat. Members of the commission who witnessed against Léon Mugesera refused to identify the diplomat who provided them with the speech. That diplomat obviously had an agenda but to this day he or she remains unidentified.
http://www.asser.nl/upload/documents/20120913T041155-Mugesera_Court_Appeal_Judgement_8-9-2003.pdf

Chapter 5

1. Gourevitch, Philip, *We Wish to Inform you that Tomorrow we Will Be Killed with our Families. Stories from Rwanda*, New York, Farrar, Straus and Giroux, 1998.
2. Interview with Faustin Twagiramungu, November 22, 2002.
3. Colonel Luc Marchal, *Rwanda : la descente aux enfers, Témoignage d'un peacekeeper, décembre 1993 – avril 1994*, Paris Éditions Labor, 2001, pp. 165-176.
4. Letter from Luc Marchal to Alain de Brouwer written in July 1998 quoted by de Brouwer in a document about the organization of International Christian Democrats and the war in Rwanda, October 2002.
5. James K. Gasana, *op. cit.*, p. 238.
6. *Ibid*, p. 232.
7. *Africa International*, May 2004; Jacques-Roger Booh-Booh, *Le patron de Dallaire parle, Révélations sur les derives d'un general de l'ONU au Rwanda*, Duboiris, 2005.
8. Gasana, *op. cit.*, p. 238.
9. Gasana, *op. cit.*, p. 237.
10. *Commission d'enquête parlementaire concernant les événements du Rwanda*, Sénat de Belgique, Friday, May 30, 1997, testimony of Faustin Twagiramungu, former Prime Minister of Rwanda.
11. James R. Mock and Cedric Larson, *Words that Won the War. The Story of the Committee on Public Information, 1917-1919*, Princeton, Princeton University Press, 1939.

12. Fred Jerome, *The Einstein File, J. Edgar Hoover's Secret War Against the World's Most Famous Scientist*, St. Martin's Griffin, New York, 2003.
13. To appreciate the power of a false story, in 2000 a group of "experts" published a book entitled *The Path of a Genocide*, still used in schools and universities, in which the January 11, 1994 cable is printed in its entirety right after the editors' preface as though it were incontestable proof of the case about to be made.
14. Interview with Boutros Boutros-Ghali, November 9, 2004.
15. The Genocide Fax, *The New Yorker*, May 11, 1998.
16. Michael Dobbs, *Madeleine Albright. A Twentieth Century Odyssey*, Henry Holt & Company, 1999, pp. 364-365.
17. Howard French, *A Continent for the Taking*, Knopf, 2004, p. 243.
18. *Ibid.* p 365. Former UN Secretary General Boutros Boutros-Ghali complained that the CIA spent as much every day as the UN in a whole year. Madeleine Albright's biographer corrected him by pointing out that it was every ten days and not every day.
19. In a sad attempt to mimic the paper trail left by the Nazis regarding their genocidal project some have conferred upon the dubious "genocide fax" and "Jean-Pierre" a sacred role in their narrative. Kofi Annan, in his ingratiating effort to maintain credibility among Western powers, quotes the fax in full in his memoirs *Interventions: A Life in War and Peace* (Penguin, 2012), as if his feigned candour could make the story true.

Chapter 6

1. On August 20, 2001, William Ferrogiaro of the independent National Security Archives published a series of decontrolled/unclassified internal Clinton Administration documents. See Chapter 7 for more details.
2. Transcript of Alison Des Forges' testimony in the trial of Colonel Théoneste Bagosora.
3. *Report of the Independent Inquiry into the Actions of the United Nations during the 1994 Genocide in Rwanda*, December 15, 1999, p. 66; authors: Ingvar Carlsson (former Prime Minister of Sweden), Professor Han Sung-Joo (Former Minister of Foreign Affairs of the Republic de Korea) and retired Lieutenant General le Rufus M. Kupolati (Nigeria).
4. *Ibid.*, p. 15.
5. David Paciocco, "Defending Rwandans Before the ICTR: A Venture Full of Pitfalls and Lessons for International Criminal Law," in *La voie vers la cour pénale internationale: tous les chemins mènent à Rome*, Les journées Maximilien-Caron Éditions Thémis, Faculté de droit, Université de Montréal, 2003.
6. Testimony of Roméo Dallaire in Jean-Paul Akayesu's trial at the ICTR in Arusha.

7. Filip Reyntjens, *Trois jours qui ont fait basculer l'histoire*, Paris et Tervuren, L'Harmattan et Institut Africain-CEDAF, 1995, pp. 46-47.
8. Charles Onana, *Les secrets du génocide rwandais*, Paris, Duboiris, 2002.
9. Speech by Louise Arbour, Paris, November 20, 2002.
10. *National Post*, Canada, March 1, 2000.
11. Testimony of Jean-Pierre Mugabe, April 25, 2000, *The International Strategic Studies Association*, Alexandria, Virginia. Please see Interview with Amadou Deme in Appendix 1.
12. Luc Marchal, *op. cit.*, p. 304.
13. Many of Paul Kagame's former comrades have confirmed that Paul Kagame was personally responsible for the assassination of the presidents of Rwanda and Burundi on April 6, 1994. These include Dr. Théogène Rudasingwa, former RPF Secretary General, Ambassador of Rwanda to the United States, and President Paul Kagame's Chief of Staff.https://www.facebook.com/notes/theogene-rudasingwa/kagame-a-tue-le-president-habyarimana/276073305750379
Although Belgian Colonel Luc Marchal (retired) is convinced the RPF is responsible for the assassination, he has made it a personal mission to have established an independent international inquiry into the shooting down of the presidential plane. In 2004 he called on Roméo Dallaire to join him in calling for such an inquiry. Dallaire never responded to his call. Luc Marchal has methodically replied to the various reports aimed at covering up for the criminals responsible. Among others, see: "Rapport d'expertise sur l'attentat du 6 avril 1994: l'arbre qui cache la forêt," 16 February, 2012 and "Analyse du rapport Mutsinzi," 1 February 2010 at the site http://www.france-rwanda.info/.

Chapter 7

1. Boutros Boutros-Ghali, *Unvanquished: A US-UN Saga*, Random House, p. 138.
2. Letter from Luc Marchal to Alain de Brouwer, July 1998. The letter is quoted in an October 2002 document on the Interationale démocrate chrétienne and the war in Rwanda. Note that Luc Marchal met the famous "Jean-Pierre" shortly after arriving in Rwanda at a time when using his own words he was still "duped by their (the RPF's) smart propaganda."
3. Maximilian Forte, *Slouching Towards Sirte, NATO's War on Libya and Africa*, Baraka Books, 2012, p. 9. For details, see pp. 247-249.
4. "Rwanda: The Art of Death," *The Economist*, May 28, 1994.
5. August 20, 2001, William Ferrogiaro of National Security Archive, published the documents on the Internet. See website: http://www.gwu.edu/~nsarchiv/NSAEBB/NSAEBB53/.
6. *Ibid.* Document uncontrolled on November 18, 1998.

7. *Le Point*, Radio-Canada, September 14, 1994.
8. Excerpted from from *Rwanda: crimes, mensonges et étouffement de la vérité* (Les Intouchables, Montreal, 2007) by Robin Philpot; full interview in Appendix 1.
9. Jacques Castonguay, *Les Casques bleus au Rwanda*, pp. 185-190.
10. Gérard Prunier, *The Rwanda Crisis. History of a Genocide*, Columbia, 1995, p. 287.
11. Pierre Péan, *Carnages, Les guerres secretes des grandes puissances en Afrique*, Fayard, 2010, pp. 306-307.

Chapter 8

1. Nicolas Bancel, Pascal Blanchard, Francis Delabarre, *Images d'empire 1930-1960*, Éditions de la Martinière/La Documentation française, 1997; Bancel et Blanchard, *De l'indigène à l'immigré*, Gallimard, 1998.
2. Dorothy Hammond and Alta Jablow, *The Africa That Never Was: Four Centuries of British Writing About Africa*, Twayne Publishers, Inc. New York (1970).
3. *Ibid.*, p 18.
4. Achebe, Chinua, *Hopes and Impediments: Selected Essays.* "An Image of Africa: Racism in Conrad's Heart of Darkness," New York: Doubleday, 1989, pp 1-20.
5. Joseph Conrad, *Heart of Darkness*, Dover Publications, 1990, p. 32.
6. In Achebe, *op. cit.*, p. 13; many contemporary writers encountered Africans as did Conrad, but few showed such visceral dislike.
7. Pierre-Damien Mvuyekure, "Philip Gourevitch's Platonic and Conradian Eyes on the Genocide in Rwanda," in Ishmael Reed's *Konch*.

Chapter 9

1. David Livingstone, *Narrative of an Expedition to the Zambesi and its Tributaries; and of the discovery of the Lakes Shirwa and Nyassa*, New York, 1866, p. 725, in Hammond and Jablow, *op. cit.*, p. 54.
2. Philip Gourevitch, *We wish to inform you that tomorrow we will be killed with our families, Stories from Rwanda*, Picador USA, 1998.
3. Gourevitch, *op. cit.*, p. 225.
4. Chinua Achebe, *Home and Exile*, Oxford, 2000, pp. 84-91.
5. India West, April 25, 1980, in Ishmael Reed, *Writin' is Fightin'*, Atheneum, 1988, p. 212.
6. Gourevitch, *op. cit.*, p. 12.
7. The Kibeho massacre occurred from April 18 through April 23, 1995, in what the RPF called Operation Homeward. International observers and many soldiers in the UNAMIR II witnessed the killing and saw troops burying

bodies of civilians as soon as they killed them. It is estimated that 8000 internal Rwandan refugees were killed during this operation. The RPF Government reported that 350 people had died. The best account is that of Terry Pickard, an Australian Medic with the peacekeeping force who wrote the book *Combat Medic, An Australian's eyewitness account of the Kibeho Massacre,* Big Sky Publishing, 2008. Following is a short excerpt about events on April 22, 1995. "As we gathered up what was left of our medical supplies and personal gear, we could see hundreds and hundreds of dead bodies littering the ground. We could hear the injured crying out in pain. But there was nothing more we could do that day to help these people. We had to get out while it was still daylight, or we might never get out at all. We could only hope the RPA would let us leave after what we had just witnessed. They had just murdered thousands of unarmed, starving, thirsty, and helpless men, women, and children. Even babies had not been spared. Some of those who had survived the lethal onslaught of 50 caliber machineguns, AK47 rifles, rocket-propelled grenades and mortars were ruthlessly hunted down and bayoneted to death where they lay injured." (p. 11)

Canadian Major General Guy Tousignant replaced Roméo Dallaire as Force Commander of UNAMIR in August 1994 and was responsible for the force until December 1995. He has received much less publicity than his predecessor, perhaps because he told what happened at Kibeho in an honest and straightforward manner in the book *La mission au Rwanda : Entretiens avec le général Guy Tousignant* (Guy Tousignant and François Bugingo, Montréal, Liber, 1997, p. 65-85). For Tousignant, Kibeho was "his worst failure."

According to Tousignant, Kagame gave the orders to attack the camp of 150 thousand refugees and killed between 4000 and 8000. Tousignant's description of how the numbers were manipulated is chilling. Tousignant's men had already reached a count of 4000 dead while the United Nations Rwanda Emergency Organization (UNREO) estimated that 8000 people had been killed. The UN Secretary General's special envoy, Shaharyar M. Khan, appeared on the scene and said, "All this smells bad. Can we not reduce those numbers?" Tousignant replied, "With all respect, sir, you are asking me to lie and I find that very difficult." Tousignant speculated that Khan was trying to "sell a somewhat acceptable image of the new Rwanda in order to please funding agencies." Shortly thereafter, the Canadian Ambassador Dussault suggested, "Why not set up an international commission of inquiry to reassure the funders who will surely use this incident to cut off funding that is already lacking?"

General Tousignant wrote, "The Commission met and submitted a conciliatory report that got the Kigali authorities out of a sticky situation." In short, the report avoided the question of numbers of dead, exonerated Rwandan civil and military leaders of any responsibility, attributed responsibility equally among the army and the refugees, and recommended that international aid be resumed.

Chapter 10

1. Carol Off, *The Lion, The Fox and The Eagle, A Story of Generals and Justice in Rwanda and Yugoslavia*, Vintage Canada, 2000.
2. Hammond and Jablow, op. cit., p. 131.
3. See chapter 6.
4. See Chapter 13, note 149.

Chapter 11

1. Gil Courtemanche, *op. cit.*
2. Filip Reyntjens, *Trois jours qui ont fait basculer l'histoire*, L'Harmattan Paris et Institut Africain-CEDAF, 1996, p. 62, note 109.
3. Aimé Césaire, *Discourse on colonialism*, Monthly Review Press, 1972, p. 53.
4. Courtemanche, *op. cit.*, p. 75. "By now Valcourt knew all to well the pleasures derived from solemn sermons, pompous speeches and long orations by so many African "intellectuals" to dare interrupt.
5. Gil Courtemanche, *Dimanche à la piscine à Kigali*, Boréal Compact, 2000, p. 118. The English translation of this excerpt leaves out the reference to the humanity.

Chapter 12

1. Luc Marchal, *Rwanda : la descente aux enfers, témoignage d'un peacekeeper, décembre 1993*—April 1994, Éditions Labor, pp. 259-260. Also interview with Gilbert Ngijol, political assistant to Jacques-Roger Booh-Booh, special representative the UN Secretary General in Rwanda.
2. Braeckman, *op. cit.*, p. 19. (Our translation and emphasis).
3. *Idem*, p. 236.
4. Raymond Tong, *Figures in Ebony*, London, Cassell and Company, 1958, p. 86.

Chapter 13

1. Interview with Ramsey Clark, New York, September 12, 2002.
2. Justice Louise Arbour refused to grant me an interview. Along with some journalists, I managed to question her however at a public meeting on November 21, 2002 in Paris where she was invited to speak about the International Criminal Tribunal.
3. Frédéric Bastien, *La bataille de Londres, Dessous, secrets et coulisses du rapatriement constitutionnel*, Boréal, 2013, p. 322. The words "constitutional coup d'État" were used by the British High Commissioner in Ottawa, John Ford.

4. Interview with Boutros Boutros-Ghali, Paris, Novembre 21, 2002. The non-membership of the U.S. has not prevented them from using the International Criminal Court to advance their own foreign policy goals. During the war on Libya U.S.Secretary of State Hillary Clinton called on the International Criminal Court to indict Muammar Gaddafi and his closest officials.

5. Richard J. Goldstone, *For Humanity. Reflections of a War Crimes Investigator*, New Haven and London, Yale University Press, 2000. Interestingly, the book is prefaced by U.S. Supreme Court Justice, Sandra Day O'Connor, a right-wing Republican in the Barry Goldwater, Pat Buchanan tradition.

6. *Ibid.*, p. 137.

7. *Le Monde*, December 15, 1997, p. 2.

8. ICTY Judge Frederik Harhoff's email to 56 contacts, June 6, 2013 (translated from the Danish – our emphasis).

9. David Scheffer, *All the Missing Souls, A Personal History of the War Crimes Tribunals*, Princeton University Press, 2012.

10. The Rwandan Genocide Seen in New Light, Gunnar Willum & Bjorn Willum, *Aktuelt*, Denmark, April 17, 2000.

11. Florence Hartmann, *Paix et châtiment, Les guerres secrètes de la politique et de la justice internationales*, pp. 247-278, particularly, 270-272, Flammarion, 2007.

12. Pierre Duclos, who was implicated in the fabrication of evidence in the Matticks Affair, was part of the team that carried out Operation NAKI in July 1997. He is severely contested by the prisoners who accuse him of using the same methods to establish the "facts" in their cases. (Specific mention should be made of the cases of former Prime Minister Jean Kambanda and Alfred Musema). See the damning report issued by Amnesty International on NAKI and the sad arrest of Esdras Twagirimana: International Criminal Tribunal for Rwanda, Trials and Tribulations, Amnesty International, April 1, 1998. (web.amnesty.org). Throughout his detention, Esdras Twagirimana requested the services of the Montreal lawyer Tiphaine Dickson, who was in Arusha and recognized by the ICTR.

13. Carol Off, *The Lion, the Fox and the Eagle, Vintage Canada*, 2001, p 320. Since Ms Arbour refused to grand an interview, it has been necessary to turn to works by people with whom she gracefully agreed to meet.

14. Carol Off, *op. cit.*, p. 333.

15. John Philpot, "Le Tribunal international pour le Rwanda. La justice trahie," *Études internationals,* Vol. XXVII, No. 4, December 1996, Institut québécois des hautes études internationals, p. 827-840.

16. David Paciocco, "Defending Rwandans Before the ICTR: A Venture Full of Pitfalls and Lessons for International Criminal Law," in *La voie vers la cour pénale internationale: tous les chemins mènent à Rome*, Les journées

Maximilien-Caron Éditions Thémis, Faculté de droit, Université de Montréal, 2003.

17. "Justice on Trial," *National Post*, December 14, 2002, B6, cited in Paciocco, *op. cit.*

18. *The Prosecutor v. Théoneste Bagosora et al., Case No. ICTR-98-41-T.*

19. See Count 1, Paragraphs 1-11, in Amended Indictment in Case No. ICTR-2001-73-I and Paragraphs 395 and 447 of in the judgment of *The Prosecutor v. Protais Zigiranyirazo, Case No. ICTR-01-73-T,*

20. Bernard Lugan, *Rwanda, Contre-enquête sur le génocide*, Éditions Privat, 2007, p. 255 (our translation).

Chapter 14

1. Chapter title adapted from *Un Canadien errant*, song written by Antoine Gérin-Lajoie, 1844, about the Patriotes from Lower Canada in the 1837-38 rebellion who were banished to penal colonies. Others were hanged. Listen to versions by Paul Robeson's or Leonard Cohen. Excerpt of poem by Langston Hughes, 1942, in *Collected Works of Langston Hughes, Volume 2, The Poems: 1941-1950*, University of Missouri Press, Columbia and London, 2001.

2. On October 31, 2013 seven Rwandans acquitted by the ICTR are forced to stay in Arusha (one man since 2004) because no country will accept them. One was acquitted in 2004.

3. Statement under oath by BBB made before Éric Thibaut de Maisières, notary at Saint-Gilles (Bruxelles). Jean-Paul Akayesu's lawyer, John Philpot met BBB for three days. The witnesses name is not revealed for his and his family's safety. The original French statement: *"Approximativement au début de 1997 selon mon souvenir, on a commencé à parler des témoins de viol. Avant il n'y avait pas question de preuve de viol. M. Karangwa m'a dit qu'il y a des veuves et d'autres qui sont faciles à manipuler pour témoigner sur le viol."*

4. Ishmael Reed, Spielberg Plays Howard Beach, in *Writin' is Fightin', Thirty-seven years of Boxing on Paper*, Atheneum, New York, 1990, p. 145.

5. Sujata MOORTI, *Color of Rape, Gender and Race in Television's Public Spheres*, State University of New York Press, 2002.

6. *Ibid.*, p. 6.

7. Nine young African American men arrested in Alabama for having raped two white women were sentenced to death. That sentence was commuted for all but won, the "Scotsboro boys" all served long sentences in prison before they were acquitted after a massive support campaign.

8. *The New York Times Magazine*, Sunday September 15, 2002, "The Minister of Rape."

9. Alexander Zahar & Göran Sluiter, *International Criminal Law*, Oxford University Press, p. 157.

10. *Idem*, p. 171.

Chapter 15

1. A very good example of the narrative or convenient fiction appeared in *The Toronto Star*, November 15, 1996, p. A24. "How the PM stirred state heads. Middle powers' backing gave him key momentum to persuade US."
2. Interview with the humanitarian worker with a major NGO.
3. *Libération*, March 10, 1997, pp 2 to 6; articles signed by Stephen Smith, later a professor at Duke University, Durham, North Carolina.
4. Interview with Raymond Chrétien in Paris, November 22, 2002.
5. Interview with the former Prime Minister of Zaire, Léon Kengo Wa Dondo, December 5, 2002.
6. "Article 33: Prohibition of expulsion or return ("refoulement"). (1) No Contracting State shall expel or return ("refouler") a refugee in any manner whatsoever to the frontiers of territories where his life or freedom would be threatened on account of his race, religion, nationality, membership of a particular social group or political opinion."
7. Jean Daniel, *Avec le temps. Carnets 1970-1998*, Paris Grasset, 1998, p. 578 (our translation).
8. U.S. implication in military operations in eastern Zaire in November 1996, which marked the beginning of a prolonged and murderous war, is widely documented. See Jacques Isnard, "Des 'conseillers' américains auraient été tués aux côtés des rebelles," *Le Monde*, March 29, 1997; "Des 'conseillers" américains ont aidé à renverser le régime de M. Mobutu," *Le Monde*, August 28, 1997. See also Wayne Madsen, *Genocide and Covert Operations in Africa, 1993-1999*, Lewiston, Edwin Mellen Press, 1999. Madsen also points to the deployment to Rwanda and eastern Zaire of American information officials specialized in propaganda.
9. Marie Béatrice Umutesi, *Surviving the Slaughter, The Ordeal of a Rwandan Refugee in Zaire*, preface by Catherine Newbury, University of Wisconsin Press, 2004, p. 120-121.
10. *Le Monde*, November 8, 1996.
11. *Le Monde*, November 6, 1996, p. 5.
12. Interview with Raymond Chrétien, November 22, 2002.
13. Pierre-Claver Ndacyayisenga, *Dying to Live, A Rwandan Family's Five-Year Flight Across the Congo*, Baraka Books, 2013, p. 79.
14. "Ottawa maître d'œuvre au Zaïre," "Jean Chrétien fustige l'inertie de la communauté internationale," and "Le général Maurice Baril dirigerait une force humanitaire de 10 000 soldats," with files from CP, AFP, and AP, *Le Soleil*, November 13, 1996.
15. Gourevitch, *op. cit.*, p. 269-270.
16. Wayne Madsen, *op. cit.*, p. 221.
17. Interview with Léon Kengo wa Dondo.
18. Roula Mouaffak, "Boutros Boutros-Ghali : itinéraire du 'frenchie'"

("Frenchie's plan"), *Magazine*, Beirut, May 1, 1998, cited in Wayne Madsen, *op. cit.*, p. 238.

19. Interview with Boutros Boutros-Ghali, November 21, 2002.

20. Declaration made on March 29, 1993, quoted in *Africa International*, No. 299, p. 31.

21. *Le Monde*, May 9, 1995, p. 8.

22. Some people counter this point by referring to Canada's refusal, along with France, to join in the invasion of Iraq. Yet it is probably the case that proves the point. In the run-up to the March 2003 U.S.-U.K.-led invasion of Iraq, Montreal, Québec was the scene of what were proportionally the largest anti-war demonstrations in the world, up to 200,000 people on some occasions at bitter cold temperatures. Québec as a whole was opposed to the war while a majority in the rest of Canada was in favour of following the United States. Prime Minister Jean Chrétien decided to keep Canada out of the war primarily to avoid having a serious political crisis with Québec. The results of the 1995 referendum had showed that Quebecers could very easily opt to separate from Canada.

Conclusion

1. Léopold Sédar Senghor, *Ce que je crois*, Grasset 1988, p 31 (our translation).

2. Gourevitch, *op. cit.*, p. 350.

3. On the "Rwandan miracle [*sic*]", see *De la révolution rwandaise à la contre-révolution* (L'Harmattan, 2003) by Albert-Énéas Gakuzi and Frédérique Mouzer. This economic and sociological analysis shows how the RPF reinstated a form of servitude of Rwandan Hutus similar to the period before the Social Revolution of 1959. Similarly, see "Rwanda today: When Foreign Aid Hurts More than it Helps," by Brian Endless, PhD, Concordia University, and Emmanuel Hakizimana, PhD, UQAM, for the Hotel Rwanda Rusesabagina Foundation.

4. See Note 1, Chapter 11.

5. Samuel Baker, *The Albert N'yanza, Great Basin of the Nile, and Explorations of the Nile Sources*, London, MacMillan, 1866, p. xxii., quoted in Hammond et Jablow, *op. cit.*, p. 54.

6. *Le Devoir*, 25 September, 2013 http://www.ledevoir.com/politique/canada/388327/le-canada-reste-engage-soutient-harper

7. Maximilian Forte, *op. cit.*, p. 239.

8. *New York Times Magazine*, Sunday January 5, 2003.

APPENDIX I

◆

Interview with Captain Amadou Deme

"Shock and Awe" in Kigali, April 1994[1]

Captain Amadou Deme[2] from Senegal was appointed by General Roméo Dallaire to the intelligence section of the United Nations Assistance Mission for Rwanda (UNAMIR), which

1. Translation of excerpts from Chapter 6, *Rwanda: crimes, mensonges et étouffement de la vérité* (Les Intouchables, Montreal, 2007) by Robin Philpot.

2. Captain Deme from Senegal spent much time in Rwanda where he held various neutral military and civilian positions as UN employee. He is among the military and civilian officials who accumulated the longest and most varied service for the UN in Rwanda. Amadou Deme was seconded in July 1993 to the Neutral Military Observer Group. When the United Nations Security Council created UNAMIR to implement the Arusha Peace Accord of August 1993, Amadou Deme briefed Force Commander Roméo Dallaire. During the crucial period of the Rwandan catastrophe, Amadou Deme was the "eyes and ears" of the UN troops in Rwanda. Captain Deme then worked as a Kigali-based investigator with the ICTR and coordinator responsible for witness protection until 1997. He participated in the investigation of the April 6 attack on the Rwandan President's plane. In 1997-98 he worked for the UN High Commission for Refugees, particularly in Goma, Bukavu, and Uvira in Eastern Congo, in Kinshasa and Kigali, in Angola and in Congo-Brazzaville. From 2000 to 2003, he served with the UN Office of High Commissioner for Human Rights, mainly in the Democratic Republic of Congo.

was established to support implementation of the Arusha Peace Accord of 1993. This interview was conducted in 2007.

Q. *What were your responsibilities with UNAMIR?*

AMADOU DEME: I was responsible for gathering information to help the Force Commander make decisions. Our intelligence network reached into all levels of Rwandan society, and more specifically:

- Monitoring of the political situation, information gathering about destabilizing elements such as violent demonstrations (i.e., places, times, resultant risk analysis, threats)
- Militia activities, training, programs, and locations
- Criminal activities, security situation analysis in order to take adequate action
- Purely tactical information on the two fighting parties, their positions, troop movements, logistics, attitude, articulation, weapons, mined areas, and capacity, and so forth
- The different incidents, mainly in the demilitarized zone (incursions), gathering and analysis of information coming from the various sectors and observers
- Illegal distribution of weapons, etc.

Q. *You were involved in surveillance of the various militias, including the Interahamwe. How would you qualify the militias?*

AMADOU DEME: The militias, whose origins are generally misunderstood, have a long history. It is often thought that the militias were created for paramilitary purposes only and that they were trained to kill and sabotage. The youth organizations go much further back. In general, they were set up first of all to organize and promote sporting events before they became affiliated with political parties starting in 1991. Ethnic background had nothing to do with them. Moreover, the Interahamwe had many Tutsis among them, including the President Robert Kajuga. I would be very careful when addressing the question of the militias and their participation in the destruction that was triggered on April 6 when President Habyarimana's plane was shot down. It is important to realize that the leaders did not have control over the youth then because they comprised more than just the militias. The youth came from all horizons. The groups were active in community work that had social and environmental objectives. Obviously, with war being imminent, the militias obviously represented a military potential. In other countries, the militias could be compared to a national guard or a civilian service. I think that in human history, given the crisis, imminent war, and long low-intensity conflict underway, no country in the world can claim that it had no militias of that type, be it in Europe, in the United States or in Canada.

Q. *Before the April 6 attack on the president's plane, did you have any signs indicating that one of the armies was preparing a major military action?*

AMADOU DEME: After the battalion of six hundred troops moved to the CND building in Kigali, we started seeing a number of incidents. The RPF started to ignore the procedures established under the peace agreement regarding the Kigali Weapon Secure Area (KWSA). They conducted ill-timed and unannounced sorties in trucks in Kigali. Troops circulated throughout the city and provoked incidents. Many RPF soldiers were extracted from the CND building and disappeared in the Kigali neighbourhoods.[3]

In addition, our observers sent to Mulindi (the RPF's base and headquarters) to escort vehicles no longer had the power to control the convoys nor the freedom to circulate in the RPF-controlled area of Rwanda. They had no access to check what was in the

3. It is estimated that some 4000 RPF soldiers were living in civilian clothing in the Kigali area in 1994 at the time the plane was shot down on April 6. That number far exceeds the 600 troops allowed under the Arusha Accord. (Serge Desouter, Rwanda: *Le procès du FPR, mise au point historique, op. cit.*, p. 155). The 600 troops were brought to Kigali under escort in "Operation Clean Corridor" on December 28, 1993 as described in Chapter 5.

vehicles in the various convoys. Many times, we received information about weapons, ammunition, and military personnel being transported by trucks coming from Mulindi and headed to Kigali.

Despite having all this information, UNAMIR was deficient in taking action to meet the problem.

Before the RPF battalion moved to Kigali in December 1993 measures were implemented to define the quantities and types of weapons that could be taken to the capital. These weapons were to be strictly organic for an infantry battalion, namely individual weapons, a few 14.5-cm crew-served weapons with possibility of anti-aircraft mountings and a few 60-mm and 81-mm mortars.

However, the RPF battalion brought more than was allowed. It had Katyusha type artillery guns, multiple rocket launchers (RPG7s), large-calibre mortar guns and more. These are battlefield saturation weapons, and not open action guns. They eat up projectiles unbelievably quickly.

Shortly after the plane was shot down on April 6, 1994 the RPF started firing its multiple rocket launchers and never stopped. The gunners had the exact coordinates of all their targets in Kigali. These were the weapons that enabled them to take Kigali and to win the war. The question is: how did they get all these weapons and masses of ammunition to Kigali? They consume enormous amounts of ammunition, which shows that a vast plan had been implemented to stock all the military materiel in Kigali before the attack on the plane.

We also had information from reliable sources that hostilities would resume imminently. Among our sources with the RPF, some had even rented hotel rooms in advance so as to be in the RPF-controlled sector when the war started up again. Eminent RPF leaders moved their families there to keep them safe and sheltered.

We also had information about major troop movements from Uganda just before April 6, logistics preparations in the RPF zone, and transport of weapons and ammunition. This information came from our observers and from officers with the Government

Forces. All these elements of information converged to show clearly that the RPF was about to resume the war. However, we did not know how they would go about it.

From the standpoint of the Government Forces, considering the political and tactical situation, peace was clearly the best option. Nobody in Rwandan government military brass would have considered that it would be beneficial to start up war again. That was the worst thing that could happen for them. At that time the Government Forces were in the process of disarming. This process was carried out openly with the help of the senior Rwandan military officers. For example, UNAMIR had managed to block shipment from Egypt of a major cargo of artillery ammunition in March 1994, even though the ammunition had been ordered before the Arusha Accord was signed in August 1993. Delivery of that ammunition ordered was allowed under the peace agreement. On one hand the RPF was carefully building up unparalleled destruction and logistics capabilities, while on the other hand the Government Forces could not even supply their units with weapons and ammunition.

Another point that is equally important is that, if the government or another pro-government political party were in fact responsible for the attack on the plane, as was alleged shortly thereafter, the Government Forces would have taken preventive action to contain the lighting attack by the RPF. That did not happen, because the attack came as a complete surprise.

Q. *The RPF massively violated the cease-fire within hours after the plane was shot down on April 6. Was it necessary to be privy to information about the attack on the plane in order for the RPF to deploy its army in that manner?*

AMADOU DEME: Absolutely! Early in the morning on April 7, the Katyushas in Kigali were thundering and they went on non-stop. Where did their ammunition come from? What's more, it is an undisputable fact that on the second day, the battalion stationed at the CND in Kigali and the battalion from northern Rwanda met up. In our opinion, they started moving before the attack on April 6. The speed with which the RPF columns reached Kigali and its surroundings was dumbfounding. The only explanation is that they were totally prepared to deploy.

The other side was not in the same state of preparedness. The Government Forces under attack had been weakened and exhausted, and their leadership and reputation undermined. They had been disarmed and the RPF had benefited from that. It was very easy for us to establish the number of soldiers, forces, weapons, and the order of command of the Government Forces. They were like an open book. The senior commanders provided us with the accurate data.

On the other hand, nobody could establish the size and capacity of the RPF army. What's more, people who try to draw a distinction between the RPF army and the Ugandan National Resistance Army are only displaying their own dishonesty and lack of reliability. It is simply unbelievable that in such circumstances, individuals, organizations, or armies can continue to give credence to the idea that the RPF conducted the war by itself.

Another important fact is that neutral representatives from UNAMIR or the Neutral Military Observers Group were never able to move about freely in the RPF-controlled zone. Even Force Commander Dallaire would never have been able to obtain such permission from the RPF. Throughout all the missions to Rwanda and along the Ugandan border, nobody was ever able to visit that zone freely. As a result, it was impossible to establish the size of the RPF army, their logistics, weapons stocking, and re-supply capabilities.

Q. *Were the embassies of the major countries aware of the RPF army's state of preparedness?*

AMADOU DEME: It would have been hard for them not to be aware. When I was with the NMOG [July, August, and September 1993], we regularly organized escorts to the RPF headquarters in Mulindi in northern Rwanda, most of the time for the ambassador of the

United States and for members of the United States State Department. These meetings continued during the UNAMIR period until April 1994, however I did not accompany those visits.

Q. *With such military imbalance, it is not surprising that the Government Forces continually called for a cease-fire immediately after the President's plane was shot down and the war started up again?*

AMADOU DEME: Exactly. When the massacres were going on, the Government Forces never stopped calling for truce to enable them to restore order. On the other hand, the RPF always refused truce because their war machine was on the move. The Government Forces were simply not able to stand up to an offensive, destructive, and fast-moving army that was well supported and supplied, while at the same time concentrating on re-establishing control inside the country and putting an end to the killing. The Rwandan army was unable to do both at the same time. Moreover, the RPF should have agreed to a truce for humanitarian reasons, considering the massive killing of people from both ethnic groups. The fact that they refused a truce is certainly a terrible crime against humanity. In a word, it was immoral.

Worse still, faced with the magnitude of the massacres, a group of government army officers including the chief of staff surrendered unilaterally in the first week in order to stop the war. The RPF however refused to agree to a cease-fire.

Q. *Did you have any idea who shot President Habyarimana's plane down at the time?*

AMADOU DEME: When it happened, my mind never once turned to the government side. I automatically concluded the RPF was responsible. That view was widely held by all UNAMIR people present. It was obvious!

What was surprising was to hear the idea that the attack might have been carried out by the hard line people in the Rwandan

Government or the Coalition pour la défense de la république, known as the CDR. UNAMIR officers were shocked and revolted to hear this, especially the African members of the Mission. It was ridiculous. I have never met a military officer, particularly among the military observers, who had any doubts about RPF responsibility for the attack on the plane.

Moreover, a colleague and I were the first to access the crash site. That day, when Major Aloys Ntabakuze from the Government Forces surprised us in the president's estate among the ruins of the plane, I thought that we were finished. Fortunately, he guided us and I was able to take pictures that were provided to the commander. Major Ntabakuze showed us the place where they found missile tubes used to shoot down the plane. He provided us with clear data on the location and on the Russian inscriptions on the tubes.[4]

Moreover, some FPR officers secretly showed that they were particularly satisfied that the attack had been carried out successfully from their standpoint. They never hid their satisfaction.

Q. *As an investigator with the International Criminal Tribunal for Rwanda, you investigated the April 6 attack. What was your conclusion? And what became of that investigation?*

AMADOU DEME: Personally, I have never had the slightest doubt about who shot the plane down. Some RPF officers never denied that their army was responsible. They were even proud of it. The problem however was to have accurate, precise, and detailed information, with an official mandate. We needed tangible information, even though everybody in the civilian and military sections of UNAMIR knew the truth, which had been provided by reliable sources.

From February 1997 on, as investigators for the Tribunal's "National Team," we began to investigate officially. We had more sources than we knew what to do with, but having sources ready to go the distance presented a problem. We obtained information

4. Judge Bruguière established that the missiles were manufactured in Russia.

from various reliable military sources who in fact had nothing in common with each other except that they belonged to the same army and took part in the same RPF offensive.

The investigation results and the evidence were limpid: the RPF carried out the attack on the plane. The information gathered was presented in a succinct report by Michael Hourigan, who was the National Team leader. After consultation with and authorization from our hierarchical superiors, the investigation commander Jim Lyons, formerly with the FBI, and the investigation manager Al Breau, formerly with the RCMP, gave us the green light. We reached the top position held by Prosecutor Louise Arbour.

At the end of March 1997 I took a plane with Michael Hourigan to Arusha. I was headed to Switzerland for a seminar on witness protection and Michael Hourigan was going to The Hague for a meeting with Ms Louise Arbour about the report on the shooting down of the plane. While I was in Switzerland, I was regularly in telephone contact with Michael Hourigan. During his trip to The Hague, Ms Arbour ordered Michael Hourigan to stop investigating the attack on the plane.

Q. *As an investigator, you also had to establish whether or not there had been a plan to commit genocide. In your capacity with UNAMIR and the NMOG, did you gather any information to that effect? If so, what?*

AMADOU DEME: We never found anything about planning by the government or the Government Forces. There has never been any evidence of state planning. The Government Forces (army, police, and presidential guard) were always on the defensive.

If there was any plotting and planning, it must be sought out on the RPF side. They had a plan with all the military mechanisms necessary to take power. However, they underestimated the magnitude of the consequences and the magnitude of the destruction.

It was a carefully prepared plan from A to Z, with all the military means necessary. It was a plan involving destabilization of the country, assassination, and massive military offensive up to and including the taking of power. The RPF had displaced nearly one million internal refugees in an area just north of Kigali. I believe that they wished to use the internal refugees as a buffer between the part of the country they were occupying and the Rwandan Government Forces.

I had a tremendous sympathy for these people who were displaced by force, pushed out of the demilitarized zone, killed, raped, and starved, even though they were totally innocent. The RPF used all possible means to prevent them from returning to their lands in order to maintain them as a buffer.

The RPF military offensive continued in the Congo after that. I had an opportunity to observe it when I was working for the United Nations High Commission for Refugees (HCR). I had to deal with the RPF army on a daily basis right into the heart of the Democratic Republic of Congo, in the Western Kasai Province, thousands of kilometres away from Rwanda.

APPENDIX II

Human Rights Watch and Alison Des Forges VS Rwandan Delegation in New York, May 1994

Human Rights Watch's Terrorist, Malicious, and Hostile Attempt to Paralyse the Rwandan Interim Government's Diplomatic Action and to Accuse it of Crimes against Humanity and Genocide against the Tutsis, in New York in May 1994

By Jérôme C. Bicamumpaka, Arusha, Tanzania, Sunday, October 20, 2013[1]

I went to New York after visiting several European countries and arrived on May 10, 1994. As soon as I arrived I began contacting

1. Jerome C. Bicamumpaka was Minister of Foreign Affairs in Rwanda's Interim Government from April to July 1994. While living in Cameroon as a management consultant professional, he was arrested in 1999 on charges including conspiracy to commit genocide by the International Criminal Tribunal for Rwanda. After twelve years and half in custody, Mr. Bicamumpaka was acquitted of all charges and was immediately released on September 30, 2011. Despite being freed, he has been forced to stay temporarily in Arusha, Tanzania, since he has not yet got a country to receive him. Alison Des Forges was the main prosecution witness in several cases before the ICTR, including Mr. Bicamumpaka's. Under cross-examination, Ms Des Forges admitted the accuracy of the facts described herein without showing the slightest sign of embarrassment

the upper echelons of the United Nations Secretariat and all Security Council members, as well as people responsible for different specialized organizations headquartered or represented in New York.

The media and various non-governmental organizations soon learned that I was at the UN headquarters and that I was making official contacts regarding the Rwandan crisis. Human Rights Watch was among the NGOs. They then launched a campaign that targeted my delegation and me, first in the media and then at the United Nations Secretariat. Their objective was to prevent me from being received by anybody in the UN and to prevent me from taking part in any Security Council meetings where Rwanda was being addressed almost on a daily basis; however no initiatives were taken to settle the Rwandan crisis. Ms Alison Des Forges of Human Rights Watch was among those who mobilized the most in this hateful and unjustified campaign, especially in light of the extreme gravity of the Rwandan crisis at that time.

All these attempts failed since I was able to take part in a Security Council meeting and be received during my stay in New York by all the people whom I had asked to meet, except for the ambassador of the United States, who pretended to apologize whereas it was in fact a refusal to meet me. Moreover, in New York, the representatives of the United States, backed especially by the United Kingdom, worked hard against the Rwandan government that I represented and sabotaged all peace initiatives that we undertook. On the other hand, they systematically supported the delegates and the proposals from the RPF, who represented an armed rebellion.

My delegation included Jean-Bosco Barayagwiza, Director of Political Affairs with the Rwandan Foreign Affairs Department since 1990 and formerly a diplomat seconded to the Secretariat General of the OAU (Organization of African Unity, now the African Union). Disappointed at not having blocked me at the UN, Alison Des Forges decided to go one step further. The day before my delegation and I were to leave New York for Africa via

Paris, Alison Des Forges, together with Rwanda's current Minister of Foreign Affairs, Louise Mushikiwabo, appeared before a judge in a New York City court to obtain a summons for Jean-Bosco Barayagwiza to appear in an emergency trial in New York during which they falsely accused him of having killed Landouald Ndasingwa. Louise Mushikiwabo is the sister of the late Landouald Ndasingwa, a former Rwandan minister (1992-94) and member of the Liberal Party assassinated within hours of the shooting down of the president's plane on April 6, 1994.

This was a frame-up organized against the Rwandan diplomat who knew Louise Mushikiwabo very well. I do not know what Ms Mushikiwabo was doing in New York then, but was told that she was studying at university. I never attempted to find out. Yet despite how false and outrageous this accusation was, the judge provided them with everything they needed to have the summons served on Mr. Barayagwiza.

In the morning on May 18, 1994, I was still in my hotel room about fifteen minutes before leaving the hotel for the JFK International Airport and Mr. Barayagwiza and several others were waiting for me in the hotel lobby. A group of at least six people along with a cameraman and a photographer entered the hotel lobby. They had likely spied on Mr. Barayagwiza so that they knew he would be there at that time in the morning.

The group actually attacked Mr. Barayagwiza, heading at him brutally, shouting, and taking pictures (he was talking casually with three or four other people while waiting for me to join them in the lobby). The people in the hotel lobby had no idca what was happening. Then a member of the group, probably the one playing the role of bailiff, threw a pile of papers at Mr. Barayagwiza while the cameras were flashing. The hotel security personnel were surprised, but quickly intervened and chased the group out of the hotel. The group left the same way they had entered, running and shouting.

Members of my delegation left the hotel lobby to try to understand who these people were and what motivated them to act like terrorists in a country that supposedly operated under the rule of law. That is when they saw Alison Des Forges, who was with the group but who had carefully remained outside the hotel, hidden in the corner of a building almost directly across the street from the hotel. Beside her was a black woman who looked like Louise Mushikiwabo, Rwanda's current minister of Foreign Affairs and sister of the late Landouald Ndasingwa.

For this group, Mr. Barayagwiza had officially been served his summons issued by a judge from a New York court to answer to accusations regarding his alleged responsibility for the assassination of the former minister in the Rwandan government from the Liberal Party.

When I arrived in the hotel lobby, the incident was over but I found Mr. Barayagwiza in a very troubled state considering what had just happened to him. He must have been asking himself many questions. I asked him what he intended to do, return to Rwanda with the other members of the delegation or remain in New York. He chose to return to Rwanda. The entire delegation then left for the airport and took off for Paris about an hour and a half later.

Mr. Barayagwiza was an excellent jurist. He quickly understood how he was being set up, and identified the many flaws in the grotesque and clearly terrorist procedure that Human Rights Watch and Alison Des Forges were inflicting on him with the complicity of an RPF personality, Ms Louise Mushikiwabo.

In short, this was one of the many strategies devised by Human Rights Watch to prevent the Interim Government of Rwanda from convincing the international community, and particularly the United Nations, of the overriding necessity to correct the error committed when it brutally withdrew two thirds of the UNAMIR troops. The correction would have involved rapid deployment of a second force with a stronger legal mandate based on Chapter 7 of the Charter of the United Nations, but also with more troops and equipment. The two-fold objective would be to save lives and bring both parties to the conflict to stop the war and try to negotiate the rapid establishment of a new government based this time on the Arusha Peace Accord, which had been seriously violated by the RPF as of April 6, 1994.

Index

MORE NONFICTION FROM BARAKA BOOKS

Dying to Live
A Rwandan Family's Five-Year Flight Across the Congo
Pierre-Claver Ndacyayisenga

Slouching Towards Sirte
NATO's War on Libya and Africa
Maximilian Forte

Challenging the Mississippi Firebombers
Memories of Mississippi 1964-65
Jim Dann

Barack Obama and the Jim Crow Media
The Return of the Nigger Breakers
Ishmael Reed

Going Too Far
Essays about America's Nervous Breakdown
Ishmael Reed

The Question of Separatism
Quebec and the Struggle over Sovereignty
Jane Jacobs

America's Gift
What the World Owes to the Americas and Their First Inhabitants
Käthe Roth and Denis Vaugeois

A People's History of Quebec
Jacques Lacoursière & Robin Philpot

The History of Montréal
The Story of a Great North American City
Paul-André Linteau